£ 9.99

INSIGHTS

General Editor: Clive Bloom, Lecturer in English and Co-ordinator of American Studies, Middlesex Polytechnic

Editorial Board: Clive Bloom, Brian Docherty, Gary Day, Lesley Bloom, Hazel Day

Insights brings to academics, students and general readers the very best contemporary criticism on neglected literary and cultural areas. It consists of anthologies, each containing original contributions by advanced scholars and experts. Each contribution concentrates on a study of a particular work, author or genre in its artistic, historical and cultural context.

Published titles

Clive Bloom (*editor*)
JACOBEAN POETRY AND PROSE: Rhetoric, Representation and the Popular Imagination

Clive Bloom, Brian Docherty, Jane Gibb and Keith Shand (*editors*)
NINETEENTH-CENTURY SUSPENSE: From Poe to Conan Doyle

Gary Day and Clive Bloom (*editors*)
PERSPECTIVES ON PORNOGRAPHY: Sexuality in Film and Literature

Brian Docherty (*editor*)
AMERICAN CRIME FICTION: Studies in the Genre

Brian Docherty (*editor*)
AMERICAN HORROR FICTION: From Brockden Brown to Stephen King

Robert Giddings, Keith Selby and Chris Wensley
SCREENING THE NOVEL: The Theory and Practice of Literary Dramatisation

Mark Lilly (*editor*)
LESBIAN AND GAY WRITING

James Aulich and Jeffrey Walsh (*editors*)
VIETNAM IMAGES: War and Representation

Readings in Popular Culture

Trivial Pursuits?

Edited by
Gary Day

se dentry
monistic

MACMILLAN 1990

First published 1990

Published by   *1630246*
THE MACMILLAN PRESS LTD
Houndmills, Basingstoke, Hampshire RG21 2XS
and London
Companies and representatives
throughout the world

Printed in Hong Kong

British Library Cataloguing in Publication Data
Readings in popular culture: trivial pursuits.
(Insights).
1. Popular culture
I. Day, Gary   II. Series
306'.1
ISBN 0–333–47522–4
ISBN 0–333–47523–2 pbk

Series Standing Order

If you would like to receive future titles in this series as they are
published, you can make use of our standing order facility. To place a
standing order please contact your bookseller or, in case of difficulty,
write to us at the address below with your name and address and the
name of the series. Please state with which title you wish to begin your
standing order. (If you live outside the United Kingdom we may not
have the rights for your area, in which case we will forward your order
to the publisher concerned.)

Customer Services Department, Macmillan Distribution Ltd
Houndmills, Basingstoke, Hampshire, RG21 2XS, England.

Contents

List of illustrations   viii

Preface and Acknowledgements   ix

Notes on the Contributors   x

1   Introduction: Popular Culture – The Conditions of
    Control?
    Gary Day   1

2   MacDonalds' Man meets *Reader's Digest*   13
    Clive Bloom

3   Acid – Burning a Hole in the Present   18
    Helena Blakemore

4   Hampton Court Revisited: A Re-evaluation of the
    Consumer   23
    Andrew Smith

5   Henry's Paperweight: The Banks and TV
    Advertising   32
    Robert M. Chaplin

6   'A Thing of Beauty and a Source of Wonderment':
    Ornaments for the Home as Cultural Status
    Markers   39
    Gwyneth Roberts

7   Pose for Thought: Bodybuilding and other Matters   48
    Gary Day

8   Dialogic Society: Discourse and Subjectivity in
    British Telecom's 'Talkabout' Service   59
    Adrian Page

9   T-Shirts and the Coming Collapse of Capitalism   68
    Paul O'Flinn

10   Recipes for Success   75
     Michael J. Hayes

11   That's Entertainment   84
     Gary Day

12   Christmas: Celebrating The Humbug   90
     Norma Wordsworth

13   War Toys   98
     Graham Dawson

14   Family Affairs: Angst in the Age of Mechanical
     Reproduction   112
     Shelagh Young

15   Is the Micro Macho? A Critique of the Fictions of
     Advertising   121
     Mary Knight

16   Pleasure and Danger, Sex and Death: Reading True
     Crime Monthlies   131
     Deborah Cameron

17   A Second Byte of the Apple   139
     Gill Simpson

18   Illiberal Thoughts on 'Page 3'   145
     Bob Brecher

19   The Golden Age of Cricket   151
     John Simons

20   Bertolt Brecht and Football, or Playwright versus
     Playmaker   164
     Barry Emslie

21   The Woman's Realm: History Repeats Itself on the
     Women's Page   174
     Ann Treneman

22   G-Men to Jar Wars — Conditioning the Public   187
     Michael Woodiwiss

23   Chaos and Order: The New York Subway   194
     Richard Bradbury

24   'And Where Did you See *Star Wars*?' — Cinema
     Going in Britain   200
     Lez Cooke

25   Museums of Fine Art and Their Public   208
     Anthony Crabbe

26   American National Identity and the Structure of
     Myth: Images of Reagan   216
     R. J. Ellis

Index   231

List of Illustrations

1. 'A Fresh Start', cover design, *Time*, vol. 116, no. 20 (17 November 1980).
2. Thomas Cole, 'Pioneer Home in the Woods', 1845–6 (Oil on canvas, 44 × 66 ins, c. 1845–46, Winston-Salem, North Carolina: Reynolds House, Inc.).
3. Thomas Cole, 'A Distant View of the Falls of Niagara', engraved by I. T. Hinton and Simpkin and Marshall, in John Howard Hinton, *The History and Topography of the United States of North America* (London: R. Clay, 1832), 2 vols, II, frontispiece. An engraving of the original Cole picture, 'Niagara Falls', 1830 (Oil on canvas, 33 × 43 ins, Chicago: Collection of the Art Institute of Chicago).
4. Emanuel Leutze, 'Westward the Course of Empire Takes Its Way', 1861 (Oil on canvas, 33 × 43 ins, Washington, DC: National Collection of Fine Arts, Smithsonian Institute).
5. George Caleb Bingham, 'Daniel Boone Escorting a Band of Pioneers in the Western Countryside' (detail), 1851 (oil on canvas, 26.5 × 50 ins, St Louis: Washington University Gallery of Art).
6. 'Dirty Ronnie', cover design: montage by Michael Bennett, *New Statesman*, vol. 101 no. 2608 (13 March 1981).
7. Anon., 'In this nuclear age can we trust leaders who shoot from the hip', CND recruitment leaflet, n.d. [1986].

Preface and Acknowledgements

Popular culture is fast becoming a widely studied subject. This volume contains twenty six essays plus an Introduction. While each essay reflects contemporary cultural theory—Marxist, feminist, post-structuralist—a number also develop original approaches to the topics they cover, thereby extending awareness of them and providing grounds for further discussion. Subjects covered range from Acid House to Hampton Court and from T-shirts to computers.

Thanks are due to Hazel Day, Clive and Lesley Bloom, Sarah Roberts-West, Malcolm Evans and Lorraine Gamman.

Notes on the Contributors

Helena Blakemore worked for several years in the record industry before returning to higher education. She has recently been awarded her MA in modern fiction at Queen Mary College, London.

Clive Bloom is a Senior Lecturer in the Faculty of Humanities at Middlesex Polytechnic. He is General Editor of the Insights Series and is the author of two books, *The 'Occult' Experience and the New Criticism* and *Reading Poe, Reading Freud: The Romantic Imagination in Crisis*.

Richard Bradbury is currently working for the British Council as an Associate Professor at the English Institute at the University of Lodz in Poland. He is also researching into American Cultural History 1941–50 for a forthcoming book and contributed to the *American Crime Fiction* volume for Insights.

Bob Brecher teaches Philosophy and runs the BA Humanities course at Brighton Polytechnic. He is interested in applied ethics and the role of philosophy in politics.

Deborah Cameron now teaches in America and is the co-author of *The Lust to Kill* with Elizabeth Frazer.

Robert M. Chaplin is an art teacher living and working in North East London. He is currently preparing his doctoral dissertation at the University of Sussex.

Lez Cooke is an Associate Lecturer in Film and Media Studies at Barnet College of Further Education. He has published articles in *Movie* and *Screen*, edited a Media Studies Bibliography and has produced various study materials for the Education Department of the British Film Institute.

Anthony Crabbe teaches History of Art and Design at Trent Polytechnic. He is a contributor to the Insights Series and is currently working on the philosophical concept of time.

Graham Dawson was for several years a member of the Popular Memory Group at the centre for Contemporary Cultural studies in Birmingham. He currently teaches Media and Cultural Studies at the University of Sussex and Brighton Polytechnic.

Gary Day teaches in Brighton and has published various articles, reviews and poetry and has co-edited *Perspectives on Pornography* with Clive Bloom for the Insights Series.

R. J. Ellis teaches English and American Literature and Cultural Studies at North Staffordshire Polytechnic. He has published a number of articles on critical theory in practice.

Barry Emslie was educated in New Zealand and returned to Britain ten years ago. He has recently completed his doctoral thesis on Marxist Aesthetics and Bertolt Brecht.

Michael J. Hayes teaches at Lancashire Polytechnic. His research interests include Disraeli's Early writings and he has contributed to the *American Crime Fiction* volume recently published in the Insights Series.

Mary Knight is a lecturer in the General Education Department of Newham Community College. She does not teach 'computer' skills. Indeed her relationship to computers is a contradictory tale of love and hate, rather than expertise. She uses one at home mainly to write drafts for her research on women and feminism in the inter-war years.

Paul O'Flinn has taught English at Ibibo State College, Nigeria, and at Trent University, Ontario and has also taught sociology at the University of Reading. He is currently a Principal Lecturer in English at Oxford Polytechnic. His previous publications include *Them and Us in Literature.*

Adrian Page is a Senior Lecturer at Bedford College of Higher Education in English and Drama. His main research interests are Twentieth Century Fiction and Drama. He is currently editing a forthcoming volume in the Insights Series on modern drama and literary theory.

Gwyneth Roberts is a Senior Lecturer in the Department of Cultural Studies at North East London Polytechnic. She is the co-author of *Outline of English Literature* and her research interests are in language and national identity.

John Simons is currently a Senior Lecturer in English and Co-ordinator of American Studies at King Alfred's College, Winchester. His publications include editions of Henry Porter's *Two Angry Women of Abington* (with Michael Jardine), and *New York: the City as Text* (with Christopher Mulvey) which is a forthcoming volume in the Insights Series.

Gill Simpson is an Associate Lecturer in the Linguistics department at Lancashire Polytechnic. Her interests include the relationship between language and power, which she is currently exploring as part of an MA in Language Studies at Lancaster University.

Andrew Smith is currently undertaking a graduate research diploma at Middlesex Polytechnic. He has also contributed to a forthcoming volume in the Insights Series on Twentieth Century Suspense.

Ann Treneman is a journalist who has worked in America and England, and currently works in London. She has a Master's Degree in Women's Studies from the University of Kent. She has written various articles on women and the media and popular culture.

Michael Woodiwiss is a lecturer in American Studies at Essex University. He is the author of *Crime, Crusades and Corruption* and has contributed articles to *History Today* and *The Spectator*.

Norma Wordsworth returned to education as a mature student and studied for her first degree in English and History at Thames Polytechnic. She is currently completing her post graduate dissertation on Women and Humour in Literature at the University of Kent.

Shelagh Young is a freelance journalist and editor of *City Limits* magazine. She lectures in cultural and media studies at Bristol Polytechnic.

1

Introduction: Popular Culture – The Conditions of Control?

GARY DAY

Popular culture is a notoriously difficult term to define particularly as definitions of an object of study largely depend on the method of study. There is, in other words, no objective reality whose nature would always be the same no matter from which angle it was approached. Many different approaches to popular culture — historical, linguistic, Marxist, feminist, structuralist and post structuralist — will be found in this volume and it is not the intention of this introduction to try and unify them into a single definition of the same. Indeed to do so would be to ignore that different aspects of popular culture work in different ways to produce different effects.

But if it is difficult, if not impossible, to know the nature of popular culture, at least something can be said about its extent. Popular culture covers so vast an area that contact with it cannot be avoided; it is there in the high street and in the home, it is easily accessible and involves mass participation, it is the mythology which gives meaning to society and through which society understands itself. Everything is pressed into the service of this mythology from house plants to fashion, from television to travel and nothing has an existence or significance outside of it. As a totality, this mythology justifies and perpetuates the social and economic relations of consumer capitalism but each individual part has its own autonomy in respect of the system it reproduces. Moreover, closer examination of the individual parts reveals how they can, in fact, oppose or deconstruct the system they support. Thus, though it may be hard to escape the combined effects of popular culture it is possible to minimise its individual effects by showing how they undermine the very things they seem to affirm. It is by proceeding

1

on this piecemeal basis that the powerful allurement of popular culture as a whole can be resisted.

It will be evident from the above that this volume attempts to move away from views of popular culture simply as a form of escapism or false consciousness. Since the development of linguistics and the growth of semiology, popular culture is no longer seen either as a deliberate attempt to hide the real nature of society or as the opium of the people. It was Barthes' *Mythologies* which first changed the perception of popular culture and he was less interested in what it concealed than how it concealed.[1] He showed how various aspects of popular culture or, to use his term 'mythologies', worked to transform historical and ideological meanings into natural ones. By the 1970s however, Barthes had abandoned this approach, he was no longer interested in analysing the sign but in dislocating it. In his words:

> it is no longer the myths which need to be unmasked [. . .] it is the sign itself which must be shaken; the problem is not to reveal the (latent) meaning of an utterance of a trait, of a narrative but to fissure the very representation of meaning, is not to change or purify the symbols but to challenge the symbolic itself.[2]

Although many of the articles in this volume show how popular culture deconstructs itself they do not wholly endorse Barthes' views here. They fissure a certain representation of meaning but they do not challenge the idea of meaning itself.

Indeed, what would be the point of challenging meaning to the point where it becomes barely possible? The desire to dismantle the symbolic, upon which meaning depends, suggests a view of meaning as oppressive. This may be true in certain cases but not all, for meaning also liberates. Furthermore, without meaning there is no concept of truth and without truth there is no way of exposing the arguments of one's political opponents. If one cannot show that these same opponents have lied about unemployment statistics or the state of the health service then there is little hope for social and economic progress which should surely be the impetus behind all analysis of popular culture.

Of course this is an extreme interpretation of Barthes' position and those who wish to come to his defence may say that he does not wish to destroy meaning, but rather show how many meanings are present when there appears to be only one. Barthes, in other words, wants to undermine the authority of one meaning by showing the presence of others. While this is a perfectly acceptable way of proceeding, particularly against the increasingly monologic discourse of Thatcherism, it does raise the question of how these meanings are to be organised in relation to one another since any relation pre-supposes some form of hierarchy to which Barthes, judging from his remarks, would seem to be opposed. This leaves meanings separate and as such they correspond to the fragmented state of consumer capitalism upon which Barthes has declared war. His analysis reproduces, in formal terms, the very thing he criticises, namely the system which he began to expose in *Mythologies*.

[handwritten margin note: Not true a all. Equal?]

But perhaps Barthes is not concerned with meaning or meanings in any analytic sense, perhaps he is concerned instead with the pleasure to be derived from moving from one meaning to another. Meaning here is a matter for play, for pleasure, for jouissance and nothing else. If this is the case then analysis becomes self-indulgence which is hardly a good basis for political progress and yet the tone of Barthes' comments seems to suggest that political progress is what is ultimately at stake. If it is pleasure that Barthes is concerned with in his analysis of cultural forms then he indirectly poses the difficult question of the relation between pleasure and popular culture: is it inherent to the *experience* of popular culture itself or does it belong to the *analysis* of popular culture?

[handwritten margin note: why nothing else?]

The problem of pleasure opens up the possibility of a psychoanalytic account of popular culture. In the discourse of psychoanalysis pleasure is discussed in terms of the repetition compulsion and repetition lies at the heart of popular culture—one thinks, for example, of the repeats on television. This leads into the question of whether or not the repeated pleasures inherent in popular culture help to condition people to the far less pleasurable repetitions of the workplace. Does repetition itself become a source of pleasure rather than what is repeated? Whatever the answer it seems certain that repetition functions to keep things as they are and as such makes pleasure a force for conservatism.

A psychoanalytic approach to popular culture would place great emphasis on how it is experienced, but an even more intriguing perspective may be to consider how far popular culture provides the conditions of experience itself. Popular culture may be something that is perceived but it is also a way of perceiving and this is

hardly surprising considering how deeply its structures have
penetrated our existence. Popular culture now touches all our lives
as religion once touched the lives of those who lived in the Middle
Ages.

Advertising offers one example of how popular culture may
structure experience. The experience of adverts is a constant one,
they are found everywhere but perhaps they are most noticeable
on television where there is a strong case to be made for saying
that they are interrupted by the programmes and not the programmes interrupted by them. After a film or a harrowing documentary
they somehow restore a sense of normality; their presence on the
screen or the street, in newspapers or magazines seems to reaffirm
a reassuringly continuous and unshakeable reality. In short,
adverts give stability. Probe a little deeper, however, and that
stability crumbles.

Advertising promotes insecurity. It encourages consumers to
believe in a state of affairs—Utopia or their own perfectability
which can never be realised. Moreover, this intense stimulation of
belief takes place in the context of a culture which believes in
nothing. It has no anchor point; God, democracy and Marx have all
faded and nothing has arisen to take their place. The habit of belief
survives and it is this which is exploited by all the sophisticated
ploys of advertising with the result that while belief is thereby
created there is nothing to which it can attach itself. This situation
is a potentially very dangerous one; it has already been exploited
by Thatcherism and there may be worse evils to come.

In as much as advertising encourages consumers to believe in
utopia or their own perfectability it can be said to orientate them
towards some future time. This future time is the locale of the
perfected consumer who has achieved that condition by purchasing the advertised product. However, no sooner does the consumer arrive at this future time than it vanishes, to be replaced by
another, equally attractive. One clear example of this is the hype
which surrounds Christmas. This usually begins in September
when cards, lights, trees and tinsel combine to present Christmas
as a time of harmony and resolution both in the family and in the
community. Advertising implies that the way to realise this state is
by spending money; you cannot fit in with the rest of the
community if you do not go Christmas shopping. Leaving aside
the question of whether this peaceful harmony can ever be
realised, 25 December, which should see the climax of all this

activity, is the very day which sees the start of adverts for the holiday season. No time is given to experience the event which has been so lavishly prepared for. Consumer capitalism goes into overdrive for Christmas but the moment it arrives it negates it by filling the television screens with information about bargains for summer holidays. This situation is typical of the way advertising works and it means either that events are never experienced or, if they are, then only as bathos.

Ironically, this orientation towards a future time, which is intended to take consumers out of their present time only succeeds in keeping them in it. Adverts make consumers desire the future but, because that future is never realised, consumers are imprisoned in an eternal present of desire. To live in an eternal present means that there is neither past nor future and this confers a kind of absoluteness on consumer capitalism, making it seem monolithic and unchangeable. Moreover, this condition destroys a sense of history, replacing it with one of myth.[3]

[handwritten margin note: in real terms no-one lives in a permanent present, psychologically impossible!]

However, though the consumer's world may be mythic in some ways it is not in others. For example the mythic world is an integrated one whereas the consumer's is not, instead it is an instant one. In such a world experiences is a product of the instant, it is not something which comes with growth and, as the instant is connected with consumption, so too by association, is experience. Indeed there is a case for saying that most experience is a matter of consumption in capitalist society; we are all constructed and addressed as consumers and our social identity is largely based on our patterns of consumption. The instant character of experience and its connection with consumption would suggest that, as with other things that are instantly available and instantly consumed, it is unique and unrepeatable. But this only appears to be the case for, in fact, it is the same experiences which are repeated over and over again. Like early man and woman the modern person is tied to cycles but they are consumerist, not natural ones and their motion is invisible.

The instant as a condition of experience means that the consumer inhabits a disparate, unconnected world where, because everything is repeated, nothing seems to happen. However, this is not how this world is experienced, it is experienced as melodrama and this gives it a kind of spurious unity. Melodrama gives exaggerated importance to quite ordinary events, a phenomenon which can be witnessed daily in the tabloid press. Their habit of dramatising mundane phenomena creates problems when something important happens for if the trivial and the significant are accorded the same treatment then it becomes difficult to distinguish between them. This sensationalising process helps to determine what is and is not relevant to ordinary lives and is therefore a subtle form of control. More importantly it establishes that what is not sensationalised is not experienced, so along with the eternal present and the instant, melodrama also becomes a condition of experience.

The technique of dramatising phenomena creates expectations of how things should appear to be. What is noticed, in other words, is the packaging and not the product. This packaging, eye-catching and dramatic, imposes a uniformity on different kinds of reality making them appear the same; thus it is expected that a politician should be packaged in the same way as a car, or a computer. These expectations of how things ought to appear mean that new or different experiences are rejected, only those which are properly packaged can find admittance into what constitutes reality which is thereby conservative. This perception of how things ought to be, what texture and significance reality ought to have, is instilled in us by advertising where the packaging process is most obvious. This shared perception is important not just for the way it narrows down reality but also for the way it establishes a ground for common values. The question of the kind of values which come from this perception is not one which can be entered into here.

Melodrama, then, offers one way in which the fragmented world is experienced as a whole one. Another way in which the world is unified is through the experience of one's own self. Everywhere through advertising, everyone encounters ideal images of themselves. These ideals are ideal insofar as they are completed versions of the 'real' self which, through advertising, is made to experience a sense of lack, or incompleteness, a state which can be remedied by purchasing the advertised product. In this situation, the incomplete self is made to desire the ideal self; the self is made to desire the self. The irony of this process is that the self one is made to desire is not the real self at all but a faceless, representative figure which is offered as everyone's reflection. A further irony is that the advertised product never confers completeness because the consumer is always made aware, through more advertising, of other products which also promise to complete. The consumer never escapes his or her lack which contributes to his or her sense of being trapped in the eternal present.

The structure of the self desiring the self serves the status quo for any attack on the existing order is, by implication, an attack on the self and must therefore be repelled. The vast and tragic narcissism which advertising creates helps to bond the social order at the same time as it fragments it. Advertising appeals to the self and not the community but the image it offers of the self fits everyone and so it manages to hold the social structure in place.

The processes of advertising, then, locate consumers in an eternal present which, despite being fragmented, is experienced as a unity. This constant orientation towards a non-existent future creates dissatisfaction with the present but precisely because everything is directed towards the future it becomes very difficult to devise strategies for coping with that present. Perhaps it is in this context that the significance of things like walkmans and filofaxs and wristwatch televisions become apparent.[4] Each of these is a way of projecting oneself elsewhere; they are distractions from the present, a means of shutting it out. This suggests that where there is no remedy for the dissatisfactions of the present there is at least escape. On the other hand, it is precisely the projection to an elsewhere that gives the present its eternal character; that escape, therefore, is illusory.

One difficulty in devising strategies for coping with the present is the way in which consumers are constructed as passive spectators. Advertising offers goods for consumers to view and the impression conveyed by this process is that the world somehow operates independently of consumers so all they have to do is buy the products they see before them. Consumers are constructed to watch the world not to take part in it, and this is a condition fostered by the ever improving technology of television. Indeed, the consumer's relation to the world is increasingly parallel to the television viewer's relationship to his or her set. On package tours, for example, tourists stare at a country through the glass of a coach window, in much the same way as a television viewer might stare at the same country on his or her screen.

Television makes the world visible and, in doing so, reduces all realities to the status of the visible. In making the world visible television generates the illusion that it is accessible: to see is to understand. This is reinforced by the way images on television are so like the images encountered in ordinary life that their veracity seems unquestionable. However, it is the very visibility of the image which conceals its significance. The visibility of the image functions to discourage analysis, the image is quite simply there and there is nothing more to say about it. The image also refutes the idea of structure or connection by announcing that it is what it is; it exists in splendid isolation without reference to anything else. The visibility of the image and its status in respect of other images implies a world that is wholly apparent, consisting of an assemblage of objects and people. And the important thing about such a world is that it seems incapable of change. *imprinting an ideology on*

In addition to making the world into a seemingly unchangeable *an o* spectacle television also provides a form for making sense of *good* modern existence, namely the soap opera. The soap opera reconciles the formless, open-endedness of twentieth-century life with a desire for form and closure by focusing on the community. The fact that the community contains a number of people allows for the development of different storylines which are never resolved until others have begun and it is this characteristic which gives soaps like *Eastenders* or *Dynasty* their open-endedness. This open-endedness is balanced by the way each storyline is resolved within the context of the community which thereby lends a kind of closure or form to the otherwise ongoing lives within it. Furthermore, these resolutions are made on the basis of traditional values which are rooted in a concept of moral responsibility that is thereby endorsed as the basis of all action. The soap opera thus has a conservative content and a progressive form.

The soap opera is one means of promoting the belief that we all share a common culture. Another is the telethon, a 24 hour programme in aid of a particular charity. In the telethon, the whole country is seen to be united by a common cause, for instance relieving the plight of the disabled or children in need. In these and other ways television tries to convince the viewer that he or she is part of the community. However the viewer is not part of the community to the extent that watching television is more of a solitary than a shared activity. Thus the actual experience of watching television is different to the experience which television is trying to give the viewer. Ironically, it is precisely the viewer's isolation that makes it easier for television to interpellate him or her and convince them that they are part of a community.

Yes—

Television assumes the viewer shares its values, values which are strengthened by constant viewing. These shared values mean that television eventually becomes a mirror in which the beholder see his or her own face. Thus the community is homogenised as an extension of one's own self and in this respect television works like advertising which confronts the consumer with his or her own reflection. Television, by offering a mirror to the viewer, somehow confirms the viewer's identity and, in doing so, dispels the need for the look of another person which is always ambiguous in that it has the potential to both affirm or refute one's sense of self. Television replaces the other's look with its own, wholly approving gaze which is really the viewer's own reflection. Television's capacity to remove the other's look is a way of both homogenising the community and undermining it since it makes the community a community of one. The homogenising function of television helps to create a culture in which class and gender divisions are covered over as they are in that much used phrase 'public opinion'. This is not to say that television necessarily contradicts real experience rather it is to suggest that television provides a condition or structure of experience which cannot register division.

Ultimately, television forces an interpretation of experience on viewers which, because of the mirror-like nature of television, they regard as their own. In this context experience is not a complex dialectic of thought, feeling and action it is something that is imposed from without. This means that it has a uniform character, a character, moreover which is the same for everyone and thus individual experiences vanish before the common one which becomes the basis of a powerful but illusory community. In this situation, where experience is imposed from without, it is difficult to learn anything new and so everything continues as it is in an eternal present.

Advertising and television create conditions of experience so that they determine not just what is experienced but also how it is experienced and this is a function of popular or mass culture generally. It is not just external but internal too and it is because it has been internalised as a condition of experience that it can act so powerfully as a form of control. Two contributors who look at popular culture as a condition of experience are Clive Bloom and Helena Blakemore. Clive Bloom, using MacDonald's as an example discusses the internationalisation of popular culture and suggests that while it reduces human stature it promotes communal security and habits. Helena Blakemore, looks at the phenomenon of Acid Houses in the context of an instant culture and shows how the conditions of experience in that culture may be changing.

The other contributors concentrate on the complex relationship between various aspects of popular culture and consumer capitalism. Andrew Smith gives an elegant account of how the Hampton Court maze calls into question the linear view of history which is implicit in the route visitors have to follow through the palace itself. Bank advertisements are the subject of Robert Chaplin's article. He argues that the images, drawn from the art world, which banks use to advertise their services, radically undermine the overt message of the advertisements revealing in the process the nature of banking itself. Gwyneth Roberts describes how ornaments are advertised in the Sunday papers noting the internal contradictions involved in the process of offering them as things which will enhance their owner's status. My own article looks at bodybuilding as an image of consumer capitalism while Adrian Page shows the paradox inherent in British Telecom's talkabout system which works to restrict communication despite its being a sign of the increased capacity for it. Paul O'Flinn takes a half-serious, half-amused look at the meaningless slogans to be found on many T-shirts which he interprets as signs of alienation and protest against a system where to do or say anything is potentially to advertise that system. Michael J. Hayes shows how power relations are to be found in so innocent a thing as a recipe while Norma Wordsworth takes a light-hearted look at Christmas saying that it almost accidentally offers us images of equable more communal ways of organising society which undermine its more evident commercialism.

Game shows are the subject of my other article in which I try to desribe the concept of knowledge which lies behind them and its implications. Graham Dawson casts his eye over all aspects of war toys. His main point, is that, unlike war toys of previous generations, today's are never sufficient in themselves. They are part of an ongoing narrative which requires the continual purchase of accessories. This not only means greater profits but, also and more insidiously, that those who use them have their fantasies constrained by the narratives which surround the toys. It is in this context that Dawson raises the issue of the ideological effects of war toys. Shelagh Young considers television counselling programmes which, she says, perpetuate the myth that problems can be solved merely by talking about them when they should really be placed in their social and economic context. She is, however, encouraged by the fewer references these programmes make to sexuality since this helps to undermine the idea that identity is determined by sexuality. Gill Simpson, like Mary Knight takes computers as her theme and asks whether or not they have come to fill the spiritual gap left by the decline of Christianity. Taking a different perspective, Mary Knight shows that, though at first computers were seen in exclusively male terms, there is now a gender instability in computer advertising which feminism can exploit to its advantage.

Deborah Cameron analyses true crime monthly magazines and argues that the murders described in them represent an act of self-affirmation or freedom which makes the murderer analogous to the figure of the free individual at the heart of capitalist ideology. Bob Brecher attacks the common argument, used to support the *Sun*'s notorious page three, that it is what people want. Brecher shows how wants are neither natural nor spontaneous but constructed. In complete contrast is John Simons' article on cricket in which he shows that while the sport is bound up with the ideology of class and imperialism there has always been an anti-capitalist strain in it, which can still provide a critical perspective on the values of consumer society. Complementing an article on cricket is one on football by Barry Emslie who provocatively suggests that Brecht's concept of theatre is more applicable to football matches where there is greater potential for Marxist action than can be found in any theatre, no matter how Brechtian. Ann Treneman gives an historical account of the women's page in the *Daily Mail* suggesting that little progress has been made over the type of issues it covers. She also notes that there is a profound contradiction on the women's page in that it questions the traditional content it affirms.

Michael Woodiwiss demythologises the popular conception of organised crime in America arguing that it is not, as successive administrations have maintained, something which is alien to American life, but on the contrary something that is intrinsic to it. In addition, Woodiwiss shows what attempts have been made to combat organised crime and what this has meant for civil liberties. Richard Bradbury is also interested in things specifically American and he considers the myth of safe and dangerous lines on the New York subway. Lez Cooke offers an analysis for the decline in cinema-going, attributing it to social and demographic factors rather than technological developments such as videos, while

Anthony Crabbe's article discusses the contradictions museums face in trying to make their exhibits accessible to the public. R. J. Ellis, in the final contribution, adopts a Barthesian approach in his analysis of the ways in which the visual representations of Ronald Reagan have created a duplicit mythic image of a modern populist-pioneer resolving the anxieties of the United States.

These articles, show in their different ways, how popular culture both reproduces and resists consumer capitalism. They are also united in the assumption that by knowing how it works the effects of popular culture can be negated. Some articles go further and imply that the forms of popular culture can be sensitive to possible changes at the deepest levels of society. It then becomes important to take the initiative and develop this situation in a radical way before these signs of change disappear or are processed by the existing order for its own benefit. Exactly how this is to be done remains an open question.

The above views are based on a conception of popular culture as external, as something outside of us and it is difficult to reconcile this view of popular culture with the one put forward in this introduction as something which is internal. There is a real problem, here, for no-one would wish to dispute that popular culture can distort reality but equally, if popular culture provides us with structures of perception, then how is it possible to get outside them so that we can make objective comments about reality? If this volume does not provide an answer to this question it is hoped that it will at least keep people talking about it.

NOTES

1. Barthes, R., *Mythologies* (London: Paladin, 1972).
2. Barthes, R., 'Change the Object Itself', in Stephen Heath (ed.), *Image Music Text* (London: Fontana/Collins, 1979) p. 167.
3. That the consumer has little sense of the past can be seen in such small things as the way in which newspapers (or indeed television) rarely follow through a story. Readers and viewers are plunged into the middle of it hardly knowing how it begins or ends.
4. Filofaxes are particularly interesting because they represent a change in the historic function of the diary which was used to record the past. The pages of the filofax, however, show the future written down before it has even happened.

2

MacDonald's Man meets *Reader's Digest*

CLIVE BLOOM

In any discussion of Western popular culture three areas always become sharply defined: what is mass or popular culture, what is American popular culture and in what ways has Europe adapted and absorbed that form of popular culture branded American, for it is this play off against Americanisation, at once so foreign and yet so familiar that is so fascinating.

In recent years the issue of popular culture has re-emerged as an important area of study for those jaded by high art and for those whose own interests coincide with the broad left interests of modern Marxism, structuralism and post-structuralism. Such an issue is a focus for considerations of taste and quality and a focus also for thoughts about traditions and what they exclude, for issues of anti-semitism, racism, misogyny and the like. This is the theoretical arena of those whose humanistic interests have opened out from specialised artistic concerns to those of a broader cultural perspective.

Before tackling the broader issue of defining mass culture we must take a glance at the history of American infiltration into Europe. Ironically, in terms of mass culture we must start with high culture. At the beginning of this century — at the point where America had already become (at least potentially) the most power-ful nation in the world with a huge industrial base, and a large naval presence, it still felt uneasy about its own importance beyond its parochial borders. At this point American artists, in order to break into the art world of London and Paris, invented a term which would coincide with mass immigration by Europeans to the United States of America and a mass exodus by American artists to Europe — the term, acting unconsciously behind American actions, was *internationalism* and it coincided with mass movements and immigrants across, and beyond, Europe and within the United States.

This internationalism which coincided with imperialist and then isolationist policies was the unspoken watchword of American intellectual and cultural exportation. To make Europeans accept the United States the United States would turn all Europe into the United States, and then give Europe back to itself now altered. The nineteenth-century prophesies of the United States as the future of the world would be fulfilled by the *internationalisation* of culture — or all culture becoming that of the United States; T. S. Eliot, Ezra Pound and Henry James saw this clearly, before them Charles Dickens, Sir Henry Irving and Colonel Cody, Thackeray, Bram Stoker and De Tocqueville. Thus a new language and a new signifying process began.

But of itself this atmosphere of acceptance, heralded by artists, writers and Coca-Cola was not enough, it required, coincidentally, the rise of new and powerful means of production, distribution and consumption. The important factor here is the growth of technological specialisation and the electric media: telegraph, telephone, and mass printing leading to the rise of the movies, radio and television.

Levi-Strauss and Henry Ford made American mass culture, as I shall define the term, possible. They created a culture which was orientated towards individualised small-scale petit bourgeois and bourgeois *consumption* which was nevertheless served by the products of large-scale industrialised production; huge conglomerate production geared towards private domestic consumption patterns. It was not the production line that made mass culture possible but the consequence and impetus of the production line, that is, the coming of *standardisation* on a *global* scale.

Take the example of MacDonald's. MacDonald's destroyed the idea of home cooking in the market place (in Britain the eel and pie shop, or fish and chip shop). These institutions had faded with the coming of the Wimpy Bar — but the Wimpy was your local quick food place, you sat in relative comfort, were served by waitresses, had the food cooked on a griddle before you and you drank imitation Italian frothy coffee. MacDonald's changed all that. You are served by automatons whose 'eat here or take away . . . have a nice day' — is learned by rote and who have no interest nor intercourse with customers — whose food is packaged beyond their view and comes in sizes from *regular* (regulation?) upwards.

You eat and then dispose of your waste without recourse to waiters. Dumb cleaners constantly patrol and sanitise your temporary living area—Tokyo or Paris or London the food is always the same. The food is good, it is healthy and MacDonald's stress the point. It is not the food that is processed but the customer. The consumer *not the consumed* is standardised. Like Ezra Pound, MacDonald's recognise the power of internationalisation as a language and as a *landscape* of signs. MacDonald's represents the pleasures of the repetition compulsion which is a name Freud gave to industrial man's automatic habits of standardisation. This is both a reduction of human stature and an elevation to the happiness and health of communal security and communal habits. MacDonald's is a *sanctuary against change*, a guarantee of conformity and the eternal Big Mac. MacDonald's in Britain was easily absorbed—we had prepared for it since the 1950s, since popcorn, DA's, Elvis, Milk Bars, Wimpys, since Birds Eye, Lyons Maid and Walls—we learned the lessons before we got the real McCoy. The products of MacDonald's are not hamburgers but *people.*

The eating of a MacDonald's meal is like the reading of *Reader's Digest*—small, easily digested, carefully processed, carefully cut down, abridged. *Reader's Digest* gives us knowledge that is easily compartmentalised, simplified, ideologically sound—All American—All European. The consuming of *Reader's Digest* (note the name *Digest*) and a MacDonald's hamburger is the same act of consumption of a landscape of significance, a locus for knowledge about the world. Both are safe, both sanitised, both proclaim the dangers of tasting outside; the world is full of sharks,—at MacDonald's we've got time for you! The big *M* in the sky, like the Coca-Cola flow-line symbol is the equivalent of *Reader's Digest's* cold-war anti-communism—homely, old-fashioned, communal, friendly, *family orientated*: mass production with private, domestic consumption values built in.

Everything I have said points to the insidiousness of goodness. This may partly be so—we desire familiar landscapes which are always happy, but this new world which is now nearly 100 years old tells us that the old humanistic concerns of inside and outside will no longer do. There is not alienation in this environment but total inclusion—a type of claustrophobia. We cannot get outside this process, but we can examine it and experience it in different ways. That is why the question of values, meaning the need to escape, will not do. We can listen to Bach in our Levi 501s without the slightest cultural migraine. Internationalism will close all the doors sooner or later and this is neither a good nor a bad thing in itself—the landscape needs to be navigated to give us back our humanity should we feel we have lost it.

All this is not a dreadful effect of American imperialism. Rupert Murdoch learnt the lessons and took over Twentieth Century Fox (he had to become an American to succeed, however). The process is now multinational and outside any individual country's cultural hegemony.

What do we want from American culture which is mass culture, lived fragmentedly? We want the old myth certainly: the desire for the exercise of the power of unlimited freedom, Levis and cowboys, but we want the other dream: the freedom of unlimited power, J. Edgar Hoover and Al Capone. We internalise and desire imperialist manners: the need to give law, to organise and administer and subjugate others, but there are no others, the others are ourselves for we internalise the disciplines of power and become the subjected subjects of our *own* responses to what *we desire* to *be given* to us in mass culture. That is why talk of Madison Avenue, Park Avenue, New York Jewish media conspiracy won't work for the *standardised need* coincides with a standardised product.

What we admire in *Dallas*, what fascinates and repels us is the *total domestic* arena for the exercise of the freedom of power and the power of freedom. Money metamorphoses into sexuality and displays of lust—money signifies only as our absence—its vastness, millions of dollars, negates its presence, but it creates a landscape, and it signifies. For *Dallas* could not work on radio where language barriers would increase differences in culture. It works on television by creating a visual image, and a *cultural gesture* that does *not* rely on any acting skills. *Dallas* is the exemplar of the new myth of information technology.

The BBC cannot help but buy *Dallas*—not merely because it is cheaper to buy in an already made product rather than produce our own, but because *Dallas* is a place of entry into a standardised consumer market place. It is not a matter of freedom of choice, for there is none. And this works both ways. *Dynasty* imported English actors to lend *class* and demonic style as did *The Colbys* and now so is *Dallas* itself. *Dynasty*—the very name undermines the American belief in democracy and self-help. Both gloat over the family as the battleground of the power of the industrial process. *Moonlighting* takes this a step further with the new male, new female—aids-conscious couple gaining wedded bliss without intercourse — babies are found at the baby supermarket.

How then can we sum up in a sentence or two a possible lead in to a definition of mass culture? <u>Mass culture is the creation of a desire and a production process.</u> It comes into being when mass production and standardisation techniques are able to find a mass urban audience whose desires are specialised, domesticised and monetarily satisfiable using techniques of cheap mass communication.

Mass culture is not a uniform block activity. It is not however folk art generated from a peasant community — it must have mass organs to promote it. Importantly it creates a petit bourgeois world of safe interiors filled with the objects we *own* — it bars the door and acts as a policeman against the world outside. It promotes paranoia at all levels. It penetrates all levels of society piecemeal and is consumed piecemeal, it integrates the highest art with the lowest because all is processed — genred, equalised. It is neither good nor bad nor a condition of modern experience for it is *the* condition of modern experience.

3

Acid – Burning a Hole in the Present

HELENA BLAKEMORE

It has been said before, and will no doubt be said again: cultural phenomena (trends, styles, fashions) do not arise spontaneously. Rather, they are either reactions against or a further development of already or previously existing phenomena (even if these were only on the fringes of mass culture or 'underground'). To become 'popular', they do not need the wholesale participation of wide sections of the community, only widespread recognition of their influence.

Acid House is one such modern phenomenon. Quite where the name originally came from remains uncertain: possibly the first single to be released was 'Acid Trax' by Phuture, and the sound originated as 'House' in Chicago, where 'acid burn' is a slang phrase for stealing—'sampling' (lifting sections of a previous record and incorporating them into new tracks) being intrinsic to Acid music and effectively stealing. In addition, the taking of the drug 'acid' (LSD) has become one of the hallmarks of the movement in mass media coverage ('Innocent face of Acid House hides a sinister drug world', headline in *Today* newspaper, 12 September 1988).

The revival of the popularity of the 1960s and early 1970s drug LSD is one of several constant elements which mark the phenomenon of Acid House. What is perhaps most interesting to consider is the way in which this, alongside the other trademarks of the movement, can be delineated into two quite specific categories. The first of these is a harking back to and revival of past trends: LSD, psychedelia, smoke machines and strobe lighting, 'smiley' badges, and a friendly 'love and peace'-type philosophy ('matey' being a very common slang phrase). The second is quite contradictory, that of futuristic high technology in the production of music (a fleet of Roland synthesisers and drum machines are the norm), programming and sampling, minimal lyrics and melody, the emphasis being on rhythm and hi-energy, and on the immediacy of the experience — 'instant' culture, elicited by means of gadgets which produce frequency changes and a pre-determined rate of beats-per-minute in a style that is constantly developing (Chicago House to the Ibizan Balaeric Beat to the English Acid House, for example). And further, the protagonists are far from the drop outs of earlier years and instead tend to be the ambitious high-achievers who have become synonymous with the Thatcherite years, the artists being not groups but individual producers and DJs, and their followers are frequently career-minded and high-earning individuals. In addition, these artists are rarely identifiable as such (with the exception of those brought into the wider commercial market, whose music is suitably moderated by the addition of additional lyrics, for example), and as a result they offer no heroes or role models, as musicians/pop stars have done in the past.

At this point, a comment about the experience of Acid House becomes necessary. Although the extent of involvement of LSD and the newer designer-drug Ecstasy remains difficult to verify (underplayed by those involved, exaggerated by the media), the effects they produce are closely allied to other elements of the phenomenon. Apart from their hallucinogenic properties, the drugs heighten the senses and give the user a feeling of increased energy and a loss of inhibitions, for up to eight hours. Acid clubs (frequently held one night of the week in already established clubs) often open their doors late in the evening, and punters will still be going strong at dawn. With the music regulated to very specific beats-per minute (122 to 135), comprising a relentless rhythm and phased synthesised sound with little form, melody or lyrical content, one track being barely distinguishable from another (any discernable change in the beat would detract from the momentum of the evening), an almost hypnotic, trance-like state can be produced in the dancers. It is undoubtedly a group rather than an individual experience (the term 'matey' re-emphasising the vital elements of friendliness, getting on with people, no hassle, no 'aggro'), but the group is not a trendy, clique-ridden one as is common in other types of club — it is more akin to the 1960s, reinforced by T-shirts sporting logos such as the familiar 'Turn On, Tune In, Drop Out', and 'Drop Acid Not Bombs', 'Have a Nice Trip' and the wonderful 'Free Your Mind and Your Ass Will

Follow', and clothes which are not elitist fashion as seen elsewhere recently but worn for comfort and freedom of movement. All in all, the end result is the submersion of the individual into a group experience which is a cross between a 'family' gathering of technologically-inspired hippies and a night out with mindless robots. This should not sound so disapproving as it perhaps does for this is not a condemnation. Instead, I am interested in an examination of what seems to be a fundamental change in contemporary cultural life, or, to be more specific, a shift in the way in which life is experienced.

Any individual phenomenon such as Acid House, seems fairly easy to dismiss in serious terms as superficial and ultimately transient. It is possible, however, to look at Acid House in terms of other popular contemporary trends, in which case it becomes evident that this is not, in fact, an isolated incident, but rather one aspect of a much larger movement within Western culture (specifically British, but extending towards Europe and the United States), of which Acid House is but one manifestation. The reason Acid House warrants such close attention is not because it is fundamentally different to the others, but on the contrary because it is fundamentally the same. Elements in it can also be found in other cultural manifestations and it is therefore possible to align these to Acid House as a central, although it would be misleading to suggest motivating or causal, phenomenon.

The most obvious features of Acid House are the combination of the revival and futuristic aspects, and the elements of 'instant culture' (music produced without pre-planning, and constantly changing). One can immediately highlight similar effects in other cultural areas: instant coffee, 'quickie' divorces and immediate access to and bombardment by information through highly developed technology are some which spring to mind. And in broader 'lifestyle' terms, it is difficult, even on the High Street, to avoid the nostalgia of Laura Ashley and William Morris or to ignore the plethora of Victorian/Edwardian fireplaces destined for painstakingly renovated city houses or the cottages of the newly-country-loving Barbour-clad yuppies. At the same time, nineteenth-century warehouses in cities around England are being gutted and filled with the latest in hi-tech furniture and appliances. They are always the latest (just as the renovated is always authentic)—last year's model may be substantially cheaper and perfectly adequate, be it a car, a computer, a hi-fi or an item of clothing, but if it is not the latest it is dispensable. Objects are not made (or marketed) to last, merely to be used until the new model is available. Who wants last year's remote control, when you can have a 'squarer, flatter screen'? Advertising consistently reflects this: the 'squarer, flatter screen' uses computer graphics, the 'appliance of science' is, the implication goes, extra-terrestrial in origin, Earth is preferable to Mars (given the choice) because it is the home of Guinness, while robots (given the option) drive Volvos. Meanwhile, Levis, Britvic, Ford and Carling all use the nostalgia of 1960s hits such as 'Heard it through the Grapevine', 'I only Want to Be with You' and 'He Ain't Heavy, He's my Brother' to sell what are effectively identical products. (One interesting result—and surely gratifying for the advertisers—is that the re-cords are being re-released, achieving success a second time around, and further adding to the nostalgic movement which includes films like 'Shag', 'Peggy Sue Got Married' and 'Buster'.)

It would be inaccurate, however, to suggest that the popularity of revivals is anything new—there have, for example, been 1950s revivals (of clothing, music and style) since the beginning of the 1960s, and James Dean and Marilyn Monroe have never ceased to be two of the most popular posters/images around. What seems to be happening now is slightly different though: the divergent trends of nostalgia and 'futurism' are leaving a gap in the present. Nostalgic revival is becoming more prevalent, and what is new and contemporary is becoming increasingly short-lived, with people always looking towards the next acquisition, the next trend, never satisfied with what is (merely) the latest available. What is 'present' thus becomes transient and ephemeral, almost unworthy of recog-nition. In the case of Acid House music, this is because the technology which permits the production of this style of music also allows for its continuous development—rock 'n' roll has always been changing, it is only quicker now because new technology allows it to be so. The improvements made in the technology during the last five years have led to massive leaps forward in its capabilities, alongside dramatic reductions in price, making it more accessible to a greater number of people.

Taking as many of these elements as one may wish to include, the conclusions do seem to imply a coherence in attitude. The use of drugs and hypnotic 'techno-psychedelic' music mean that the present is experienced in terms of sensation rather than anything more tangible; houses and jobs are viewed increasingly by the young in terms of an ambitious means to an end rather than enjoyment, satisfaction or long-term security; education is becoming increasingly industrially or commercially orientated, whilst those in the arts are having to defend in commercial terms their function, purpose and even the place the arts have in the community, no longer being accepted as a necessary part of the cultural life of the community.

The implications of this change in the nature of experience would seem to be closely tied in with our experience of time. Acid House is but one example of the way in which the past is being resurrected and appropriated by means of modern technology, which at the same time is altering it in such a way that what is manifested becomes not 'the past' but effectively a mere imitation of it. While our experience of the present may become increasingly rich in acquisitive material terms, from an aesthetic, sensual or intellectual point of view it seems there is less that is specifically set in the present, and that which *is* fixed appears to be for instant consumption and assimilation rather than considered appreciation. Current television programmes such as Network 7 and Wired, for instance, exemplify and promote contemporary cultural trends, broadcasting in short bursts and quick flashes information which has to be instantly absorbed, not allowing for questioning or debate. As with Acid House, the information is experienced rather than considered. And as with other phenomena, the items in question are transitory, the information disposable.

Quite what effect these new ways of experience will have is unclear. On the one hand, it is certain that they are part of the long-term development of human experience/communication as a whole, which has moved from the spoken to the written word and more recently to visual images, each requiring more sophisticated skills. On the other hand, however, it would appear that the late 1980s are lacking a constant identity (as compared to the 1940s, 1950s or 1960s, for instance), and this further suggests that there is also a lack of stability. If our experience is indeed that of either a nostalgically-revived past or of a transient, insubstantial and forward-looking present, and bearing in mind that the medium of experience is time, then the implications may be that as time is being destroyed, so experience is lost also, and life becomes a series of rose-coloured memories and yearnings for Utopian futures — and that would be a shame.

4

Hampton Court Revisited: A Re-evaluation of the Consumer

ANDREW SMITH

The Palace

Hampton Court is not for the hurried visitor. A treasure trove of royal history, architectural gems, great paintings and stunning gardens, its delights are best experienced at a leisurely pace, with frequent rests along the way, simply to take stock. Whether a student of history, a lover of beauty or a keen gardener, there is something for everyone, which is why many visitors come back time and again. Hampton Court grows with the knowing. [An official guide book.[1]]

The Hampton Court maze survives as a relic of the Wilderness Gardens created by William III's royal gardeners in the 1690s. Its status in relation to the Palace is a peripheral one, its current survival based on the assumption that it functions as an idiosyncratic quirk in contrast to the organised sedentary of the main gardens. However, in one important sense the maze, or more exactly the idea of the maze, signifies at a cultural level; and this is manifested through the way in which the deceptions, reversals and trickery of the maze apply to the ways in which knowledge is consumed within the Palace itself.

In effect the maze makes this explicit in that not only is the consumer ultimately deceived about his/her relationship to the forces of consumption, but this deception becomes disguised as an act of fun. What is required in the maze is not the idea of an idealised product to consume, but an ideal of what comes to constitute the idealised consumer, who is granted this status in being able to effectively map his/her route, to follow the signs so that discovery and completion become dependent upon acceptance of a formal set of unspoken rules. Added to this there is a search for a regularised consumer who can also function within a desired ethical code ('Do Not Litter', 'Keep Off The Grass') and who in effect can operate as self-policing.

At Hampton Court, the experience of the maze is thus to formalise many of the conceptions about knowledge, and the way in which it is to be consumed, that are expressed within the Palace itself. Any deception which takes place within the use of knowledge, is not here defined in terms of there potentially existing an authentic knowledge which is being disguised, but that it is the relationship between the consumer and the product which is being disguised.

What is sold in the Palace is history, and by extension value. The way in which this is achieved is through a two-fold process, namely authenticity and consensus. The visitor is confronted with a myriad of bedchambers, halls, closets, dining rooms and lobbies, all of which attest to some genuine historical feature; such as the Wolsey rooms, King William III's bedchamber, George I's private chamber, the Prince of Wales' appartments, Queen Mary's closet. The attempt is somehow to bring history to life, to make it as colourful and 'realistic' as possible, the paintings in these rooms reflecting their respective occupants (an exaggerated example of this process can be found at Hever Castle, where wax works of Anne Boleyn and her family are used for similar ends). The enterprise is thus not solely dependent upon revealing these rooms as testaments to sovereign rule, but as literal portraits of specific historical characters.

In one sense there is a certain cultural schizophrenia bound up in this process, in that the consumer is asked to assimilate extreme historical shifts. This is possible because there is the implication that somehow the knowledge which is on display is 'permanent', it is read from one selective direction, whilst paradoxically being 'court-up' within the frames of many histories. It is this suggestion of permanence, of a monistic approach, which becomes reinforced in the idea of a genealogy of sovereign succession of an inevitable and so unavoidable train of cause and effect. Thus any idea of history as being created and formed through antagonisms, through any kind of process of historical materialism is a priori precluded. It is in this sense that the information becomes selective and this idea of selectivity is reflected not only in the notion of royal selection of descent and ascent, but also in the formulation of a hierarchy which is reflected both internally (spatially) and externally (architecturally).

In touring the building there is a route which the consumer is required to follow, this route is in fact the same route which any of the sovereign's subjects were required to follow when it was a royal residence. Each room which is entered is more exclusive than the one which preceded it; so that the route goes via (in the case of the King) a staircase, a Guard chamber, the King's First Presence chamber, King's Second Presence chamber, to the King's Audience chamber; after that the rooms become increasingly exclusive to the degree of their personalisation, with the state bedchamber, the dressing room through to, but not open for the public, the King's writing closet. The attempt here is to reveal two sides to an abstract personality, the official royal process juxtaposed with the intimate and private. This operates on the level of 'King' as an abstract concept; abstract to the degree that it is a theory of hierarchy which is being sold here, which has the effect of transcending the historical portraiture in its overall view of the royal process. In effect because it is abstract it fulfils the idea of social distance from his/her subjects required of a palace, whilst simultaneously providing accessibility to a general theory of social mobility uninterrupted by intrusive personal detail.

This ideal is reflected externally in terms of the hierarchal use of window space, as one guide book puts it; 'Wren's building was conceived not in isolation but the centrepiece of a vast formal landscape in which buildings and garden were carefully integrated to form a unified whole'.[2] The large sash windows for the state appartments are given greater architectural significance than the smaller windows used to light the lodging rooms for court members, so that the shape, size and variety of the windows reflects the internal planning of the palace itself, and by extension the internal mechanism of any social discourse constructed in hierarchical terms. What the ideal consumer is being asked to buy, is not here solely a ready made history of the Kings and Queens of England, but a general theory of systems of domination which are revealed to be resonant with historical forces. In effect the consumer is being asked to accept two basic premises, and it is here that the idea of consensus succeeds or fails, one is that systems of domination constructed in terms of ultimate power (and here Henry VIII's marital history is used to significant effect) offer stability and the second is that this process is historically inevitable and in itself desirable. There is thus a reification of domination at Hampton Court which is not solely confined to its celebration of sovereign rule, but is heavily grounded in the processes of capitalist enterprise itself. This is because what the regularised, calculable, consumer offers is an acceptance of domination inherent in the relationship between consumer and economic and cultural consumption, and it is because of this that 'meaning', as Raymond Williams says, is 'never simply expressed', but 'produced',[3] that is it has to become defined in terms of an ideal manifestation, which is produced within the consumer, who to some degree consents to this; that is to say there is an element of ideological allegiance at play here which takes on the form of a directly social and political consensus about the functioning of systems of domination.

This process is based on the acceptance of certain features to do with 'court etiquette' and 'sovereign privilege', and this is reflected in certain of the exhibits, as in the tapestries in the Great Watching Chamber, three of which depict episodes from Petrarch's Triumphs; significantly they are that of Death over Chastity, Fame over Death and Time over Fame. Individuals become irrelevant to historical forces, they are caught up in the supposedly autonomous, but shaped, lumbering expressions of history. Individuals are thus shaped by history not vice versa or even by negotiation, in the same way in which the visitor is defined in terms of his/her ability to consume, not his/her ability to produce. Thus the problem of sovereignty in a consumerist culture:

> . . . serves only to mask the real transformation in the operation of power which takes place with the emergence of the bourgeois state: it conceals the expansion and consolidation of a disciplinary power, and of an ever-tightening coercive control of the body and of normalising 'technologies of behaviour'.[4]

The visitor's route is pre-planned, regulated, a 'personal' tape recorder offers the myth of individualism (of 'free enterprise'), whilst simultaneously guiding the consumer in specific directions, formulating specific conclusions about the inevitability of political and social hierarchy, which ironically, as suggested, lampoons the very status of the visitor through the process of the selective dissemination of knowledge.

This means that any idea of historical investigation on the part of the consumer is chanelled in regulated directions, and there are prohibitions in operation in order to enforce this. The curators within the palace do not function as guides so much as a means of the enforcement of the 'tour', ensuring that consumers follow the correct directions making it impossible to backtrack. Exhibits are distanced, sanitised (removed of context) and labelled for easy consumption. Consumers are permitted only to see so much, the writing closet in the King's dressing room, at the centre of personal sovereign disclosure, is not open to the public. Likewise many of the less grandiose aspects of the palace, such as the Master Carpenter's court, the King's beer seller, and the Privy Kitchen are made inaccessible, in effect two aspects of hierarchy are evaded here, in terms of what the palace has to offer, the ultimately personal and the idea of labour which has sustained this hierarchy.

This works at a cultural level only if the consumer agrees that both are irrelevant to the maintenance of systems domination; the process is thus politically sanitised to the degree that the idea of manual labour remains hidden. By removing the idea of manual labour from the context of hierarchy it becomes possible to avoid any formulation of exploitation, and by keeping the King's inner sanctum secret, it supplies power with an inaccessibility which gives it the desired political mystique and social distance.

The abstract idea of hierarchy is further developed through an approach to culture, in which the palace becomes a bastion of 'high art' paradoxically at odds with its sub-textual reliance on capitalist popular-culture as a means of support. The palace associates itself with Pope's 'Rape of the Lock', suggests that Shakespeare may have acted there in *Measure for Measure*, other references are made to Skelton and Morden.[5] The effect of this is to develop in the consumer a sense of social and cultural awe; and it is here that paradoxes about knowledge begin to surface.

The consumer is asked to share in the abstract celebration of systems constructed in terms of domination, whilst simultaneously being inculcated with the idea of social and class distinctions from which they are necessarily precluded. As one guide book reminds the consumer; '. . . Hampton Court Palace remains a royal palace and is used for state and other functions by members of the royal family.'[6] In effect there opens up a paradox in the formulation of the regularised consumer in that they are being asked both to participate in, to share in its celebration of social divisiveness, and to act as voyeur to that from which they are excluded.

The production of knowledge at Hampton Court begins to take on an increasingly contradictory character, and this is in part bound up with its multiple identities. Hampton Court can be identified as part palace, part museum, part castle, part architectural period piece and part medieval folly; meaning that knowledge becomes packaged in many forms but is sold as one, it is 'a harmonious blend'.[7] This attempt to sell many identities contemporaneously is reliant upon a conceptualisation of the consumer as ultimately exploited by many forces. Hampton Court is thus not only a celebration of hierarchies, but extracted from this is the reification of a market economy in which the consumer is able to consume promiscuously and unreflectively. One spin-off of this is shown in the varied form which souvenirs take, as in jig-saws, key rings, finger-puppets, pencils, 'cartoon histories' and pop-up cut-out characters, none of which as objects are relevant to the internal organisation of Hampton Court but which become expressions of the consumer's ability to consume.

This multi-packaging of knowledge, of historical, social, cultural and political forms can be best explained via the notion of 'bricolage', which is of significance here because in it lies the possibility of altering the existing construction of knowledge for radical ends. In bricolage:

> Together, object and meaning constitute a sign, and, within any one culture, such signs are assembled, repeatedly, into characteristic forms of discourse. However, when the bricoleur relocates the significant object in a different position within that discourse, using the same overall repertoire of signs, or when that object is placed within a different total ensemble, a new discourse is constituted, a different message conveyed.[8]

Thus the question becomes one of re-alignment, in which the relationship between consumer and capitalist is altered. One method of approach would involve attacking some of the basic precepts about knowledge and its relationship to history which is the essential product that Hampton Court has to sell. There is the suggestion at Hampton Court that somehow knowledge is permanent, and this is a useful idea (or ideology) to propagate because it creates and caters for a convenient regularised consumer, being regularised, defined, precisely because it becomes unnecessary to introduce any notion of historical fluctuation or historical discontinuity, which is not so easily assimilated. So then, there is the creation of a regularised consumer who is sold a regularised, easily assimilated product and, as suggested, it is easily assimilable because there is a consensus and an ideological rapport with such ideas in a money-based, consumer orientated society.

At Hampton Court then, there exists the myth of a permanent (in capitalist terms ideal) history of succession and accession which is manifested through its privileging of the notion of hierarchy. To attack this formulation of knowledge thus becomes an attack on hierarchy itself and by extension on the relationship between consumer and capitalist.

To achieve this it becomes necessary to change the way in which knowledge is packaged. If the experience of Hampton Court is to suggest that the more things change the more they stay the same, it means that to modify this it becomes necessary to de-formalise many of the knowledge claims that operate to sustain this mechanistic process.

The manner in which hierarchy is celebrated through the use of selective historical detail, requires in some fashion to be reshaped, resulting in a redefinition of the forces of production. It is here that the ambiguity within the theory of the maze begins to reassert itself, because what the maze suggests is that signifying practices are to some extent open, in the sense that it is possible to read, to redirect, to traverse and to hesitate over the process of signification, or to produce meaning through activity. With the maze although there is one 'conventional' reading, that discovery and completion of the maze is dependent upon an understanding of its purposefulness, nevertheless what the idea of the maze introduces is a theory of deliberation; and although in the palace there is the idea that it is, 'best experienced at a leisurely pace . . .' this is starkly at odds with the way in which history is conveniently packaged; the tape-recorded tour lasts for an hour in which, 'to experience nearly five centuries of English history',[9] or as the Tower of London boasts in its advertising 'see 900 years of history in 3 hours'. Information is necessarily condensed to the degree to which it is simplified for easy consumption.

The absorption of this knowledge, through its catering for a hypothetical regularised consumer is dependent upon it not drawing attention to itself through the introduction of historical alternatives, through avoiding any suggestion that a signifying practice can in some fashion be open to different approaches. So that in the palace, unlike the maze, the consumer is not lead through a labyrinth of possibilities, because its celebration of historical fact precludes any notion of possibility. The problematic of reclaiming this knowledge for radical ends thus entails translating some of the cultural premises of the maze to the palace itself, whilst attempting to avoid the notion of a 'correct' reading which the maze has as its ultimate option. This is itself in some degree paradoxical in the sense that the maze produces the idea of choice whilst simultaneously directing it in certain ways and this is intrinsic to its basic structure, its basic purpose. It thus becomes necessary to transpose what is useful from the maze for radical ends, and if what the maze has to offer is at heart consumer choice, then what is also required is a re-appraisal of the forces of production.

The problem then becomes one of creating a knowledge from within the process of production which is in some way open-ended, which is simultaneously reflective and self-reflective and it is possible to achieve this through a conceptualisation of knowledge which is in Althusser's terms 'overdetermined'[10] and there exists within the palace the possibility of achieving this through its multiple identities, which are condensed to the extent that they all become part of the same product, being all packaged as one identity. By redefining these identities, by making them distinct, it necessarily reintroduces the idea of historical relativity; each identity can in some fashion thus be seen as somehow determining and being determined by the other identities which are on offer; non-identity can also function in this process so that that which is excluded (the idea of ultimate sovereign privacy and the extreme economic and social opposite of this in manual labour) becomes significant.

This in turn redefines the consumer as being a free agent in this process, to the extent that it re-introduces the idea of history, and by extension knowledge, as being created through forces and pressures which are not necessarily its own. This also has the effect of radically altering the consumer and capitalist relationship, because the consumer begins to take on an active role in the process of interpretation which such an open-ended approach to knowledge would stimulate. The consumer would then cease to be defined as a regulatable entity and would become actively involved in the process of production itself. It opens up a cultural space in which the consumer is able to assimilate knowledge in terms of social and political negotiation. Juxtaposing the respective claims to knowledge which the varied identities suggest, and thus broadening the context in which history, knowledge and value is produced.

There thus exists at Hampton Court the concrete possibility of re-aligning its knowledge claims for radical ends, freeing the consumer to become an active participant in the interpretive process and thus introducing the idea of the consumer not as a passive unit of productive forces but as a reflective historical investigator. 'Hampton Court grows with the knowing.'

NOTES

1. Oughton, E. et al., *Hampton Court Palace* (London: The Department of the Environment, 1988) p. 26.
2. Chettle, C. H. and J. Charlton, *Hampton Court Palace* (Edinburgh: HMSO, 1982) p. 30.
3. Williams, R., *Marxism and Literature* (Oxford: Clarendon, 1978) p. 166.
4. Dews, P., *Logics of Disintegration: post-structuralist thought and the claims of critical theory* (London: Verso, 1987) p. 161. Please note that Dews is here less expressing an opinion than passing comment on M. Foucault's concept of the subject via a critique of power and discourse.
5. Oughton, E. et al., op. cit. see pp. 4, 8, 12, 17.
6. Ibid., p. 23.
7. Ibid., p. 5.
8. Clarke, J., quoted in D. Hebdige, *Subculture: the Meaning of Style* (London: Methuen, 1986) p. 104.
9. Oughton, E. et al., op. cit., p. 5.
10. Althusser, L., *For Marx*, translated B. Brewster (Harmondsworth: Penguin, 1969) pp. 87–128.

5

Henry's Paperweight: The Banks and TV Advertising

ROBERT M. CHAPLIN

The homeless and the bootless; what is their place in the high-consumption, self-serving, money-oriented, property-owning democracy of late corporate capitalism? The easy answer is none, they have no place and no place can be made for them in a non-society where each member stands or fails by his or her own efforts. So perhaps it should be a surprise to see just those homeless[1] and the bootless[2] parade across the television screen promoting a bank's services. It is not only these disenfranchised that are pressed into promotion of the financial institutions; monsters snap and guzzle a path across a desolate landscape;[3] paranoiac visions crash and threaten their way across the corner of our living rooms;[4] a game of amusement arcade skill and dexterity is played across the façade of a high street bank.[5] All these are linked by a curious relation of borrowing and exchange, of money and imagery.

What is being chosen to represent the financial institutions forms a fascinating mix of the popular, the fantastic and the highbrow. Where they are brought together, and what brings them together, is television. Television has a great appetite for all things imaginable. Its dubious achievement is to reduce all imagery to one condition of perception, the immediate, which is the image of television. This is to abbreviate all those sources which the medium uses and deal only with the superficial, the easily assimilable or already digested. By the same token it displays a careless power of collage. The exclusive energy of this activity makes it discontinuous; the substance of the object remains intact in the transfer of surface. The concept of transfer and transference[6] has psychoanalytic implications which are not to be lost in this discussion. Alongside these there will also arise the notions of the palimpsest and the 'mystic writing-pad'.[7] The irruptions in the palimpsest and the ghostly scribbles which appear on the pad occur in the coincidence of messages, of one breaking into the other and forcing a misreading. The clear text is undone as other partial texts are revealed in the fabric of its structure.

The overlaying or interweaving of texts in our examples are those of popular entertainment, sculpture, the financial system and television itself. A peculiar feature of the medium is its narrative flair, it can tell a story about anything, and it can sell anything, and these two characteristics meet in the commercial. The reputation of British television in this field is unequalled, if at times derided as being more concerned with entertainment than the product, which is still nonetheless generally obliged to make some appearance. This poses a problem in our examples, what is the product? It is the invisible operation of banks, the movement of money and the making of money, loans and borrowing, investment and interest. The advertisers concentrate their efforts on the human, visible transactions of banking, the customer-bank exchange. And what do they make of it? In one instance of fugitive client is persistently deflected from satisfaction by a series of aggressively inquiring others from whom he is seeking aid. In another, an emaciated figure in a land of equally malnourished natives is blessed by the loan given by a bank to manufacture and sell shoes. Yet another instance has a rural family group driven by the extreme conditions of their existence to call upon a bank to salvage their lives with a loan for shelter. As a contrast another client enjoys the electrifying sensation of playing the money game as pinball.

These scenarios are derived from, respectively, a film based upon a science fiction novel, a Giacometti-like sculpture, a Henry Moore-like sculpture and a particular scene from a film of a 'rock opera'. In the last the player instigates the game via the cash-dispenser set in the bank's wall. The two sculptures are animated in short narratives while the first is a lengthy evocation of the mood of the film. None of these are current images, they are recalled from a recent, or the not so recent, past. The pinball wizard from *Tommy* is some 15 years old now, the Giacommetti and the Moore look-a-likes perhaps forty, the film *Bladerunner* from 1982. It is a curious mixture and one with no obvious connections.

Why these images? In the instance of the Giacometti how can an effigy of deprivation become a symbol of opportunity? The figures which stride rather aimlessly to a jolly tune in the advert were wrought in the angst of Existentialism. Giacometti, a friend of Sartre, once more turned away from the model in 1940, away from realism toward a relation with reality, to the fact of one's existence. In this second phase of his career the forms began to shrink, attenuate and rarefy. Despite the artist's repeated attempts to return to the full figure he was terrorised by the shrinkage of the form; size and volume were reduced until the continued existence of the piece was threatened. These eroded creatures cling to their space in an atmosphere which seems itself corrosive of their substance. The lonely introverted symbols which the sculptures become occupy a world devoid of passion or purpose except that of being, of existing. What other form is conjured up by this wasted figure? What other group of figures wanders stick-thin and fragile across our screen? What other group has such a perilous and delicately balanced existence as this twig-like population? Any news broadcast from the Third World will show them to us; the dying peoples of sub-Saharan Africa.

Contemporary with Giacometti and now united via the ad-man's ingenuity is Henry Moore. On a storm-swept hillside a monumental family group is sufficiently discomforted by conditions to seek shelter. They stir their massive forms and stomp off down the hill and after suitable negotiations take up residence in an unoccupied dolmen. The familiar group is typical of Moore's post-war bronzes, large, public and thematic. Persistent in this is a 'truth to material' which is a peculiarly British doctrine and continues through the work of Barbara Hepworth. In this tradition are concerns of Truth, Substance and Scale, which contrast neatly with the existentialist doubt, withering and shrinkage of Giacometti's work. The tottering gait of the stick figures is contrasted with the purposeful progress of Truth on the move when the monument of the family comes home to the megalithic shelter against the exigencies of the world. A criticism of Moore's later work is that it pursues the masterpiece, the definitive and the final, that it closes on the movement of enquiry. Even his open works turn in on themselves, the within is firmly part of the enfolding form, without being introspective, merely contained; the combining forms are neatly interlocking and exclusive. The works seem resistant, but when threatened turn to a reassuring fundamental, the origin one could say, the truth of material, the very stone of truth. The monument which houses the monumental family is not hewn or fashioned, mediated, but remains true and singular. The truth to material maintains this integrity, man's mediation is within and sympathetic to his origin. The journey from hilltop to home is a return to true nature.

A series of oppositions can be made here; of monument and relic, the durability of the first and the fragility of the second; the metaphysics of origin and the existential condition; substance against decay; truth against doubt. All are contained, in the overall strategy of the advertising campaign, within a structure of exchange and of value; that is the banking system of the Capitalist Western world. This is no place to go into the whole dynamics of that system but the operations of the banking system bear heavily in this argument. Rex Butler writes of the 'debt bomb' in 'Buying Time'[8] where he likens the Third World operations of the Western banks to that of the balance of terror tactics of nuclear deterrence. The final exchange, nuclear or financial, when the debt is finally called in, is devastating and all are losers. Ultimately the banks can do nothing about debt on the scale of Third World, except to keep the debt going. Their own, and the whole of Western society's best interests are served by lending more to pay the interest on the loan. The paradox is that the strength is now with the weak, if the creditor nations called in the debt or the debtor nations were allowed to default the whole system would collapse as confidence fails. The only way the strong remain superior is to allow the new distribution of power, to lend more to pay old debts. A significant proportion of Western bank investments are made as loans to developing countries, what began as risk venture has become crisis management.

Which returns us to the television campaign and the pinball-bank where, to an accompaniment reminiscent of The Who's tune 'Pinball Wizard', the whole edifice flashes as the bank is 'played'. It is best to be reminded that the hero of this rock opera was severely disabled; deaf, dumb and blind, a naive and abused child whose singular talent was to play the pinball tables. The game, a combination of chance and skill, could act as a metaphor for the actual operation of the banks as players in the real game of international finance. The ball that must be kept in play is the burden of debt, whether local or international, it is the only way the score of interest is accumulated. The customer who introduces the debt which energises the entire structure is the one who maintains it with further demands. Tommy, the pinball wizard, is helped to the table, 'becomes part of the machine', 'plays by sense of smell'[9] and amasses the highest score. The mechanism of the machine is mysterious while the player is further disadvantaged by a complete inability to comprehend the operation of the machine on even the most basic level. He cannot see, hear or question, his sole abilities are touch and smell. The game is played, the score piles up and to maintain any sort of creditability the player must continue increasing the score. Who is the player with his finger on the button of the bank credit machine?

The fun of the game, the pleasurable diversion it affords, is paid for when reality impinges on the illusion, when the delusion of power is overtaken by the delusion of persecution. Philip K. Dick the author of *Do Androids Dream of Electric Sheep?*,[10] filmed as 'Bladerunner', is most concerned with reality and illusion, authenticity and the fake. The film concerns the pursuit and capture of escaped androids, perfect replicas of humans, and the confusion this causes. What is reality and what false is the theme of the film where scepticism turns to paranoia and threats abound as the secure is shaken by doubt. The mood of the film is established in the scenes of a decadent near-future, anxious, menacing, ominous. The same atmosphere is created in another advert, with no disguise of its source. A customer, seeking an authentic response to his enquiry, is met with a series of various negative reactions. The client is constrained in a paranoiac *Weltraum* of fear and anxiety, only relieved in an abreactive exchange with an apparently kindly bank employee in pleasant, recognisable and comfortable surroundings. But what is the authentic response, allowance or refusal, pleasure or reality? Where does the fear properly reside and where should scepticism be directed?

A particular image is being sought in these commercials using already established imagery which bring a burden of significance which cannot be shed in a shift of context, indeed as a palimpsest it operates to subvert the context and expose other readings. These exchanges between surfaces reveal a process where the financial system plays out its actual condition in relation to certain chosen objects which represent that real situation. The smoothness of the television advert is broken up as these borrowed images disrupt its surface. What emerges in the overwritten surface is the experience of repetition, as the banks compulsively repeat the repayment of a debt established in a false reality. The false reality is that of money itself, the self-referential body. The removal of control in 1968 with the departure from the gold standard allowed this speculation, the mistaken inflation of image to substance. And what television deals in is the image from the ether, the insubstantial medium. What is concretised in the overlay is the recall to reality and the exposure of the false condition. A kind of stereoscopy is induced whereby, in a shift of vision, image is transformed in its substance.

What does this stereoscopic vision reveal in these adverts: a Third World largely untouched by the power of the West; a deep-seated anxiety over the continuing ability of the banking system to prevent its own and the industrialised world's collapse, and a slide into post-industrial corporate paranoia; a longing for a security which refers to a past of simple truths; a recognition that the operations of international banking amounts to no more than the blind accumulation of interest? Only by their own ingenuity can the Giacometti puppets escape the folly of providing shoes for the hungry while Western economies demand cash crops from the starving. As more and more power slips into fewer and fewer hands a new democracy arises wherein individual responsibility and accountability replaces social obligation and collective action. The escape from the harshness of existence is made only into the more problematic construct of society, the dolmen may be rough and unhewn but it represents, like the family itself, a structure in which we must all make ourselves. There is no return to some metaphysical truth or origin. The edifice of the high street bank is exposed as a front to a speculative if skilful game whose only prize is that the game continues.

The relation of television to these observations has not yet been analysed; what role does it play? Is it merely the hard surface over which these scribbles are made, or is its role more intimately connected with our analysis? The choice of television as an advertising medium is made for many and varied reasons, the most obvious being the scope and size of the viewing audience. However the reasons for advertising may be more complex than the simple selling of a product, bank services or whatever. The wish-fulfilment appeal of so many advertisements is obvious and quite frank, but why in our chosen instances is there the use of imagery with which a great proportion of the viewers are probably unfamiliar, or whose connection is tangled? Perhaps, as the wishes of the buying public are courted in the playing out of scenes of sexual or power relations, the television is also the scene of transference for the crisis of corporate identity. The images we see are the images, good and bad, which are projected onto television as the resemblance of the primary situation; the inflation of image to substance. The mass medium of television has become the private arena where corporate business works out its relation to society.

NOTES

1. This is one of a series of commercials devised for the Royal Bank of Scotland by the agency Boas-Massini-Pollit.
2. Op. cit.
3. Op. cit.
4. A short series of commercials for Barclays Bank through the Yellowhammer agency. The film *Bladerunner* (Warner Bros., 1982) and these commercials, which draw so heavily on the scenario and set design of that film, were all directed by Ridley Scott.
5. An advert devised for NatWest by the J. Walter Thompson agency.
6. Laplanche, J. and J.-B. Pontalis, *The Language of Psychoanalysis* (London: Hogarth Press and Institute of Psychoanalysis, 1985) pp. 455–61.
7. Freud, S., *On Metapsychology—the Theory of Psychoanalysis* (London: Pelican Freud Library, 1985) vol. 11, pp. 427–34.
8. Grosz, E. A. (ed.), et al., *Future Fall: Excursions into Post-Modernity* (Australia: Power Institute of Fine Arts, University of Sydney, 1986) pp. 52–63.
9. Townsend, P., *Pinball Wizard* ('Tommy', Polydor, 1974).
10. Dick, Philip K., *Do Androids Dream of Electric Sheep* (London: Panther Group, 1972).

6

'A Thing of Beauty and a Source of Wonderment'[1]: Ornaments for the Home as Cultural Status Markers

GWYNETH ROBERTS

'A rare and exclusive edition of Collectors' Pieces for you', shouts the headline. *'Each perfect miniature is meticulously crafted and painted by hand. A unique collection to grace and enhance your home and with a numbered Certificate of Authenticity.'*[2] The advertisement, for a group of three-inch-high pottery Historic Houses, typifies the come-on for ornaments for the home by mail order: the ornaments are invariably 'rare' and 'exclusive', even if the 'Limited Edition' turns out to be 'limited' to 25 000 (there are sometimes dramatic accounts of how the mould will be broken in the presence of highly respectable independent witnesses after the limit is reached, no matter how many desperate collectors—or, variously, connoisseurs—beg for a chance to be included among the select company of owners). There is always emphasis on perfection of detail, frequently at the cost of the makers' mental equilibrium ('Dedication to accuracy became compulsion ... compulsion became obsession',[3] pants an advertisement for a model sports car). They are always 'miniature' and occasionally 'tiny', but never small (the measurements are usually omitted, and the scale can often be judged only by a comparison with the human fingers reverently holding them). They are never merely *made*, but lovingly 'crafted' by dedicated artisans with generations of experience using time-honoured methods and scrupulously following the design of the artist or sculptor, other of whose works are owned by Emperors and Presidents: the buyer's home will be made a richer and rarer place and thus score points over the neighbours ('these miniature

39

works of art will bring hours of pleasure to you and an understand-
able degree of envy from your friends and acquaintances' says an
advertisement for fifty-one pendant miniatures of the World's
Favourite Dogs 'in a style that would have delighted George III',[4]
although this powerful endorsement is weakened by its not
specifying whether the king would have needed to be mad at the
time). The object's rarity and fidelity in detail is supported by a
piece of paper saying so. (The passion for authenticity sometimes
manifests itself in bizarre ways—details of a china figure of the
young Queen Victoria are drawn from 'research into archives'[5] and
as a result her necklace, ruffles and footstool are based on those in
three different contemporary portraits: but in the quest for accuracy the world-famous sculptor gave less attention to the figure's
face, which looks rather less like contemporary portraits of the
young Queen Victoria than a Barbie doll.)

The art objects are sold only by mail order, so that the advertisements need to make sufficient impact on readers to produce an
immediate sale, and typically appear in mass-circulation magazines aimed at the middle class and a middle class clearly insecure
in its artistic taste and knowledge of current cultural fashions.
Since the qualities with which the advertisements invest the
objects are part of what is being sold, the advertisements are very
revealing when looked at in large numbers ('When advertising is
great advertising, it fastens on the myths signs and symbols of our
common experience and becomes quite literally a benefit of the
product.'[6]). Whatever the individual advertisements are for—china
figures of cute Victorian waifs, a bronze figure of Henry VIII
mounted for no discernible reason on a block of Brazilian onyx, a
lovable fox cub in pure crystal—the same paradoxes are apparent
in the copy; the objects are rare, yet available in large quantities:
hand-crafted, yet mass-produced, works of art only for the discern-
ing, yet available to anyone who can pay for them.

The advertisements present several very revealing assumptions
about the perceived functions of such ornaments and the attitudes
of their owners, and others, to them. Firstly, and perhaps obviously, they are intended only for display, not use. Even those based on
originals made to be used are precluded from this by their size or
material: plates, jugs and teapots are far too small to use (often,
almost too small to hold safely); thimbles are made of smooth china
(sometimes with additions which would render any attempt at use
even more ludicrous, such as a baby animal from the Scottish

Highlands perched on top); dolls wear diamonds and sapphires, and come with a display stand. Even books are to be bought as physical objects and not for their content. 'Just think how beautiful these books will look on your shelves, with their rich Burgundy leather-like binding and gold tooling'[7] says an advertisement for a collection of classic novels, which goes on to emphasise that 'the stories . . . have *already proved* themselves' (their italics) so that the buyer is relieved of the necessity to exercise personal daring and can take refuge behind the parapet of established opinion. Interestingly, the phrase suggests that the stories have achieved their place in the rankings by their own enterprise.

An advertisement for original oil-paintings by 'talented but unknown artists' (translation: you won't have heard of them but you'll have to take our word that they're good) stresses that the pictures would be 'a perfect gift for anyone who appreciates the finer things of life' not because they are good pictures but because each is 'superbly mounted in an antique-look oak frame'.[8] Sometimes the physical appearance of the object is intended to impress more crudely: a Cinderella doll (dressed for the ball rather than the grateside, naturally) wears 'twenty-seven genuine hand-cut sapphires'.[9]

Secondly, these ornaments are advertised as objects which will reveal the taste and cultural awareness of their owners. By buying them, the owners will be transformed into serious collectors but with the sweat taken out of the act of collecting. This type of collector can dispense not only with knowledge and critical judgment but also with the effort of tracking down new items ('Your friends may think you acquired them one at a time over a period of many years. But you can obtain this collection far more easily and conveniently.'[10] This transformation into connoisseurs and those who appreciate the finer things of life is achieved simply by filling in a form and sending off a cheque sooner than the rest of the population who are not so quick off the cultural mark ('only a fraction of the many people who appreciate its extraordinary veracity of technique and detail will ever be able to own this')[11] or who can't afford a week's average industrial take-home pay to achieve this status. Also, of course, the collector will not be using the money to back his or her own taste, since there is a constant appeal to authority on the object's cultural rightness, either through the artist's standing (which is proved by a quotation from the artist which demonstrates overriding devotion to his or her art, usually expressed in terms of the time spent on it, and clinched by the high social position of those who own his or her previous work) or of its cultural or historical importance.

Thirdly, many such objects are based on historical artefacts or figures, and the Certificate of Authenticity and laborious research in (unspecified) archives are cited to guarantee that the objects are historically accurate in form as well as being made by historically accurate methods by craftsmen with generations of experience. When ivory carvings for the white market constituted a major source of income for Eskimos near Hudson Bay, the white agents of the dealers didn't merely reject some carvings as 'not authentic', they destroyed them so that the credentials of their own trade wouldn't be compromised.[12] The result is that the object 'comes with its own history'[13] and that when you as the owner hold it 'History is in your hands'[14]—that is, you haven't just bought a piece of culture but a piece of history as well. History—in the form of objects—is thus not only made accessible and purchaseable, it becomes in a sense continuous with the present, since what is being bought and sold is not in fact an ancient artefact but a recent recreation to suit modern tastes using traditional techniques: history can thus be recreated to infinity.

Fourthly, the advertisement offers not merely a chance to own a piece of recreated history, which is presented as being indistinguishable from the historical history, but an opportunity to 'possess' the emotions associated with it. This is particularly noticeable in advertisements for ornaments which involve representation of the human figure: the advertisement sets up an imaginative recreation of the character's feelings and then implies that buying the figure will enable the owner to enter into those feelings. So the future owner is invited to identify with the hopes and fears of the Edwardian young lady of fashion going to her first ball, the Victorian street urchins envying 'the important dignitaries in their tall top hats and frock coats',[15] the picturesquely nubile country girl thinking of the village lads whose hearts she's about to devastate. It is as if owning the objects extends to owning the characters they represent, who are always reassuring in their physical attractiveness, often youthful vulnerability and cosy conformity to bourgeois standards of acceptable appearance. Even the Victorian street urchins have exquisitely-shaped clean bare feet on the picturesque cobblestones, and the girls have snowy-white lace-trimmed petticoats debouching from under their uncreased calico skirts. They are all cutely chubby-cheeked Anglo-Saxons, usually with blond hair and large dark appealing eyes and the opportunity to enter vicariously into their imaginary lives makes them even more attractive as objects, so that they provide their owners with emotional as well as cultural satisfaction. Advertisements for figures of winsome small animals — a large section of this market — have to work to simpler demands and need to play heavily on the emotions aroused by the real-life equivalents, so that these can be transferred to the pottery pieces. The advertisements therefore emphasise the life-like qualities of the animal figures, which are sometimes presented in habitat, from which they can emerge to strike up a meaningful relationship with their owners ('Each woodland animal will be happy to come out [of its tree trunk, cave or lily-pad] for a visit . . . with a little nudge you'll even have the baby bear eating from the palm of your hand.').[16] The comparison with video baby, cat or dog is inescapable: a make-believe relationship which avoids the demands and mess of the real thing.

Fifthly, the object's owners are buying the creative inspiration of the artist who designed, sculpted and drew it (although the artist's inspiration has to work within strict bounds: one of the most frequently repeated praises of the ornaments and pictures is that they are 'life-like'). Readers' responses to the artist are manipulated by the use of adjectives such as *renowned, world-famous* and *celebrated* and sometimes, particularly in advertisements for the more expensive objects, a short biography is provided, which features the awards won and commissions gained from prestigious institutions or individuals as well as the saleability of his or her work ('art dealers from Dusseldorf to New York are competing enthusiastically for the privilege of showing his beautiful paintings.')[17] The emphasis throughout is on the artist as producer, hence the need to establish his or her trade credentials. Some advertisements are accompanied by Market Analysis Reports which chart the increase in the price of work by the same artist over the previous years and then imply that the same percentage increase will apply to the object now being offered for sale, which can thus 'offer an important financial advantage for the knowledgeable'[18] (the owners will thus have demonstrated their financial as well as artistic judgement).

This view of the artist as a producer of objects with investment potential presents a very different concept of the relationship between the artist and society from the traditional Romantic image of the artist as a visionary and seer, able through inspiration to tell truths about life, love, death and the universe to illuminate the lives of the duller and more conventional members of a society which marginalises him or her. The two approaches are brought into strong contrast in an advertisement for a set of twelve medals based on details of works by Van Gogh. The medals are in high relief, of 24 carat gold on bronze, and it is difficult from the illustration to imagine the mind-freezing effect of seeing, say, 'The Potato-Eaters' transmogrified in this way, not only because so much of the stunning effect of the original lithograph comes from the sharp and dramatic black and white contrast of light and shadow (from the light cast on the faces of the potato-eaters seated around a table by the lamp hanging above it) but because of the obscenity of rendering an image of grinding poverty in gold. While the copy is able to describe the work of the medal-makers as full of investment potential, the references to Van Gogh can hardly follow the established pattern, since any suggestion that his curriculum vitae included commissions from crowned heads or an eager line of art dealers from Dusseldorf to New York would clearly be a non-starter. Van Gogh is therefore described in terms of the Romantic artist ('sensitive . . . tormented . . . yet incredibly brilliant . . . he created some of the most powerful work of all time')[19] so that potential buyers can be sure they're getting the real thing—artistic genius—although at one remove, while the fact that the man and his torments are safely dead mitigates his neglect of market forces.

As so many advertisements make clear, there's no point in possessing an awareness of the products currently riding high in cultural and artistic stock markets, and having the money to buy them, if no one else knows it. The advertisements make clear that a major function of the art objects is to excite the interest and envy of others: a set of eighteen one-inch-high pottery jugs is sold as 'a thing of beauty and a source of wonderment' not because it will give aesthetic pleasure to its owner, but because it will act as 'a tremendous talking-point amongst your family and friends'.[20] The home which has such objects on display is thus transformed into a museum or art gallery, echoing the setting of the originals. It is therefore no surprise that many of these ready-made collections come with a 'free' glass dome, case or display stand, and that the owner's role is that of museum guide or curator: 'Because we send you background notes, you'll be able to talk knowledgeably about your cherished collection.'[21]

The home has therefore stopped being a private place in which to relax and escape from the outside world, and has assumed a public function. It has become yet another stage on which to impress an audience, with the difference that what is here being displayed is not any of the public attributes of the owner (those connected with his or her work or public persona) but the so-called private self: 'see what, in the privacy of my own home, I am really like—culturally aware, aesthetically discriminating, and with a high credit rating'. The advertisements make it clear that the art objects in such a home will not be there solely because they give pleasure to the people who live there but, more importantly, because they reflect the owner's income and awareness of current cultural fashion. The home thus becomes a place where a constructed and edited 'private' self is presented for public consumption, a concept carried to its logical extreme in some middle-class European homes where there is a 'public' sitting or drawing room (antique furniture, expensive pictures and china) and a 'private' equivalent in which the family actually lives (comfortable beat-up furniture and the TV).

The owner's so-called private and individual self is thus doubly a pretence: it is presented for public approval, and it is constructed from pre-fabricated sections chosen by others. (Although etymology is always less significant than current usage, it's worth noting that 'person' and 'personality' derive from the word for the mask, portraying one strong characteristic emotion, worn by Roman actors.) It is the decorative objects in a home that are more often regarded as a give-away of the owner's character and private interests, in the same way that leisure interests are often regarded as better indicators of the 'real' people than their paid occupation; since for most people work is uncreative and its content and priorities are determined by others, it is the things they do but don't need to (their leisure interests) and the things they own but don't need to (decorative objects) which are held to reveal 'what they're really like'. To make such an object is possible for few; to commission such an object to one's own individual taste is given to hardly more; for most people, the nearest they get to this sort of freedom is to choose something already made and mass-produced because it means something to them as individuals—because the shapes, colours, textures give them pleasure, or because it reminds them of a particular moment, person or feeling, and is charged with an entirely personal significance because of it.

If instead they choose an object because it is socially acceptable and feel that by doing so they are buying the individuality and creative emotion of the person who designed or made it, the con is not that they are buying an object identical to those bought by thousands of others while feeling it is unique to them, but that their so-called private and individual self has been taken over to such an extent that it is in danger of becoming as mass-produced as the artefacts they are buying.

It is therefore not just the fact that a social bargain has been struck: that as members of our society we are governed by its myths (in the Barthesian sense), which underpin the basic structures of our lives, operating within the boundaries of what our society regards as acceptable, and that in return we are then allowed minor and trivial opportunities for the expression of individual interests in the interstices of our public lives (and, of course, these expressions of 'individuality' are heavily constrained—it is socially acceptable for me, as a member of Western bourgeois society, to choose between gymnastics and stamp-collecting but not shrinking my dead enemies' heads or coprophilia). It is rather the case that even minor personal interests are just as mass-produced, just as impersonal and just as characterless as the major social structures within which we live. It may be covered by the wolf-pelt of individualism, but underneath there is the same old socially-conformist sheep.

NOTES

1. *Sunday Express*, 2 August 1987.
2. *Sunday Express*, 28 February 1988.
3. *Sunday Express*, 16 August 1987.
4. *You (Mail on Sunday)*, 6 September 1987.
5. *Sunday Express*, 7 June 1987.
6. Blonsky, M., 'Endword', in M. Blonsky (ed.), *On Signs* (Oxford: Basil Blackwell, 1985).
7. *Observer*, 28 May 1978.
8. *Sunday Express*, 5 July 1987.
9. *Sunday Express*, 13 September 1987.
10. *You (Mail on Sunday)*, 28 August 1983.
11. Publicity Flyer from *Bradford Exchange*, Autumn 1987.
12. Graburn, N., 'The Eskimos and Commercial Art', in M. C. Albrecht

et al. (eds), *The Sociology of Art and Literature* (London: Duckworth, 1970).

13. *Sunday Express,* 28 February 1988.
14. Ibid.
15. *Sunday Express,* 9 August 1987.
16. *Sunday Express,* 23 August 1987.
17. Publicity Flyer from *Bradford Exchange,* Autumn 1987.
18. Ibid.
19. *Observer,* 9 April 1978.
20. *Sunday Express,* 2 August 1987.
21. Publicity Flyer from *Franklin Porcelain,* March 1988.

7

Pose for Thought: Bodybuilding and Other Matters

GARY DAY

Bodybuilding has become big business in recent years. Most cities and towns now boast at least three or four gymnasiums which incorporate all the latest technology of weight training. There are also numerous magazines such as *Bodybuilding Monthly, Muscle and Fitness* and *Flex* which give advice on diet and training as well as keeping the reader informed of the increasing number of competitions which he or she may enter. Of course bodybuilding has been around a long time but in the past it was linked to displays of strength like the circus strong man's ability to bend iron bars or pull heavy weights using only his teeth and a rope. The attraction of the circus strong man however lay in his being different, even somewhat freakish; his very costume, the traditional leopard skin leotard, signified his being closer to primitive rather than modern man and so the spectacle he provided reassured his audience of their sophistication at the same time as it entertained them. Outside the circus ring bodybuilding was aimed at those who did not want sand kicked in their face. The implied promise of Charles Atlas and others was that by following a prescribed course the purchaser would never again suffer intimidation. Bodybuilding was thus seen as a way of dealing with a hostile world and to that extent it had a rationale, however questionable.

The position now is somewhat different for the link between bodybuilding and both self-protection and feats of strength no longer seems to exist: the field of self-protection today belongs to the martial arts while the displays of strength are the province of men like Geoff Capes, 'The Strongest Man In The World', whose mountainous physiques very definitely proclaim that they are not bodybuilders. But despite its apparent purposelessness bodybuilding is more popular and widespread than ever before. The reasons for this are many and varied but one is surely the illusion of power it gives to those who have none; for bodybuilding is primarily a working-class pursuit and they are precisely the class who, through unemployment, have lost political ground over the last few years. Another reason is the shifts in sexual morality and the consequent change of fashion, particularly those which have emphasised the male body in a way that only the female body used to be emphasised. Thus it is quite common to see male bodies being used in an overtly sexy way to advertise shampoos, deodorants and jeans. The use of the male body in the selling process has further heightened awareness of it and so contributed to the burgeoning of the bodybuilding industry.

The results of bodybuilding can be seen by the adoption of specific poses which show whether the adopted exercises have succeeded in enlarging and pronouncing the muscles to which they were directed. When the bodybuilder is satisfied with the standard he or she has reached then he or she is ready to enter a competition which calls for a whole repetoire of gestures whereby their achievements can be admired and assessed. But, there is more to looking at the bodybuilder than admiring or appreciating how much more developed he or she is than the other competitors for in many ways the bodybuilder is an image, sometimes iconic, of of aspects of the consumer society of late capitalism.

At a very general level bodybuilding is part of an overall focus on the body which permeates every aspect of the media and represents consumer society's concern with the outside rather than the inside, with surface rather than depth. This general emphasis on the body has to be seen in conjunction with a technology which makes everything visible; the microscope and the camera combine to make the world the sum of its appearance. One effect of this is to banish interiority, pursuits associated with the inner life start to vanish; one notes, for example, the disappearance of philosophy departments in polytechnics and universities. With the 'loss' of the inner life comes a realignment of subjectivity which is now centred on the body.[1] Subjectivity becomes visible in such sayings as 'you are what you eat', or 'you are what you wear'. Moreover, the change from inner to outer puts pressure on subjectivity to be visible and this may be one explanation for the emphasis on size in bodybuilding. In addition, bodybuilding concentrates on sculpting and shaping *muscles* which would otherwise remain unseen, for example, the neck is usually on view but its muscles are hidden and the desire to highlight the muscles, to bring them into relief also shows bodybuilding responding to the need to make the invisible visible, to produce the unique features of a particular body, its subjectivity.

The transfer of subjectivity from the inner to the outer, from the mind to the body, connects it with sensation so that subjectivity now partakes of the instant, and is thereby enabled to function in a culture of fast foods and instant credit. The instant is momentary, promises instant consumption and becomes ultimately, the condition for experience which, in consumer society is always defined in terms of consumption. Subjectivity thus becomes linked with consumption, further eroding the possibility of an inner life based upon reason and imagination which are more geared to production.

The tendency of everything to become visible puts a stress on appearances which, as a form of compensation for the loss of the inner, somehow have to suggest a depth they don't actually have. This is achieved by the polished surface of consumer goods and one has only to look at certain television adverts, for example, Guiness and Castrol GTX, to see the importance given to texture which is made to signify richness, roundness and completeness. The bodybuilder suggests the same by the curvature of his or her muscles, and in competitions, when oil is rubbed onto the body, it takes on the glossiness of consumer goods in general. In having a surface sheen which seems a reflection of depth the bodybuilder's body itself becomes a commodity along with other commodities. The bodybuilder thus shows one way in which the body is integrated into consumer society. Furthermore just as the bulk of the bodybuilder is a sign of the disappearance of interiority with a consequent diminution of both the capacity for and the quality of experience, so too does the body as a commodity mark a further degeneration in this area.

To see the body as a commodity is ironically, to abolish the difference between bodies which, as has been seen, function as the site of subjectivity. As a commodity, one body is no different to any other. In addition the emphasis on an ideal body, which occurs not just in bodybuilding but also in most adverts, encourages the spectator to think in terms of one type of body, all others being a deviation from the ideal. In bodybuilding this abolition of the difference between bodies occurs even at a biological level for women are judged according to how far they can develop male physiques. Like men they should also have large biceps and pronounced pectorals. This trend toward uniformity in respect of the body parallels the process of consumerism where the trend is always towards sameness. Fashion, for example, works on the principle that everyone is unique, but the fact that it is mass produced makes a mockery of this idea. At a political level the pressure to conform is more obvious. Opinion polls are one example of this, while dissent on issues such a nuclear power is intolerable to the extent that it's very nearly regarded as treacherous. One thinks back to 1983 when the Government accused CND of having communist links.

Another consequence of seeing the body as a commodity is to see it, in common with other commodities, as something that must be possessed in order to complete the self. All adverts work on the principle that life will be better when you buy the particular product being advertised or, as John Berger has it, publicity offers the spectator 'an improved alternative to what [she or] he (*sic*) is'.[2] Of course bodies are not for sale in a literal sense but they are nevertheless presented in such a way that they are felt to be the consequence of purchasing the product with which they are associated. Adverts in slimming magazines are the most obvious example here where it is suggested that if an overweight woman eats Ryvita as a part of her calorie controlled diet she'll actually look like the model in the bikini whose expression makes the biscuit seem delicious as well as slim inducing. The advert makes the woman dissatisfied with her own body so that she desires another. This process is at work in less obvious ways in other adverts where the spectator is persuaded to buy the product because of the desirability of the body with which it is associated. The advert makes the spectator dissatisfied with his or her body to the extent that they want a new, model body and this can be clearly seen in adverts for bodybuilding with their characteristic before and after pictures. In the sense that it completes the spectator like other commodities, the other's body becomes a symbol of unity that the spectator feels will overcome the lack in his or her own.

Subjectivity then may be centred on the body but the consumer is always made to feel dissatisfied with his or her body and consequently to desire, mostly in an unconscious way, a different one. This distancing of one's self from one's body takes a specific form in bodybuilding where the bodybuilder is encouraged to take an objective attitude towards his or her flesh. This is apparent not only in the technical language that is found in bodybuilding magazines but also in the bodybuilder's attention to diet and its effect on muscle development and in his or her concentration, when training, on only one or two groups of muscles at a time. This represents an objectification of the body which is in direct contradiction to its being the site of subjectivity. The bodybuilder's objectification of him or herself merely repeats the way the body is objectified in a more general way in advertising, as an ideal.

The bodybuilder also objectifies his or her body through the look, though here the situation is a little more complicated. Round the walls of most gymnasiums are mirrors which allow the bodybuilder to see how he or she is progressing. Thus the bodybuilder regards his or her body in the same way that a craftsman would look upon a piece of work that's not quite finished — admiring, but aware that there's more to do yet. But mingled with this objective assessment is an element of narcissism which is not only evident in the presence of the mirrors but also in the very nature of bodybuilding itself. Bodybuilding it must be stressed, is not a sport — if by sport is understood a skilled activity which involves both competition and co-operation. It may be true that bodybuilding involves competition but the important fact is that it need not do so for it is not necessary to enter competitions to be a bodybuilder. The bodybuilder is always an isolated figure, he or she does not need anyone else and lifting weights cannot really be regarded as a skilled activity. Bodybuilding is centred exclusively on the self and the bodybuilder's motive for developing his or her physique is one of self-gratification. The mirrors are there not just for the bodybuilder to admire the size and shape of his or her muscles but also to do away with the need for the other's look which, though potentially threatening from a psychoanalytic point of view, is also available as a means of confirming one's sense of self. By gazing appreciatively at his or her own reflection, the bodybuilder becomes his or her own other. If he or she should enter a competition then it is only in order that the self-approving look can blend with the approving look of the judges. Another kind of look which the bodybuilder may seek is the envious one, the look of those who would like their own body to be like the body they behold; in this instance, the body builder's sense of self comes from making other's aware of their lack. Ironically, however, the bodybuilder is here looked at in precisely the same way as a commodity so that, in the end, the other's look confirms the body builder only by objectifying him or her.

The bodybuilder's separation from others is similar to the consumer's position for he or she is mostly addressed without reference to other consumers. The consumer is encouraged to think only in terms of his or her desires and thus the consumer is ultimately set apart from human relations, instead, he or she is orientated towards commodities in the same way that the body-builder is orientated towards his or her weights. Also, both are on a treadmill, the consumer consumes without ever being satisfied while the bodybuilder, in the end, is reduced to lifting more and more weights merely to stay as he or she is. Finally, just as the bodybuilder solicits the envious regard of others so too does the consumer who, through what he or she consumes, wakes in others those feelings of incompleteness which he or she experienced when looking at the commodities which he or she now possesses.

The bodybuilder is an image of the consumer in his or her separation from others, a separation which perhaps can be ulti-mately characterised as self-absorption. But this self absorption does not signify that the bodybuilder is at one with him or herself. On the contrary, he or she is alienated through an identification with their mirror reflection which confers a false sense of unity.[3] Moreover the ultimate source of this mirror reflection is not the bodybuilder him or herself but some ideal body to which they aspire. Thus he or she constitute themselves in accordance with a picture in a magazine or an image on a screen and so they are always, in some profound sense, going to be other to themselves. The bodybuilder's relationship with his or her mirror reflection also describes the consumer's relation to adverts which offer him or her an ideal image of themselves to which they can have access through purchasing a particular commodity. Both the bodybuilder and the consumer identify in one form or another with the image of a body and that may be because the body symbolises unity in a world that is experienced at other levels as being radically divided. Whatever the merits of such a view it is at least true to say that the bodybuilder is not an aberrant figure, as his or her grotesqueness would seem to suggest, but one who is a fitting image of some aspects of consumerism.

The bodybuilder believes that his or her body is something to be developed and thus he or she conforms to an ideology of progress.

However, it could be argued that the development of the body is nothing more than its distortion. The lifting of heavier and heavier weights on a daily basis results in grossly inflated muscles which may perhaps be taken as an oblique comment on over production in the capitalist system as a whole. The muscles seem to stand out separately and have no relation to those around them or indeed the whole body. The body thus fails to be an image of unity and its individual parts become the object of fetishistic attention: a part or parts of the body become a substitute for the whole. This divided body, whose parts seem greater than the whole, is an apt image for a country divided between north and south, a division that is in no small part due to the economic policies of the past few years.

Another way in which bodybuilding seems to reflect the economy is in its purposelessness. There is no point to bodybuilding for the strength that the bodybuilder acquires is never needed either at home or at work. Furthermore a bodybuilder is never required to demonstrate his or her strength in competitions so it remains a superfluous quality. In this bodybuilding resembles the economy which also produces what it does not need, for example weapons, while not producing what it does, for example housing.

Technology is an important aspect of bodybuilding as it is of the economy. The bodybuilder can rely on and relate to technology in a manner that is almost a satiric representation of his or her relationship with others. Nowadays the bodybuilder, particularly in America, can be coaxed and criticised by the computerised equipment which he or she uses and which, by giving advice and encouragement, replaces the human coach or trainer. The bodybuilder's relationship with technology is not surprising in a society where most people have a television and where videos and computers are becoming more common. Perhaps it is even possible to suggest that these same people are becoming more orientated to technology than they are to each other. One thinks, for example, of the old-fashioned complaint that television undermines family life.

It may, however, be more instructive to see technology as mediating human relationships rather than replacing them. For instance how far does the ability to programme a computer or change a television channel instill a feeling of control which may then be carried over into a relationship with others? Indeed, how far does living in an 'instant culture', itself the product of technology, affect relations with others? Ought they also to be instant? Perhaps our relationship with technology, which is increasing all the time, subtly engenders in us the belief that we are in control and that things exist for our pleasure and convenience: the television is there to entertain and if we do not like one programme we can always turn over to another. Technology appears to serve our needs and this expectation, which is constantly reinforced by the appearance of each new labour-saving device, perhaps permeates our relations with others; a process made easier by the fact that technology has separated us from one another, it has broken down old ways of relating and constituted new ones. One political consequence of this is that people are easier to control. The less they rely on each other the more they rely on technology and this makes them malleable particularly as regards information and opinion. It is not only technology, however, which puts people in this precarious position for so does their status as isolated consumers. Cut off from others as a consumer and relating to them through technology which yet only intensifies that separation the individual is easier to influence than if the opposite were true.

The bodybuilder, however, is more than a mere reflection of the process whereby people appear to relate more to technology than to one another for he or she has a specific relationship with it that may or may not have a wider application. In the first place the bodybuilder's art can be regarded as an assertion that it is both heroic and useless. The bodybuilder's physique seems to announce body power at a time when it is not needed: technology does more and more of the work that the body used to do. Thus through the bodybuilder the body comes into prominence at the moment that it disappears from the sphere of labour. Another way of looking at this is to say that as it is no longer geared to manual work the body is free to be developed as an aesthetic object. And it is as an aesthetic object that the bodybuilder becomes a sign of human presence in a world where, ironically, the focus is moving away from the human to the marvels of technology. Films are a good guide here particularly science fiction ones where plot and character are often subordinated to spectacular special effects.

It has been mentioned that technology perhaps mediates relations between people with the effect of alienating them from one another; it encourages, in other words, an objectification of one person by another. However, although technology is connected with alienation it can also be interpreted as that which completes, which ensures that the human is, in fact, human. This can be seen in a variety of ways. For example, cars are advertised in a manner which suggests that it is they which give the best expression of what it means to be human: they are associated with freedom and power, the very qualities needed for full self-realisation. The *Rambo* films also present a character who is defined and fulfilled by his technology, it is that which enables him to cope with the world and to overcome his enemies and it is in both these respects that he is realised as a human character. The bodybuilder too appears in magazines either with simple weights or with more sophisticated equipment without which he would not *exist* as a bodybuilder. Technology, then somehow enables the human being to be human, it increases human capacity in the world thereby extending the definition of what it is to be human at the same time as claiming that the possession of technology ensures that that definition is realised. Perhaps the most extreme case of technology 'completing' the human being can be found in children's toys, derived from cartoons, like Centurions and Transformers where the characters are actually articulated with pieces of machinery that enable them to function in superhuman ways and it is precisely these characters whose appearance on the screen is offered as an ideal with which to identify. As regards the bodybuilder, his or her relationship with technology detracts from the aesthetic effect of their physique for insofar as it is associated with technology it loses the all important aesthetic quality of unity; it refers to something outside itself and, in the process, reveals its mode, if not condition, of production. The bodybuilder's relationship with technology shows, moreover, that he or she has not entirely escaped it. The inflated flesh may be a sign that technology has liberated the body in one respect, only to enslave it in another.

But the bodybuilder's relationship with technology goes even further for it is possible to suggest that technology has, in some sense, come to stand in for the lost interiority mentioned earlier. The bodybuilder signifies the interior made exterior and as that exterior is dependent on technology so too is the interior which it has become. Through being externalised the interior is mechanised. Inner life is thus not only made visible but it is also, through its association with the mechanical, made predictable and regulatable. Of course this is not to be understood in any literal sense and it certainly requires further development. However, it is worth noting that in psychology, at least one branch, behaviourism, is concerned to transcribe the inner, to reduce it to that which is observable so that it can be predicted and catalogued. Such an approach once more draws attention to the inner being made visible and there are increasing pressures on it to be so in a society where surveillance is growing. Cameras record from motorway bridges and strategic points in shopping centres. The mentality behind this process, no matter how disguised by the language of bland officialdom, ultimately assumes that whatever is unseen is suspect. The interior thus has to become exterior and the bodybuilder is an image of one small part of this process.

Technology as inner life, the relationship between technology and the body and the place of both in consumer society are questions which await further development. At present, their significance and implications remain somewhat hazy but it is at least clear that bodybuilding offers a partial expression of these problems. It is therefore important to see not just how bodybuilding but how any aspect of popular culture represents, in microcosmic form, the whole of which it is a part. Seeing things as a whole is, of course, an anathema to those critics who stress division and fragmentation but it is only by seeing things as a whole that relationships are clearer and our chances of doing something about are them increased. Furthermore, to see things as a whole is to recognise the importance and relative contribution of everything that makes up that whole. In this perspective, nothing is ignored or dismissed — a fatal error, for capitalism can use what is ignored or dismissed to perpetuate its ideology and even, perhaps, increase its appeal thereby undermining whatever gains have been made elsewhere. In addition, to ignore something like bodybuilding maybe to miss what is not apparent anywhere else, so it is necessary to understand it, therefore giving more force to one's opposition to the system.

To see bodybuilding as a reflection of consumer capitalism is, however, only half the task. The other half consists of reappropriating it so it can be used against that system. Thus one can note how the bodybuilder's muscles represent the sort of accumulated profits of the capitalist economy, but what should be stressed is the futility of these muscles and how they correspond to the nonproductive nature of profit itself. Seeing the bodybuilder in this way is to show how the images of capitalism — in this case the strong individual — can be made to reveal their shortcomings.

It is possible, then, to see the bodybuilder as an ironic image of capitalism, one which seems to trumpet its virtues but which also discloses its vices. But in order to appreciate the irony it is first necessary to see how the bodybuilder reflects consumer capitalism and this essay has made a few suggestions on that point. Ultimately, the bodybuilder with his or her imposing physique is a reminder of the power of human potential but also of how it can be grotesquely distorted. The challenge is to release that potential, redirecting it against the system which frustrates and thwarts it. This is a task requiring vision and imagination; unfashionable words but they offer more hope than some recent critical theory with its emphasis on how human projects are always doomed to deconstruct. Such pessimism can only gladden the hearts of those who wish to keep things as they are.

NOTES

1. I use the word subjectivity to designate a sense of self, nothing more. It is an immensely difficult term that has connections with psychoanalysis and linguistics which it is not my purpose to comment on here.
2. Berger, J., *Ways of Seeing* (Harmonsworth: BBC, 1977) p. 142.
3. For an account of 'mirror relations' see 'The mirror stage as formative of the function of the I as revealed in psychoanalytic experience', in Jacques Lacan, *Ecrits: A Selection*, tr., Alan Sheridan (London: Tavistock, 1977).

8

Dialogic Society: Discourse and Subjectivity in British Telecom's 'Talkabout' Service

ADRIAN PAGE

The radio would be the finest possible communication apparatus in public life, a vast network of pipes. That is to say, it would be if it knew how to let the listener speak as well as hear, how to bring him into a relationship instead of isolating him.[1]

When Brecht expressed this opinion in the early 1930s he was principally concerned that the radio audience should not be passive recipients of this 'apparatus for distribution'. His solution was that the listeners should themselves produce radio transmissions in order to transform the medium into an instrument for communication. This proposal for what Raymond Williams has called 'free communications', however, is not simply a call for democratic participation in the means of production. As Brecht also says, the outcome of such a reciprocal network should be an increase in the opportunities to engage in a wider range of inter-personal dialogues which enhance social relationships and ultimately, perhaps, reinforce a sense of community. The example of British Telecom's Talkabout service illustrates the point that increased participation alone does not necessarily achieve the aim of reducing isolation.

Since Brecht wrote, there have been a number of technological developments which have enabled individuals to take part in broadcasting. Although it has been possible to own and operate the very expensive 'radio ham' equipment under licence since 1949, this has never become an option for the general public. The radio phone-in, which originated in 1970, created the impression that the audience could overhear a debate between experts or celebrities and the nation. In reality, phone-ins are very carefully orchestrated to provide a 'balanced' debate, and often reserve the right to leave a short time-lag between receiving and broadcasting calls so that unacceptable material can be deleted. The phone-in did not cater for the desire to be able to initiate conversations over the airwaves rather than merely responding to a public invitation.

Many people found this desire was satisfied by the Citizens' Band radio (CB) equipment which began to be used illegally in this country in the 1970s. CB enables anyone to make a narrowcast, a transmission over a short range which will reach anyone who is listening in. The device became popular with American truck-drivers as a means of evading police speed-traps and of alleviating the boredom of long-distance driving.

The history of CB radio in this country provides an interesting example of political responses to the concept of free communica-tion. In 1978 the Labour government voiced grave doubts about the principle of permitting free communication at all, arguing that the participants would feel they had 'the right to rape, pillage and steal'.[2] By 1981, however, the Conservative government had acceded to a massive public outcry by the CB lobby and legalised the equipment on restricted wavelengths and within a limit of ten miles radius. Licences were introduced and penalties remained for using equipment which did not meet the Government's specifica-tions.

Raymond Williams predicted such developments some time ago when he wrote, 'It will be widely argued that the old choice between "public service" and "commercial" broadcasting is now outdated by the new technology, and that we can move beyond both to community services'.[3] Williams also warned, however, that 'community services' could become purely commercial ventures rather than socially useful projects inspired by communities them-selves.

The Talkabout service was begun by British Telecom in 1983 in Bristol, shortly before it became a private company in August, 1984. By dialling a certain number, anyone could be 'dropped down' into a conversation between up to ten others who were on the line at the time. For the first time anyone with access to a telephone could enjoy all the excitement of CB radio without the need to purchase the fairly expensive sets. By early 1988, however,

Talkabout was discontinued, partly in response to a storm of controversy about the activities of young people in particular who used the services. There were allegations that young people used the service to arrange sexual liaisons and to plan illegal activities such as drug-pushing, as well as running up enormous bills for their parents. In other European countries such as France similar problems were encountered with the Minitel service which also had to be banned when young people began to dabble in prostitution.

Free communications has therefore shown itself to be a potentially subversive concept which has had to be repressed in capitalist societies, but is this because the access to forms of communication has been as completely free as Brecht wanted? In the limited ways in which access to broadcasting has been allowed, the opportunity to establish relationships is often denied or at least hindered. On Talkabout, for example, any attempt at arranging meetings was censored by the omnipresent 'monitor', a BT employee who co-ordinated the service and attempted to prevent any salacious conversation by listening in and cutting off the guilty party.

Far from the serious business of forging new social networks, Talkabout and the similar services which have followed in its wake present themselves as the ideal trivial pursuit, neither advice line nor message service but 'a party on the phone'.

The question which Talkabout raises, therefore, is how such an apparently innocuous diversion could give rise to such a degree of socially unacceptable behaviour. Was this upsurge of youthful rebelliousness an indication of the radical social change which free communications might lead to, or was it an example of a commercial interest unwittingly promoting dissatisfaction through the form of its service? In either case it is clear that increased 'free' access to telecommunications did not produce 'the finest possible communication apparatus.'

If there is a modern myth of telecommunications, it is that they serve as a neutral media through which autonomous individuals express themselves fully, thereby 'putting people in touch'. The greatest accolade that the manager of Bristol's Talkabout could claim for the service in an interview on Radio 1 was that it had led to three marriages. This model of telecommunication relies on what Bakhtin calls monologic language: as in poetry, the language is thought of as expressing unique thoughts which can only be

fully comprehended by a sole authority, in this case the individual
who uses them.

Bakhtin, however, argues that no language can be fundamentally monologic discourse; all languages consist of a number of
socially-recognised languages which need to be understood by
reference to each other. CB radio discourse, for example, contains
the '10 CODE', the International Q Code and the American
truck-drivers' jargon. In order to understand any discourse completely, therefore, classical linguistics is not enough, since what is
needed is a sociolinguistics which will be able to explain how what
is said relates to the complete social context of utterance, or its
'heteroglossia' as Bakhtin calls it. Rather than expressing ourselves
uniquely, our choice of language is 'populated with the intentions
of others'[4] and the socially-determined aspects of our discourse
can only be revealed by examining discourse's dialogic structure.
Dialogic discourse is that language which implicitly recognises the
existence of other discourses as the context in which it must be
understood.

In everyday communication subjectivity can be revealed
through the speaker's ability to refer to the heteroglossia, the social
context which is necessary to establish meaning clearly. On
Talkabout, however, many references which will accurately identify the speaker are outlawed, hence the voices are divorced from
any social context at first and conversation is a struggle to
construct the social dimension which clarifies meaning:

Gary	Rachel, where d'you come from?
Rachel	Who's that?
Gary	Gary.
Rachel	Gary, how old are you, Gary?
Gary	Fifteen.
Rachel	Where d'you come from?
Gary	Derby.
Rachel	I come from Derby. What school do you go to?
Gary	Finnistone.
Rachel	Finnistone?
Gary	Yes.
Rachel	You're the one in the fields aren't you, with Timmo and that lot?
Gary	Yes.

Rachel	I phoned Timmo at work, and I asked him if he knew who you were, and he said he didn't know a Gary or nothing.
Gary	Well I know him.
Rachel	He didn't know you, 'cos I couldn't get your phone number off him.
Monitor	You weren't Rachel?
Rachel	You what? Who said that?
Monitor	The monitor.
Rachel	Oh no, I wasn't really trying to get his number [sarcastically].
Monitor	Do you go to the same school then?
Rachel	Oh no, I don't go the Finnistone, I go the Beryl.
Gary	Oi Rachel, do you live in Chiltern then?
Rachel	Yes.

In this conversation Gary finds that he is not entitled to use the word 'know' as he pleases. His relationship with the celebrated 'Timmo' seems to have implications for his status in Rachel's eyes, but whether he 'knows' Timmo in the sense that they are friends, or merely knows who he *is*, is a matter that Rachel decides by reference to the social context. The context, in fact, has primacy over the text as Bakhtin maintains: it is more important to find out whether Gary's relationship with Timmo is mutual than to understand the words he uses.

Ironically, therefore, this most intimate closed circle of speakers are compelled to resort to socially-determined codes of meaning rather than seizing the opportunity to differentiate subjectivity through language. Meaning is not explored by directly referring to the subject of utterance, even though the opportunity to do so is clearly present. Understanding the language of Talkabout means understanding contemporary social codes, not each other.

The attraction of this phenomenon is illustrated by the popularity of the game show, 'Blind Date' hosted by Cilla Black where guests are invited to choose a partner for a romantic holiday. The man or woman who is allowed to choose can put three questions to each of three would-be partners who remain hidden behind a screen. Here again the subjectivity of the would-be partners is approachable only through discourse. Attempting to discover something about the person responding to the questions is a matter of understanding the *language* they use, independently of any supporting social context. In this situation, the person choosing a partner has to acknowledge and understand the dialogic nature of the answers they hear. As Bakhtin says 'Consciousness finds itself inevitably facing the necessity of *having to choose a language*'.[5] The questioner has, then to understand both the type of language used and the possible reasons for choosing it. Grasping subjectivity for Bakhtin means appreciating the balance between the centripetal tendency, which moves towards the the unified, monological subject, and the centrifugal tendency which disperses meaning and opens up a wider range of socially-determined strata in a dialogic relationship.

On Blind Date, for example, the questions are clearly put to the participants well in advance, and the result is that the answers are often ingenious double entendres. The choice for the questioner, on having decoded the ambiguity and its sexual connotations, is to decide whether this response is an indication of, for example, passion, or wit and playfulness. The audience of Blind Date derive a great deal of their obvious pleasure from witnessing the questioner stumbling over the ambiguities of discourse.

At this point the language of Talkabout appears to provide an ideal illustration of the poststructuralist divorce of signifier and signified. In the absence of heteroglossia, signifiers can only arbitrarily be made to coincide with signifieds, and the impression that communication is taking place is an illusion, since listeners can create a coherent position for the speaking subjects by rearranging verbal signifiers to suit their own preconceptions.

If there were all that would be said about Talkabout, however, its considerable social impact would remain a mystery. The service was not felt to be harmful because the participants lapsed into private fantasies, but because of the effect they had on each other. As Julia Kristeva has pointed out in her essay, 'The System and the Speaking Subject',[6] to reduce the phenomenon to a coherent linguistic model in all cases is to ignore the specificity of Talkabout, its particular social effects and the reasons for them.

Bakhtin's theories are enthusiastically supported by Kristeva because they acknowledge the social character of language yet also retain the idea of the speaking subject as a unique point of origin of language. In order to understand the Talkabout phenomenon completely, we would also have to understand the complete social context of the subjects who expressed their personal desires through this medium.

In general linguistic terms, the specificity of Talkabout derives from what Bakhtin would have called its carnivalesque qualities. The carnival represents for Bakhtin the ultimate scene of the dialogical nature of language where each carnival-goer adopts a language of their own and celebrates the diversity of social languages and their contrast with the monological language of authority. It is essentially a playful attitude towards language and identity since 'all such languages are masks and no language could claim to be an authentic, incontestable face'.[7] On Talkabout the choice of a language acts as a mask, yet subjectivity is not the reality which lies behind it but the process of selection.

One effect of engaging in the carnivalesque discourse of Talkabout, therefore, is that the participants can lose their sense of individual identity which monologic discourse confirms. Kristeva remarks that 'A carnival participant is both actor and spectator; he loses his sense of individuality, passes through a zero point of carnivalesque activity and splits into a subject of the spectacle and object of the game'.[8] When wearing a mask it is all the more obvious as Lacan says that the pronoun 'I' can refer both to the person who speaks or the subject about whom he speaks, his adopted persona.

Ultimately, therefore, Kristeva describes carnivalesque discourse as 'a social and political protest'[9] since in denying the authority of grammar and semantics carnival is also threatening to destabilise all authority. The following encounter from Liverpool Teenage Talkabout provides an example of carnivalesque atmosphere.

Monitor	Yea, who's shouting the monitor?
Mandy	How come all our calls have to be monitored?
Monitor	How come what?
Mandy	How come all our calls have to be monitored?
Monitor	Because, you see we've been getting a lot of bad people on the line who've been swearing, making dates and giving phone numbers out, and have you heard it on the news and in the papers?
Mick	Yes, the monitors wouldn't have a job, and they'd be on the dole just like us. Yea.
Mandy	Like if you didn't drop litter or . . .
Monitor	Well you'd better start behaving yourself 'cos you know if you don't behave yourself and every one starts

carrying on the way it is then it's going to get closed
down.

Mick	Hey Gypsy.
Monitor	Yea.
Mick	Just think I get promoted next month.
Monitor	Very good.
Mick	Good eh? [sniggers]
Mandy	Hey monitor, you sound like my games teacher.
Monitor	Do I?
Mick	You never know. She might be moonlighting.
Pete	She's a real bitch.
Monitor	I am, you wait.
Mandy	Is your name Mrs Mitchell?
Monitor	It is, yea.
Mick	Ooh you little liar.
Mandy	What's your maiden name, then?
Monitor	I'm not telling you.
Pete	Her name's Mrs Mitchell because she's got a tyre for a stomach.
Monitor	No because it's not Mi . . . Pardon? [laughter] You've been cut off.
Mandy	Hey monitor we caught you laughing there.
Mick	Ooh that was cruel that one was.

On the radio phone-in the diversity of voices may sound dialogic,
yet they are all ultimately contained within the monologic discourse of the broadcasting authority which is presenting a 'balanced view' of the spectrum of opinion. The anarchic spirit of
carnival on Talkabout, however, shows here how even the monitor
who represents the monologic voice of authority, can become both
'subject of the spectacle and object of the game'. As the monitor is
drawn into the banter, she begins to participate by assuming an
identity. At this point she is no longer a detached outsider but the
object of the mockery which the callers hurl against her as a figure
of authority. Her authority is rapidly lost as she exchanges the
language of adult common sense for that of the callers themselves.
The entry into dialogism also marks the transition from subject to
object.

   This example shows that the subversive effect of carnival is the
fact that it is infectious. A common media image of carnival in our
society is of a policeman smiling broadly as he receives a garland or

a hug from a throng of carnival-goers. One significance of such a picture is that the spirit of carnival excites a desire in us all to shed our normal roles. The truly challenging issue for future research on the Talkabout phenomenon, therefore, is to explain how and why such desires arise in individual subjects.

Kristeva's answer would be to return to psychoanalysis of the individual, but there are some theoretical factors which point towards an explanation. An attractive analogy for Talkabout is that it represents the polyphonic state of the juvenile id. Released from identity and the ego, the unrepressed desires conflict only with the super-ego as personified by the monitor. On Talkabout the unconscious appears to the manifest rather than latent as participants attempt to whisper the occasional unacceptable remark such as a sexual invitation when they hope the monitor is not listening. In Lacan's terms, Talkabout's discourse resembles the entry into the symbolic order when the unconscious finds a language, yet one which already enshrines the categories of authority such as the notion of parents.

The prohibition of Talkabout against the use of surnames invites the conscious splitting of the subject which results in a newly-chosen language-mask, and with this partial disguise, the callers are free to express their unrestrained desires in the face of authority. Although access to Talkabout did constitute a two-way form of telecommunication as Brecht wanted, its characteristics did little to foster the development of subjectivity or social relationships. As he wrote, 'In our society one can invent and perfect discoveries that still have to justify their existence'.[10]

NOTES

1. Willett, John (trs.), *Brecht on Theatre* (London: Methuen, 1987) p. 52.
2. Ainslie, Alan C., *The UK CB Handbook* (Frome and London: Butterworth, 1982) p. 9.
3. Williams, Raymond, *Television, Technology and Cultural Form* (Bungay Suffolk: Fontana, 1974) p. 148.
4. Bakhtin, M. M., *The Dialogic Imagination* (Austin: University of Texas, 1981) p. 294.
5. Ibid., p. 295.
6. See Toril Moi (ed.), *A Kristeva Reader* (Oxford: Blackwell, 1986). ch. 1.
7. Bakhtin, op. cit., p. 273.
8. *A Kristeva Reader*, p. 49.
9. Ibid., p. 36.
10. Op. cit., p. 51.

9

T-Shirts and the Coming Collapse of Capitalism

PAUL O'FLINN

To start with a couple of brief scenes. It was my birthday in April and Deirdre asked me what I wanted. 'I don't know ... Oh, yes, I need a T-shirt or a sweatshirt. See if you can get me a plain one without advertising or some dud slogan on the front.' After all, I was not keen to appear at a lecture with a chest that announced VIRGIN or HAWAII BEACHBOY to a group of students with a healthy disrespect for their elders, students who in the past have been known to heckle a colleague in an ill-advised wig. I was told later that it took a couple of deeply dispiriting Saturdays trailing round the shops before something as apparently simple as a plain sweatshirt appeared in amongst the racks of 83M AMERICAN SYSTEM and MID PACIFIC CARNIVAL. Next year I'll ask for some handkerchiefs.

The second scene. I am walking up the stairs at the Poly. Coming down towards me is a young Italian, about 14, over on a basic English language summer school course. Her jacket says TEAM RACING USA. What team, I wonder as I pass her—Ferret Breeders, perhaps? No use asking her because she doesn't know the language. And so I turn the corner puzzled as to how it comes about that an Italian in England silently offers me a message that neither of us understands but which seems to be about something American and was probably made in Taiwan, and is this what Marx really meant by alienation?

Two trivial moments from everyday life, and yet moments worth thinking about because of their paradoxically immense significance. Clothing represents, after all, along with food and shelter, one of the three basic requirements for human survival and it is therefore around the production and distribution of those three that all conceivable forms of society take shape. And then again cotton, the raw material for most T-shirts, was the commodity at the heart of the world's first industrial revolution. Not only was its manufacture the world's first large-scale capitalist industry but it remains arguably the most typical of all because, linked with the discourse of fashion, it is the industry where planned obsolescence is most overt, where today's exclusive designer wear is next season's sales bargain and next year's jumble sale offering. It is not a coincidence that as the cotton industry grew at the end of the eighteenth century so Britain's illustrated monthly fashion magazines began to appear.

Allied to these facts is the whole question of clothing as an aspect of culture. The way we cover our bodies sends out a host of signals to other people about our sense of gender and morality, about our class and income, about our notions of style and taste. And while we are all in theory quite free to wear what we choose those choices are very insistently conditioned. (You can prove this for yourself by closing this book for a moment and having a look at the men going past in the street outside. It is a fairly safe assumption that nearly all of them will be wearing trousers and not many of them will have, say, a pencil-slim skirt with a fetching slit up the side.) Those deeply determined choices lock the people who make them into a range of identities and self-definitions, into particular manufacturers and suppliers and into a greater or lesser dependence on imported goods and the imported values that go with them. Nothing is more symptomatic of the profound changes taking place in China at present than the disappearance in the past few years of the once ubiquitous boiler-suits and the appearance instead of a mass of bureaucrats in grey flannel, ties and white shirts looking like investment analysts and with politics to match.

Clothes of that sort speak their own coded language, but what is different about the slogans on T-shirts and jackets is that here the message is foregrounded in letters six inches high. These messages can be categorised in various ways. A rough list of some of the main divisions amongst mass-produced items that I would like to examine would seem to me to include the following: the overtly political (FREE NELSON MANDELA or NICARAGUA MUST SURVIVE); those worn by fans of various kinds (MUFC or MADONNA); those implying the higher status or exotic experience of the wearer (OXFORD UNIVERSITY or IT'S BETTER IN THE BAHAMAS); those that are straight forms of advertising (NIKE or BENETTON); and those that are apparently meaningless

(BLUE CODE ENERGY or 225 AWARD).

The case of the first category, the overtly political, is fairly simple and commendable. The bearers regard their chosen cause as humanly necessary but in most cases neglected by the media and therefore offer their bodies as a means of communicating that cause to the public at large. The second category, the fan's T-shirt, performs a not dissimilar function. About the third category — the slogan that testifies to the experience or the status of the owner — we need not say anything except to hope that it won't be too long before the people behind them hit on a more fulfilling and socially valuable sense of self-worth. It is the last two categories — the T-shirt as advert and the meaningless T-shirt — that raise the most revealing and disturbing questions.

Let us begin with advertising. When the first casual clothes prominently displaying the name of the manufacturer started to appear a few years ago most people assumed that the wearers were being paid for their trouble. They seemed to be a modern version of sandwichboard men, those hapless souls removed by a law of 1853 from the pavement to the gutter where they earned an inadequate living humping big signs proclaiming THE END OF THE WORLD IS NIGH or EAT AT JOE'S. It therefore came as something of a shock to discover that people similarly touting ADIDAS or PRING-LE on their sweaters, far from being rewarded with a modest sum for consenting to the exploitation of their person, were in fact subsidising their own degradation at £39.99 a time. It is one of the more bizarre and depressing triumphs of capitalism in our time that large firms no longer have to buy their own advertising but have discovered a bovine army that is happy to pay a lot to do it for them.

This strange fact is only one symptom of the way the market is invading every aspect of social life. Its colonisation of sport, for example, is now complete, so that within the space of months the old Football League becomes the Canon League becomes the Today League becomes the Barclays League, and no professional soccer player is properly dressed without the name of a product positioned squarely for the television cameras. Indeed, to hawk only one product is a little reticent: Steffi Graf managed three (ADIDAS, BASF and OPEL) on her tennis shirt at the Wimbledon 1988 final. The prize is taken by Grand Prix drivers who these days look less and less like human beings and more and more like colour supplements tossed into a food mixer by mistake.

A generation ago Raymond Williams offered this analysis of the expansion of the advertising industry:

> The extension is natural, in a society where selling, by any effective means, has become a primary ethic. The spectacular growth of advertising ... has behind it not a mere pressure-group but the whole impetus of a society. It can then be agreed that we have come a long way from the papyrus of the runaway slave and the shouts of a towncrier: that what we have to look at is an organized and extending system, at the centre of our national life. . . . It is increasingly the source of finance for a whole range of general communication, to the extent that in 1960 our majority television service and almost all our newspapers could not exist without it. Further, in the last forty years and now at an increasing rate, it has passed the frontier of the selling of goods and services and has become involved with the teaching of social and personal values.[1]

Williams's reference here to 'teaching' has recently taken on an extra resonance that even he can scarcely have anticipated with the Manpower Services Commission's Enterprise in Higher Education Initiative. In return for £1 million per university or polytechnic over a five year period these institutions will be expected to 'develop competencies and aptitudes relevant to enterprise' amongst students, in which process 'employers shall have a clear stake ... and provide resources on a partnership basis'.[2] The extent to which society has changed in less than twenty years can be gauged by the fact that this Government bribe has been met with some enthusiasm and little resistance in higher education, whereas in 1970 E. P. Thompson could edit a successful Penguin called *Warwick University Ltd* based on the premiss that links between higher education and employers, far from being socially desirable, amounted to a squalid scandal.

In the course of the same essay Williams goes on to offer some intriguing asides on the way capitalism encourages people to accept partial definitions of themselves, as 'hands' or mere producers in the nineteenth century and as 'consumers' or mere stomachs in the twentieth. This saves having to negotiate with a full humanity and its awkward range of desires, needs and dreams. He concludes:

The consumer asks for an adequate supply of personal 'consumer goods' at a tolerable price: over the last ten years, this has been the primary aim of British government. But users ask for more than this, necessarily. They ask for satisfaction of human needs which consumption, as such, can never really supply. Since many of these needs are social—roads, hospitals, schools, quiet—they are not only not covered by the consumer ideal: they are even denied by it, because consumption tends always to materialize as an individual activity.[3]

We can now see as we move towards the 1990s that the processes Williams describes have moved several stages further on. It is, for example, no longer the task of higher education to aim for the realisation of a full humanity, to produce people capable of developing their unmanageably diverse potentials, to facilitate the emergence of a critical citizenry. The function in future will be to train entrepreneurs with 'competencies and aptitudes', a partial but revealing echo of the 'accomplishments' that women in the nineteenth century were offered as a substitute for genuine learning. In such a culture we can then recognise the T-shirt-as-advertisement as both symptom and facilitator. It is at once a sign of the times and one of several ways of accustoming people to their own robbery, the robbery of (amongst other things) their right to a real education as opposed to some form of meretricious indoctrination. After all, if you already pay ADIDAS to advertise on your chest, how can you possibly object if ASDA offers to buy up your brain?

The last category of T-shirt described earlier, namely those with apparently meaningless slogans on them, could be seen as a tiny protest against this advertisement culture. A top that declares YOU GRIND or 42 SWEATS is used to express nothing rather than sell something; these are signifiers that do not signify, words subverting their own communicative function. Sometimes they are not even words but a jumble of initials and abbreviations. There is a chain store tracksuit that affirms NMAA ASSOC. PHYS. DEPT. EST. 88 and recalls Herbert Marcuse's analysis of the terse, acronymic language of one-dimensional man.

To purchase such a top might indicate a promising restlessness on the part of the buyer with mass-produced uniformity, a desire to say something distinctive, but its distinctiveness is soon lost when we remember the identical hundreds on department store racks. The buyer is thus caught by the primary contradictory swindle that lies at the centre of fashion, namely the anxiety on the one hand to be in tune with contemporary developments and therefore like everyone else and, on the other, the aspiration to be special and therefore unlike everyone else.

Hence it becomes possible to argue that what apparently meaningless T-shirts that state cryptically M or SC in fact represent are new manifestations of alienation. It is alienation still rooted in the old truths about class, ownership and control, but alienation growing out in fresh, monstrous shapes. These are clothes that claim to express you, that make a statement about your identity and yet at the same time force you to bow to the market and participate in the circulation of gibberish. As I type there is a row of sweatshirts on sale in Selfridges which announce HEET CO. LTD. and then, in smaller lettering, go on: 'We are trying to find out a better way so life HEET experimental eo. LCD real taste'. What has happened here? Did the designer's word processor jam? Or is it a strangled cry from a sweatshop in the Philippines, as some half-starved seamstress's hazy grasp of English spins off into a demented shriek? Does anyone know? Does anyone care?

Just as disturbing are those shirts which use language with only the slightest denotative content but with powerful connotative implications. Many of these seem to be linked more or less directly with US imperialism. Some gesture towards North American sports and lifestyle (STATE OF THE ART SURFWEAR or BEST MONTANA CANADIAN HOCKEY) while others have a vague military menace (COMMAND OFFSHORE or BG MARINES SQUADRON). All can appear, in paranoid moments, to be designed to recruit the world's youth for the CIA, equipping them with uniforms which proclaim and contribute towards American cultural hegemony and military domination. The purchaser shares vicariously in that power by buying the slogan and then contributes to its entrenchment by parading it down the High Street.

At this point the primary need that clothes seek to meet—to provide us with warmth and covering—has almost disappeared behind a range of signifying practices developed by what can loosely be called publicity. Publicity not in the specific sense of advertising a particular brand, but publicity for a whole economic and political system. Far from being meaningless, what the apparently meaningless T-shirt in fact marks is the collapse of the local, the distinct, the different, the strange, the unique, the parochial and the eccentric, all absorbed into a world market which seeks to obliterate cultural specificity, regional variety and national tradition in order to function more efficiently. You can begin to glimpse a world with no jerkins, blouses, saris, kimonos, dungarees, caftans, boleros, togas, cardigans, blazers or tunics; everyone wears a sweatshirt that says 21 SAN FRANCISCO TOYBOY.

But if you set paranoia aside for a moment and substitute simple observation, you notice something quite cheering. People do not wear these sweatshirts. The shops may be full of them, but if you look around the streets in between those shops you will see that most men and women are still dressed in odd, plain, daft, impractical, dogged, ordinary or outlandish ways. They seem to be able to hunt out from somewhere clothes that are not overt adverts for a company or covert adverts for a 'lifestyle'. There is an unacknowledged, mulish rejection of these uniforms of domination and exploitation. It parallels the instinctive refusal of the vast majority, in spite of strenuous appeals, to drink fizzy beer, vote Conservative, buy shares in British Gas or take out private health insurance. It is on the rock of that splendid and stubborn good sense that resistance and then social transformation will eventually be built.

NOTES

1. Williams, R., 'Advertising: The Magic System', in *Problems in Materialism and Culture* (London: Verso, 1980) p. 184. Article originally published in *New Left Review*, 4, July–August 1960.
2. *Guardian*, 20 June 1988.
3. Op. cit., p. 188.

10

Recipes for Success

MICHAEL J. HAYES

We spend our lives interpreting, or as Barthes would say 'reading', not only the language but also the objects, actions and activities that constitute our environment. If somebody says they are going to have an aperitif we know they are going to have a certain kind of drink as a prelude to a meal. The use of the word 'aperitif' and the actual drink they choose, be it whisky, sherry or white wine and cassis, further reveals something of their lifestyle. If, moreover, they should give a self-consciously exaggerated pronunciation to the word 'aperitif' itself, we would suggest they are aping their own pretensions to the lifestyle announced by using the word, or even parodying that lifestyle in order to distance themselves from its social implications. They might be saying something such as 'we like the drink but don't want to be associated with the social conventions it implies'.

In this latter case the speakers are demonstrating an awareness of the ideological significance of what they are saying and doing. They are going beyond the surface or 'natural'[1] meaning in order to invoke consciously the hidden order of meaning. It is not the place here to summarise theories about meanings which derive from philosophy and linguistics, suffice it to say that meanings are created by and carry with them the whole history of people's relations with each other. Among the principle factors governing people's behaviour towards each other is the power relationship. The 'reading' we started with can, at a certain level, be seen as a reading of the history and practice of power relationships.

This interpretation of everyday language and occurrences as part of a power struggle is often easier to see when looking at cultures other than our own. Frake in his excellent 1964 article, 'How to Ask for a Drink in Subanun', says, for travellers who might have ventured to that part of the Philippines

The strategy of drinking talk is to manipulate the assignment of role relations among participants so that, within the limits of one's external status attributes, one can maximise his share of encounter resources (drink and talk), thereby having an opportunity to assume an esteem-attracting and authority-wielding role.[2]

In other words the drinking party Frake is discussing is an occasion specially designed for the individual to assert himself among his peers. He does this with a view to gaining approbation as a result of which he increases his personal authority and prestige. He concludes his article by writing 'In instructing our stranger to Subanun society how to ask for a drink, we have at the same time instructed him how to get ahead socially.'[3]

The Oxford English Dictionary defines the culinary meaning of 'recipe' as 'A statement of the ingredients and procedure necessary for the making or compounding of some preparation, especially of a dish in cookery: a receipt.'[4] It is the purpose of this article to look at ways in which cookery recipes are as much instructions on 'how to get ahead socially' as asking for a drink is in Subanun.

When Reay Tannahill published her *Food in History* in 1973 she expressed some surprise that, given the fundamental significance of food for the human race, nobody had produced such a work before. The search for sources of food, the development of new methods to improve cultivation of food crops and the battles for good food-yielding lands have been primary features of the human struggle. That power struggle found expression in the type of fare that different orders and classes of people were able to provide. Not for nothing does the Prodigal Son scrabble with swine for husks to illustrate how far he has declined, and have his return and rehabilitation signified by his father's killing a fatted calf for a feast.

Of course in more sophisticated societies than are figured in the world of the parables the struggles enacted on the table take on different significance. In her introduction to that monument to Victorian family life Mrs Beeton writes,

Men are so well served out of doors—at their clubs, well-ordered taverns, and dining houses, that in order to compete with the attractions of these places a mistress must be thoroughly acquainted with the theory and practice of cookery, as well as be perfectly conversant with all the other arts of making and keeping a comfortable home.[5]

Even if we ignore the possible ambivalence present in the word 'mistress' (and its secondary meaning has been in use since the fifteenth century), we still see the wife as having a duty to compete with the attractions outside the home. The key to maintaining the home as the primary focus of the husband's attentions is the provision of good food. In the struggle between domestic and public life a varied and interesting menu is an important weapon in the distaff armoury. But if the implied position of the woman is interesting, though conventionally fitting-in with our stereotypes of the Victorian wife, the man's position is equally interesting though less conventional. The man is seen not as a moral being but as one prey to his own desire for ease and comfort. His decisions are not seen as stemming from convictions but rather as weak, selfish inclinations to be manipulated. If we were to read Mrs Beeton's *Book of Household Management* (cookery did not figure in the original title) carefully we would discover a great deal more than simply what to eat and how to cook it! But in a field as vast as the ideological implications of cooking instructions (!) the scope of material for study has to be narrowed, in this case by focusing on the present day. Before coming right up to date, with a look at the cookery recipes given in the Sunday papers on 10th July 1988, it is worth considering for a moment the work of Elizabeth David, who has been a major influence on modern cookery writing.

The terms basic to cookery recipes involve ingredients and procedures, and we are concerned with the ways in which these terms are used as indicators of power relationships in social life. These basic terms are augmented by a range of subsidiary terms that in themselves can be interpreted as indicating underlying cultural realities. So Mrs Beeton, in her apparently commonsense way incorporated details of cost, numbers of servings and the seasonableness of the various ingredients. I use the phrase 'apparently commonsense way' because, whilst such information is certainly practical it is evident that it also had financial, social and even class implications.

Elizabeth David in addition to manipulating the basic terms involving ingredients and procedures also gives numbers of servings and three types of signification which I shall informally call internationalism, sophistication and literariness. It is these three which particularly signal the underlying meanings of the recipes.

Certainly the praise that Elizabeth David has attracted from a wide range of sources is deserved in that, those with the authority to say, attest that her recipes work. Moreover her blending of the ingredients with the mode of preparation rather than simply listing the constituents and following them with instructions makes for fluency and vivacity. This articulacy contributes to the sense of literariness which makes her books enjoyable browsing for some who rarely, if ever, attempt the dishes described. This literariness of her work is also advanced by her discussions of ingredients, her revelation of sources and her ability to locate the dishes in their places of origin whether they be France or Italy. We not only get the recipe but the story to go with it.

However this combination of literariness and internationalism, this evocation of experiences in foreign places, this easy familiarity with foreign living as distinct from merely foreign travel immediately privileges the few. It is the few who have either enjoyed similar experiences or who have the background sufficient to recognise the experiences who can enjoy the recipes. The structures of meaning are such as to include the few and exclude the many. Inclusion is based on a level of appreciation which is primarily located in class determined attitudes, experiences and perceptions. These features, generally identified as internationalism, sophistication and literariness, can best be developed by looking at a particular recipe. Choosing fairly randomly from *Italian Food* we have the recipe for Ragù. As Elizabeth David says 'This is the true name of the Bolognese sauce which, in one form of another, has travelled round the world.'[6] The authenticity of the name is the first play in attesting the absolute authenticity of this particular recipe against rivals which appear 'in one form or another . . . round the world'.

This easy familiarity with what is foreign not only yields information interesting in itself but its trustworthiness can be used to validate accompanying information. So far we are observing only that the truth of the name, ragù, is by implication validating this particular recipe, but potentially such validation can be used to assert anything, even particular designer life styles. Here we are concerned only with the dish itself, though we note in passing the transferable power of authentication.

Sophistication derives in part from that sense of special knowledge, here deriving from internationalism, also from the fluent blending of ingredients and procedures. It is true that, 'The ingredients to make enough sauce for six generous helpings of pasta are'[7] sequentially listed. However the main source of sophistication is to be found in the elaboration of either ingredients or procedures. So we find 'Another traditional variation is the addition of the ovarine or unlaid eggs which are found inside the hen, especially in the Spring when the hens are laying'.[8] The secret ingredient lies hidden in the hen. Ready access to ovarine eggs is, one would suppose, limited, if you are among the chosen and able to draw on the secret ingredient the result will be 'small golden globules when the sauce is finished'.[9] For the initiates it is not just special knowledge which is important but the implied power over the processes of nature. In the struggle for food resources the ability to utilise rare or specially cultivated ingredients is an assertion of power over both nature and one's rivals in the contest for food.

The third feature I have chosen to identify, literariness, arises as I have suggested from the recipe as narrative, in many cases narrative as folk-tale. We have already pointed to the implied magical properties of ovarine eggs. Now let us look for a moment at the last paragraph of the recipe. Zia Nerina is the actual source of the recipe but her reputation is mythic. As in the best folk stories she is 'renowned far beyond the confines of her native city'.[10] Indeed Elizabeth David herself has become a part of the myth in that it is she who has returned with the magic recipe. Unfortunately turning people into fictions can be demeaning, Zia Nerina is 'a splendid woman, titanic of proportions but angelic of face and manner'.[11] The fictionalising and mythologising with its juxtaposition of the pejorative 'titanic' with the ameliorating 'angelic' is unpleasantly condescending. The literary sensibility at once enhances the scope of the writing, it adds context to the bare recital of ingredients and procedures, but in reducing a real person to a few glib phrases denies her right to a truer presentation.

As the conventions inherent in particular kinds of writing undergo changes there are both losses and gains. There appears to have been a revitalising of cookery writing in the 1950s. As to Elizabeth David's role in that I am uncertain, what is certain is that her writing exemplifies features which are open to manipulation and abuse. In the third part I shall look at cookery writing in the Sunday papers particularly those of 10 July 1988.

There is something contradictory in the concept of newspapers. They are intended for the day but their use of written language propels them beyond the moment. This contradiction is in part resolved in the Sunday papers by the production of magazine sections and colour supplements, both of which aspire to a life longer than the day. As one would expect recipes, with their need for prior planning and purchase of ingredients, require a longer time span so are usually to be found in the magazine sections or the supplements.

So far I have tried to establish that recipes, like other languages carry messages of power. Moreover as the conventions of recipe writing have been extended the potential for ideological manipulation has been increased. In looking at the cookery writing for Sunday 10 July 1988 we can see both the manipulation of the messages and the corruption of those genre features informally identified in the writing of Elizabeth David.

If one were, on the basis of the discussion so far, to predict where most of the food and cookery writing would occur it would be in the so-called quality papers and that, as we will see, is the case. But before looking closely at them we will look at the offerings in the other papers.

The *People* is interesting in having a regular recipe column in the 'Go' magazine section. On a page that has a small motoring column, a crossword and a gardening column it devotes a few inches to the 'Recipe of the Week'. This recipe eschews all but the basics, it gives the ingredients and the method of preparation. For 10 July it was a 'Fruit crumble pudding'. No attempt is made to do any more than give practical cooking instructions for one dish each week.

The other papers in this group with their specifically colour supplement offerings, as opposed to the *People*'s magazine section that has the same format as the paper, manipulate the genre more determinedly. The *News of the World* on this particular day has part one of a 'Pub Guide' giving locations and a few lines of description, included in the guide is a list of '100 Best Beers and Lagers'. Another relevant feature is an article about a young woman who goes on a diet, her aim in doing so is to be recognised, 'to be somebody' as she says. This ambition can be realised by being sexually attractive, a goal expressed by becoming a glamour model. My analysis is concerned with the use of recipes and food writing more generally to promote power and authority structures. Such structures obviously, in our present cultural situation, have sexist dimensions. While not being primarily concerned here with that aspect it must be remarked that this feature in the *News of the World* is a particularly blatant example.

Neither the *Sunday Express* nor the *Mail on Sunday* have recipes as such though both have food writing in their supplements. The *Express* has an up-market version of the good pub guide in its series 'A Taste of Summer', advising on places to eat. Dinner, apart from three reasonably priced suggestions, comes out at an average of £19 per person—one way of blowing unemployment benefit! Another *Express* series is called 'Out to Lunch', it features a restaurant and a star, in this case Lesley-Anne Down. Basically it is an opportunity to interview the star with minimal comments on the food being served. A reminder of Lesley-Anne Down's cockney origins are mixed in with reference to the 'asparagus with its chervil and beurre blanc sauce'[12] which she is eating. The genuine internationalism of Elizabeth David has succumbed to the authority of glamour.

The *Mail's* version of this authoritative glamour of food is an interview with the head of a champagne firm Claude Taittinger. Like his glamorous product Taittinger epitomises authority. When his wife and daughter join him and the interviewer 'The respect they showed for Taittinger was impressive. Whenever he spoke they were absolutely silent and only offered additional comment when he or I referred to them directly.'[13] While there is a certain ambivalence underlying the interviewer's stance, likening Taittinger to Blake in 'Dynasty' for example, there is little to suggest that this quotation is intended to be taken ironically.

When we move on to the *Telegraph* Sunday Magazine there is no such ambivalence. Robert Chalmers article 'Culture on a Plate' is a generally caustic article on the cafés and restaurants attached to various theatres and galleries. Again the food is discussed but there are no recipes. However in the women's section of the paper there is an article devoted to cooking with apricots. 'I always associate apricots with my childhood in Syria . . . and the best taste of all is if you can pick and eat the fruit still warm from the sun on its branch.'[14] The rather pretentious internationalism of the opening is followed by a variety of recipe suggestions for using apricots. But the assumed audience for these recipes is most definitely not that for the *People's* fruit crumble. For spiced pork 'an iron casserole' is specified, and when we read, 'If you have an icecream maker you can puree the stewed apricots', I am tempted to reply 'we have, but it's his day off'.

The epitome of sophistication as self-indulgence is the dinner party in the *Observer*. Here the director of the Chichester Theatre is entertaining a number of stars, such as Donald Sinden, from this year's company. The format is a good deal of gossip with some commentary on the food and wine being served. Where the article differs from the Express 'Out to Lunch' feature, which the following week starred none other than that bon viveur Donald Sinden, is in actually giving a recipe. Here the first course gazpacho is featured. The recipe itself just has ingredients listed and simple instructions for preparation. Nothing is made of the internationalism of the gazpacho, in the face of sophisticated glamour that has become unremarkable. As for the literariness commented on earlier that has become the rather banal retailing of self-congratulatory theatre gossip. The narrative context for the recipes has become the weekly construction of a media event, glamorous figures eating.

The search for new culinary secrets for the initiates has become more taxing. If ordinary Sunday papers can get by with simply repackaging their food writing, the 'qualities' have actually to give their readers new information. The *Sunday Times*, on its 'Food and Drink' page discusses the wine to go with chocolate while in the *Observer* Raymond Blanc determinedly elaborates the simplicities of the new cooking, counterpointed by Paul Levy's frequently pretentious commentaries on various aspects of food, wine and which restaurants to go to.

What I have tried to show in my analysis is that just as control of food supplies is obviously a source of power so writing about food entails a rhetoric of power. When a mass medium, such as journalism, gets hold of this rhetoric its endless repetitions create distortions. By selectively imitating its own borrowings it ends up parodying or even attacking its own substance. Of course as the power of the old rhetoric declines a new one emerges; 'Oh we have that, but we call it "bubble and squeak".'

NOTES

1. Barthes, R., tr. R. Howard, 'The Kitchen of Meaning', in *The Semiotic Challenge* (Oxford: Blackwell, 1988) p. 158.
2. Frake, C. O., 'How to Ask for a Drink in Subanun', in P. P. Giglioli (ed.), *Language and Social Context* (Middlesex: Penguin, 1973) p. 91.
3. Ibid., p. 93.
4. The Oxford English Dictionary (Oxford: OUP, 1961).
5. Beeton, I., 'Preface to first edition', reprinted, *Mrs Beeton's Cookery and Household Management* (London: Ward Lock, 1961) p. 5.
6. David, E., *Italian Food* (London: Barrie and Jenkins, 1987) p. 190.

7.   Ibid., p. 190.
8.   Ibid., p. 190.
9.   Ibid., p. 190.
10.   Ibid., p. 190.
11.   Ibid., p. 190.
12.   *Sunday Express* Magazine, 10 July 1988, p. 62.
13.   You Magazine, (*Mail on Sunday*) 10 July 1988, p. 80.
14.   *Sunday Telegraph,* 10 July 1988.

11

That's Entertainment?

GARY DAY

The number of quiz shows on television is a testament to their popularity. They enjoy consistently high ratings and not an evening goes by without at least one, with all its accompanying razamattaz, appearing on our screens. But why do people watch them, what is their appeal and do they serve any other purpose apart from that of entertainment?

There seem to be two kinds of show. The first and more serious, of which the paradigm is 'Mastermind', tests the general knowledge of the contestants while the second, for example 'Play your Cards Right', measures how far the contestants' views conform to the public's on such matters as the proportion of husbands who help their wives with the washing-up.

At present, there are more shows of the latter type than the former, though each has its own appeal. The straightforward quiz allows the audience to pit their wits against the contestants and arguably has more drama for, as the questions get harder, the prizes get bigger. The other kind of show, however, which might be termed the 'fun quiz', has an altogether more frenzied atmosphere, which in part derives from the personality of the host, in part from the trivial and slightly risqué nature of the questions and in part from audience participation. In addition to these individual qualities, both kinds of show contain elements of fantasy which makes them an ideal form of escapism. Their glossy formats, the fact that they are open to all and the seemingly inexhaustible supply of easily available luxury goods, offers an attractive alternative to the real world which, with all its problems, is dull by comparison.

But although quiz shows function as a refuge from reality it is also true to say that they help mould it, since their values and structures draw on and reinforce certain aspects of capitalist ideology. Most obviously, both kinds of quiz encourage the values of acquisitiveness and competitive individualism, without which capitalism couldn't function. However, there are other, more subtle, ways in which the quiz show shapes and underpins the capitalist view of the world.

To take the second type of quiz first. Here contestants are told, for example, that a hundred people were asked to name a vegetable beginning with 'T'; the contestants are then asked to do the same and the person who gives the most popular answer, according to the show's poll, is the winner. Bob Monkhouse, who used to host 'Family Fortunes' sums up the philosophy of such shows when he tells the contestants to think of the 'obvious'. The obvious, however, is always an ideological concept. What appears to be natural, spontaneous and self-evident is in fact a product of a particular way of looking at the world. To say it's obvious that people aren't equal is to forget how far such a statement serves the interests of capitalism. The obvious is never just obvious, it always has a use. The fun quiz, by reinforcing the idea of the obvious helps to reinforce the ideological experience itself which is never felt as ideological but always as obvious or natural; indeed that is precisely where its power lies, for the obvious, as Althusser and others have noted, obscures those very things it supposedly explains.

Trying to make people think of the obvious is an essential part of what the fun quiz is trying to do, namely encourage contestants to respond in the same way as members of the public did when they were asked to name a vegetable beginning with 'T'. The question itself is important only in so far as its inanity deflects attention from its real purpose, which is to elicit a set of standard responses. The contestants who give the most popular answer, according to the sample of people questioned, are rewarded, while those who give the least popular answer, again according to the sample, are penalised. In other words, the winners of such shows are always those who respond as the majority respond.

This attempt to make individuals conform is not confined to the fun quiz for it can also be seen in the vast number of public opinion polls which are so ubiquitous nowadays. These, it may be said, do not reflect the public opinion so much as influence it, since those who read them are, in fact, being pressurised to think like everyone else. In both the fun quiz and the public opinion poll the individual is being asked to submit to the authority of the group; a group, moreover, that he or she knows nothing about and whose existence is entirely statistical. By preying on the human fear of not belonging, the fun quiz and the public opinion poll help create a climate of conformity which politicians can exploit to their advantage. In such circumstances the definition of democracy is narrowed to agreeing with the views of an abstract majority on pre-determined issues which may not be of the least importance to those questioned about them.

Sometimes, however, as in 'The Price is Right', the public is not a statistic but a concrete reality. The audience in that show play an active part throughout, shouting advice at the contestants with the result that, in the end, the latter have no choice but to yield to group pressure and give, not their own opinion of the price of an item but the audience's.

The now defunct 'Generation Game', though not strictly a quiz show, offers another example of how entertainment works to preserve the status quo. One of the highlights of this show was the introduction of a person skilled in some particular field which could be anything from cake decorating to morris dancing. The expert quickly demonstrated his or her particular skill and then the contestants were invited to 'have a go'. Needless to say, their bungling attempts to make, say, a corn-dolly, were a source of much amusement. The laughter, however, derived from the idea, perfectly consistent with class society, that everyone has their place and function and to try and step outside them is both foolish and ridiculous. In this way the 'Generation Game' helped to produce a static view of the world which is, among other things, exactly what the serious quiz shows do, though by a different means.

To begin with the serious quiz promotes a particular use of knowledge, one which serves the all-important ethic of acquisition. The contestants in these shows are rewarded, not according to how much their view conforms to the majority view, but according to how much they know. Knowledge is judged quantatively rather than qualitively and this, together with the fact that it is exchanged for goods, means that it functions like money, for like money it is used for the pursuit and possession of commodities. The more you know, as it were, the more you win. The fact that it's the cumulative value of knowledge that's stressed in shows like 'Sale of the Century' is surely significant in a society whose aim is the accumulation of capital as profit. One definition of profit, perhaps, is money that's removed from the processes of production to benefit the individual rather than the community. If this definition is acceptable, then it can be seen that knowledge behaves in more or less the same way, for it too is removed from production by being part of a programme which is meant as entertainment. It is not bound up with research, nor does it have any larger practical purpose nor, indeed, is it used in any of the ways that one expects knowledge to be used. It benefits no-one but the contestant, exactly as profit benefits no one but the isolated individual. What counts in the serious quiz then, is not knowledge *per se*, but the use of knowledge since that reinforces the use of money as accumulation and profit and as something for the purchase of goods, all things on which capitalism depends.

One of the basic assumptions of the serious quiz is that for every question there is a right or wrong answer. Perhaps the effect of such an assumption, transmitted nightly over a long period of time, is to encourage people to think in terms of absolutes, to see only one side of an issue rather than to recognise its complexity. Such a perspective would certainly help to reinforce certain myths that abound unchallenged in our society including, among others, Soviet ambitions in the West and the power of the unions.

Myths, of course, stand in opposition to history and therefore have a timeless quality. They present a static view of the world which is not dissimilar to the way the serious quiz presents knowledge. What it suggests is that knowledge is a body that's already complete since all that's required of the contestant is that he or she reproduce it, not add to it. There is an answer to every question the host asks even if the contestant doesn't know it and it's this principle of the answer already being known that helps generate the sense that the body of knowledge is complete. What the serious quiz ultimately, yet insistently, urges is that there's nothing more to know: the contestants regurgitate what they already know and the body of knowledge is complete to the extent that they are only ever tested on it. This idea, never articulated but constantly implied, naturally precludes the possibility of discovering anything new and thus the serious quiz artfully cultivates a passive attitude toward knowledge. Enquiry and exploration are superfluous if everything is already known and so these two intellectual activities, which are in an indispensable relationship to knowledge, are divorced from it. Speculation is unnecessary where there is a right or wrong answer to every question, and so eventually, the activity of speculation, except in rarefied circles, becomes devalued as something which has no practical purpose.

The serious quiz's tacit conception of knowledge as something that's complete and either true or false is echoed in the way news is reported on television and in the press. Behind the emphasis on factual reporting, irrespective of whether or not it's achieved, lies the assumption that there is a true or false description of events and the true one is that which contains all the facts. The news is a representation of the world based on these assumptions which it shares with the serious quiz. Both are concerned with what rather than why. The news is about what happens, while the typical question in the serious quiz runs something like this: 'What is the capital of Peru?' or 'Which composer was thought to have been poisoned by a rival?'

Just as the serious quiz encourages a passive attitude to know-ledge so does the news to the event it portrays. The various institutions of the media work less on the basis that people make the news than that they need to have it brought to their attention. The audience, in other words, is allotted a passive role. All it's required to do is witness events without either necessarily under-standing them or taking sides. By developing a passive attitude to the world, the news reinforces that passivity to knowledge de-veloped by the serious quiz. Together they create a view of the world as given and fixed, making it difficult to either conceive of change or imagine how it may be brought about.

A further way in which both the news and the serious quiz secure this effect is by suppressing connections between items of information. The answer to one question in a quiz will not do for the answer to another question. Each one is complete in itself and has no reference to any other, even though they may both relate to the same topic, as they do in a programme like 'Mastermind'. The aim is not to discover any relation between either the questions or the answer on a particular subject but to answer more questions than the other contestants. Similarly, news items appear in the press or on our screens one after the other, without any apparent connection between them. In a single news bulletin the viewer may see pictures of riots in South Africa and hear about virginity tests at Heathrow Airport yet not make the connection between them because the news, in virtue of its structure, does not allow that connection to be made.

The viewer receives information about the world a piece at a time, therefore he or she cannot form a whole picture of it, which is absolutely necessary if he or she is to analyse and understand it. In presenting knowledge and events in this sequential, unconnected fashion, the serious quiz and the news once more support each other and make it difficult for people to make connections between what they know in order to criticise and challenge the society in which they live.

Although the news has a structured similarity to the serious quiz in the way it presents things, it is also related to the fun quiz for it is true that news is slanted and, to that extent it is, like the fun quiz, attempting to create a consensus. But the news is not just related to the quizzes, as the appearance of bingo in most of the daily papers shows. Bingo differs from the quizzes in that it has nothing to do with guessing or general knowledge, it is purely a matter of luck. The people who play hope to win that magic million which will change their lives, but they put their faith in chance rather than in their own efforts and this is precisely what bingo encourages, trust in forces outside the self. In this, it underscores that very passivity of the individual which is produced by the quizzes and the news.

What all this amounts to is that the distinction between news and entertainment is not as marked as the pages of a newspaper or the *TV Times* or *Radio Times* would have us believe. They complement one another in the way that they structure our perceptions of the world so that we see it from one point of view rather than another. This structuring process is not obvious and perhaps is all the more effective for that; it has to be uncovered in a manner analogous to that of literary criticism which attempts not to lay bare the inner, essential meaning of a work, but to recognise its multiple meanings and see how they are produced.

Cultural analysis of this sort is not to be dismissed as an elitist activity practised by academic Marxists for it is an indispensable tool in the fight against capitalist ideology. Its use is all the more necessary as leisure time increases, for with it so do the number of quizzes and games. Not only do these need to be understood, but so too does the present trend towards home-based leisure, for as more people remain indoors with their videos and computers, the more vulnerable do they become to manipulation by that very technology which is now in danger of becoming the new opium of the people.

12

Christmas: Celebrating the Humbug

NORMA WORDSWORTH

There has always been a certain section amongst the Left who have been ill at ease with pleasure and enjoyment. It is almost as if poverty and pain were the essential ingredients in the fermentation of revolutionary fervour, as if, somehow, it was counter-revolutionary to laugh. Such activities that might lighten the load and make living more bearable are viewed with suspicion and more than an element of disdain. George Orwell for one, in his treatise on the working class *The Road to Wigan Pier* stated, 'It is quite likely that fish-and-chips, art-silk stockings, tinned salmon, cut-price chocolate ... the movies, the radio, strong tea and the Football Pools have between them averted revolution'.[1] Although I've never been entirely sure why strong tea should have been singled out in this way the message is clear enough. Watching 'Eastenders', listening to Boy George and reading Mills and Boon might well prevent you from building the barricades. They are thus consigned to the dustbin of false consciousness. Regarded as mere sops for the unaware and uninitiated they seem almost to have replaced religion as the opiate of the masses, at least in the minds of those most influenced by the Frankfurt School of aesthetics. As a consequence Socialism has become devoid of the ability to engage with those very aspects of living that people most enjoy.

The good news is that people need no longer feel quite so guilty about indulging in the latest Stephen King offering or staying at home to catch the omnibus edition of 'Brookside'. Soap opera, romance stories, indeed genre fiction as a whole, popular music and cinema have all been re-evaluated and taken out of the 'dope for the dopes' strait-jacket of more orthodox criticism. If they have not been universally reclaimed as 'legitimate' pastimes then at the very least they are being debated. What is slightly less gratifying though is the silence over those areas of our material culture which refuse the neat categories of 'leisure' or 'entertainment'. I'm thinking here of those aspects of our life which are more specifically ritualistic in nature and of which Christmas is a prime example. Neither hobby nor activity it is nevertheless part of our lives and some sort of indicator of the state of our personal and social relationships. Christmas may only come once a year but it has a long established place on our agendas dating back to the pre-Christian era and it deserves a little reappraisal, if only to expunge some of the guilt that seems endemic whenever 'that time of year' looms ahead.

The immediate problem is of course that Christmas carries with it such strong overtones of commercialisation that much of the criticism about it seems perfectly valid. An ever increasing circle of people I know regard it as something to be suffered rather than celebrated. Each year these same people promise themselves that this year will be the very last year, that they will not be inveigled into posting cards and stuffing turkeys and, as you may have guessed, I have counted myself amongst these number. But, come December the temptation to stuff the cards and post the turkey has been abandoned, laid to rest, murdered by an overkill of advertising hype and inter-personal pressure. Not that the impulse to flee the festivities goes to its grave willingly. But, confronted with 'what about the kids?' and threatened by 'it's only once a year', the urge to ignore the yule-tide junket shuffles its way to the scrapyard of what-might-have-been and awaits resurrection to the clarion call of Christmas-Next Year. It is a brave individual who swims against the tide and I am not one who has ever been accorded that particular description. So, bearing it, if not actually grinning I, along with the rest of the populace, begin the Long March to supermarket and chain-store.

I may be imagining it but as I get older the countdown to The Big Day starts a little earlier each year. Christmas now seems to arrive in September, albeit imperceptibly. Its presence heralded, not by angels, but those 'Buy Now—Beat The Rush' holly-decorated stickers that are emblazoned on the windows of the more market-minded stores. By November 'Xmas' is in full swing, along with the interminable, inevitable office party and occasional intrepid carol singer. Where only yesterday shop fronts were stressing the delights of Factor 19 cucumber sun tan cream and the luxury of the individual, inflatable beach pillow, they now extol the necessity of possessing monogrammed Y-fronts, exotic lingerie, perfumed pom-poms and other assorted trinkets from tinsel town. In the force fed world of consumer and consumed there are no rules for the natural seasons, except those of the seasoned campaigner in search of higher profit margins, naturally. In the merchandisers' scenario summer springs effortlessly into winter paying only lip-service to autumn with those 'Back to School' advertisements and a thank you nod in the direction of Bonfire Night. Where would November sales be but for Guy Fawkes? Ironic, really.

By the end of November the advertisers have gone into overload. Television commercials assume an air of Messianic zeal and manic frenzy. 'There's never been a better bargain in your life' jostles for position alongside 'Your child will love you for buying My Little Puppy—it walks, talks and sings', does everything in fact bar mess on the carpet. The choice before the consumer is simple; purchase and be loved for ever more, resist and be eternally damned; the spectre of Scrooge hangs heavy over every parental head. So it comes to pass that by December the shops are burgeoning with the new life of those curiously ephemeral consumer durables. They appear as if by magic overnight, destined for the Christmas market, an ad-person's fantasy land populated by fictional families of high wage earners with limited sensibility incomes. These families know that 'The Special Day' will not be special unless they are the owners of the variable speed, voice-activated carving knife which tells not only the speed at which you carve but also the time in ten different countries. But, it is a curious fact that I have never, to this day, met anyone willing to admit ownership of an alpine-spa foot massager or an electronic car key fob which whistles when you clap your hands. Presumably though there must be those in receipt of such items; closet owners of things best kept in the closet.

In this never-never land of consumerdom the fairy lights always twinkle, the goose always lays a golden egg before laying itself in the oven and Bing Crosby ever croons 'White Christmas' outside the window whilst Santa gives out the presents. But, as the critics of Christmas point out, Supplementary Benefit doesn't stretch to a goose, golden or otherwise, the homeless have no windows for Bing to sing outside of and there is little cause for the unemployed to celebrate when Santa proffers an empty sack. So why bother? Why do people continue to go through with this peculiar ritual each year if Christmas is only about fantasy goods for fictional families?

For Christians perhaps the occasion is not as laden with misgivings as it might be. At this time of year personal belief and community celebration coalesce, become intertwined in a festival that is a witness to their faith. Certainly there are Christians who equally deplore its commercialisation but, at the end of the day, there is still some point to it all. The excesses of consumer materialism can be regarded as just that, the regrettable consequence of a secular world. For those with a vested interest in the machinations of the market economy there is also every reason to celebrate. Christmas is truly the season of good cheer and glad tidings to all men, the ringing of the tills foretells yet another profit and a still more healthy bank balance. But for the rest of us, those who are uncommitted to Christianity and unconvinced by Conservatism, why do we bother?

Part of the answer to this must rest with the fact that the scenario of Christmas as a capitalist con-trick played by the captains of commerce on a passive population just doesn't work. There is nothing inherently 'wrong' with consumer durables. They are not 'bad' by some mythical socialist yardstick. As far as I can tell, the acquisition and redistribution of shop bought goods, that is giving presents, doesn't in actuality mitigate against socialism. Rather, the impulse to give might be seen as subversive to that capitalist ethic which suggests that you can't get something for nothing. This may sound somewhat specious since presumably the essence of the antipathy towards Christmas resides in its being a commercial manipulation of the genuine desire to give. This is true to a certain extent but it also begs the question as to how we are to define 'genuine' desires. We can't, however much we try, lift ourselves out of the social and political nexus unscathed and point to an a priori genuine person with unmediated desires and demands. Although capitalism may seek to channel human behaviour in an effort to buttress its own foundations, our needs and impulses are not in themselves symptomatic of the drive towards capital accumulation, and not wholly under the control of the business barons.

It seems to me that the real problem for those most suspicious of Christmas rests not so much with the fact that people consume but rather with the nature of that consumption. In other words people buy things for others that they don't 'really need', that the entire process is a waste of money. I would have thought though that this lack of obvious utility was one of the aspects of Christmas that gave substance to the occasion and accounted for its longevity of tradition. I remember that as a child the presents I loved the best were not the essential shoes or warm jumpers but the plastic farm animals and glittery tinsel-topped jewellery that served no ostensible purpose in life other than that they made me happy. These were the gifts that delighted most and that they did so was partly to do with the fact that I didn't need them to survive. They were not reminders of an external reality that I had constantly to negotiate in order to find where I fitted but sources of pleasurable fantasy in which I could construct myself at will. Now that I'm a 'grown up' this joy in non-essentials hasn't changed. It's just that I feel guilty about it because of the awareness that superfluity signifies such a range of negative attributes, of which greediness and wastefulness are but a few.

I suspect that what lies at the heart of this anti-consumerism form of critique is a type of patronising conceit. As Beatrix Campbell has pointed out, 'the complaint from the moral school of socialism against material goods is always about the working class having them. Presumably if they were going to the opera on HP instead of buying automatic washing machines, there wouldn't be a problem.'[2] I have my doubts as to whether opera on HP would be any more acceptable to those of the 'moral left' than the purchase of a washing machine. Nevertheless Campbell has pin-pointed the area that gives rise to considerable misunderstanding regarding consumer goods and the nature of their consumption. In point of fact an object is never just an object and is always mediated by the methods of production. But there is an immense difference between what people own in their personal lives and the means by which these goods are manufactured within society. No one gets richer by possessing a washing machine, only the owners of the plants and factories where they are produced. Those childish impulses, those 'child-within-us-all' desires for novelty, surprise and enjoyment are not activated by the market. Rather a symbiotic tension exists between our desires on the one hand, and on the other the goods in the warehouses that business wants to sell to us. Admittedly the match is never very even; what we are left with a week after Christmas is the aftermath of badly made things that were *almost* what we wanted. But, given that this is the case it should not lead us to the position where we abandon Christmas altogether when it is the method and means of marketing which need overhaul rather than the occasion.

Possibly the most injurious criticism voiced about Christmas is that it reinforces those notions of the family which are retrogressive in their insistence upon it as a self-contained, self-serving unit. That in fact it is this more than anything which leads to the alienation of those who find it difficult to participate, either through lack of money or because they are on their own. That in effect Christmas leads only to a retrenchment of their position as 'outsider'; isolated financially and/or emotionally Christmas is just another exclusion zone and an additional burden to shoulder.

What tends to be forgotten in all this is that Christmas can be a time when the usual definition of family becomes distended so as to encompass those not normally within the confines of its parameters. Indeed friends, neighbours, even distant relatives are often a more vital part of the proceedings than immediate family. Even that curious phenomenon the work-place party gestures some way towards breaking the demarcation line between the personal and the formal relationship. If Christmas is a time that doesn't actually shatter the myths surrounding the family at least it can allow a glimpse into the possibilities of different ways of connecting with others. Sometimes this alternative vision of what might be possible shifts from the realm of the imagined and becomes a lived reality.

During the recent miners' strike Christmas could have been yet another burden to be shrugged off. That it wasn't was due to the efforts of both the miners' families and the wider community which supported them:

> ... more and more of our time was spent getting ready for Christmas. We were receiving massive support. Presents for the kids were pouring in ... the other side of the preparations, the preparing of food, was also a massive task ... Every woman will know how much work it takes to prepare for Christmas. We prepared for a monster Christmas and the work involved was monstrous. But we did it willingly and happily, we were so surprised that the support had been so generous to us. We'd expected the worst Christmas of our lives and now it seemed we were going to have one of the best.[3]

This repays close reading, not the least in its acknowledgement of womens' extra labour during Christmas. It also succeeds in making a nonsense of the notion that such a festival has no place on the calendars of those least in a position to celebrate it. Denied a more conventional Christmas the mining communities created their own and by so doing strengthened their own sense of individual worth and collective identity:

> The pit always held a Children's Christmas Party and this year none of us had been invited so we held our own. It was fantastic, the kids had a ball. Father Christmas came and bought them all a little present . . . Christmas day itself was fantastic. We hadn't been able to find out exactly how many people were coming, in the end there was just over a hundred of us. Christmas dinner was as elaborate as any we've had, we went without nothing. Supporters had bought us food, drinks, Christmas crackers and cigarettes, as well as the presents.[4]

It is instances like this that illuminate how such occasions can break the insular definition of family and suggest a broader, more encompassing network of community. It might be argued that this widened sense of family and community was already in place, produced not by any wish to challenge the normative values of society but by the exigencies of the strike. However, the decision to strike was, in itself seen by the government as a challenge to its right to rule and therefore a challenge to the normative values of society. In any case what is important is that as the mining communities discovered that they could not rely on such institutions as the press they had to develop new means of organising. In a situation where they had to question those aspects of life normally taken for granted, such as the role of the family, they were able to place Christmas as a celebration of and testament to their new sense of community.

Another often overlooked factor about Christmas is that even within the strict definition of family it can offer one of the only times when collective activity can become a possibility. It was for instance that rarest of occasions when my mother enjoyed being in the kitchen. Surrounded by both sisters she enjoyed a sense of mutual support not normally on offer during the rest of the year. It would of course be absurd to suggest that Christmas can transform the nature of our relationships or of our society. Such events are not agents of change and are always open to manipulation. But at a time when the ruling powers are distinctly unhappy about business and industry shutting down for the Christmas week then its about time we started to question and define such events on our own terms. Part of Christmas may indeed be fantasy goods for fictional families but that's not all of the picture and need not lead us to relinquish it wholesale. Even when the barricades have been erected I suspect that there will still be the need for community celebration of some sort and always the desire for the non-essential and frivolous. If we ignore this part of ourselves then we also run the risk of denying the dynamic within us that ignites personal and political change. If Christmas as it stands is not entirely satisfactory then neither is it completely beyond the pale. Personally I think Dickens and Disney have a lot to answer for but, as Emma Goldman is reputed to have said, 'if I can't dance its not my revolution', and if I can't indulge then it's not my insurrection. Always remember it was that arch capitalist Scrooge who said of it 'Bah—Humbug!'.

NOTES

1. Orwell, G., *The Road to Wigan Pier* (Harmondsworth: Penguin, 1974) pp. 80–1.
2. Campbell, Beatrix *Wigan Pier Revisited* (London: Virago, 1984) p. 226.
3. Beaton, Lynn, *Shifting Horizons* (London: Canary Press, 1985) pp. 249–50.
4. Ibid., p. 251.

13

War Toys

GRAHAM DAWSON

'A toy, simply, is something to have fun with.'
Leslie Daiken, *Children's Toys Throughout the Ages.*

With only 64 shopping days to Christmas, 'Toys for 1988: the
Gamleys Christmas Catalogue' landed unsolicited on my doormat.
It was a reminder that the toy industry trades in wishes and
desires. The front cover photograph features a Christmas morning
scene with tree and presents, bathed in golden light, that is gazed
at from the shadows in the doorway by a boy and a girl with their
backs to the camera. The presents themselves are not wrapped up
as gifts, but displayed as they would be in the shop, in attractive
packages with brand names facing the viewer: 'Kongman', a 'Tiny
Tears' doll, 'Le Mans Scalextric' — and an 'Action Force' helicopter.
Within the catalogue, these toys are sorted into sections. At the
front, you immediately discover 'Action Figures, Cars, Trucks,
Robots, Trains and Science', featuring on the first page the 'Action
Force' series of 'fully poseable modern army figures' and their
range of military vehicles. At the back, after some hunting, you will
find 'Soft Toys, Around the House, Dolls and Accessories'. Predict-
ably, all six illustrative photos in the 'around the house' section
feature girls, and all four in the 'action' section feature boys. The
organisation of desire here is gendered, and a classic dichotomy
reproduced, whereby girlhood is associated with domesticity and
the private world, and boyhood with adventure and the public
world. One of the central themes in this play world of boyhood
adventure is, of course, war.

Toy soldiers and other war toys have attracted much criticism
over the years, and continue to do so. Three different grounds can
be identified. Since the 1930s, a movement for educational toys
informed by psychoanalysis has criticised a general tendency
towards increasingly representational toys.[1] The argument goes

that non-representational toys without a fixed form allow freer reign to the child's creative imagination: so small figures unmarked by occupational or other codings are preferred to, say, toy soldiers or farm workers. In a connected although different argument, accurate representational detail in toys is thought to interfere with a child's developing capacity to distinguish between 'fantasy' and 'reality'. Detailed toy guns, in particular, have been criticised on these grounds, and banned in some European states. Much of the news coverage of the Hungerford massacre in July 1987 drew on the notion of psychotic confusion between fantasy and reality in attempting to make sense of Michael Ryan's psychological make-up and motivation. Connections were made between his adult fascination with guns and his absorption since boyhood in a fantasy world of military adventure.

The Ryan case also provided a focal point for another critique of war toys and fantasies, when he was described as a 'Rambo' figure, and his crimes explained as an expression of a particular form of masculinity, that has been encouraged, legitimated or even produced by popular cultural forms. This line of criticism, deriving from feminist theories of sexism and patriarchy, has placed war toys and fantasies in the context of a peculiarly masculine fascination with war, whereby 'manly virtues' such as toughness and aggression are valorised and valued above other qualities and attitudes. The popularity of war forms within boy culture can then be explained in terms of gender stereotyping and socialisation into boyhood, or alternatively in terms of a child's attempts to secure an appropriate 'masculine' identity through identification with representations of masculinity. Figures like Ryan can then be seen either as typical products of this culture of masculinity, or as extreme cases, where something has gone seriously wrong. In a further extrapolation, war itself may be explained as a comparable manifestation of masculine violence and aggression, and fairly direct connections made between playing at war and fighting real wars. At this point, feminist arguments begin to overlap with a third line of critique, developed by successive peace movements.[2]

In this approach, disapproval of war toys and other forms of war culture is grounded in the belief that they generate interest and excitement around military personnel and technologies, and that this helps foster a militaristic spirit without which wars fought for national or imperialist motives would not receive popular support. Arguments like this, revived in the anti-nuclear movement of the early 1980s and sharpened by the South Atlantic adventure in 1982, have their origin in opposition to the militaristic and imperialistic popular culture that flourished in Britain from the 1880s through to the First World War. This was the culture that spawned the Boy Scouts and a host of similar organisations; produced a literature of military adventure involving new kinds of soldier-hero, targeted explicitly at boys; propagated a notion of 'moral manhood' based on physical fitness and exemplified in the new image of the soldier and the army; and stimulated demand for the new model toy soldiers, produced for a mass market for the first time by Britains Ltd in 1893. By 1905, Britains were producing over one hundred different figures and casting five million of them each year; toy soldiers had succeeded the train sets whose gauge they copied, as 'the most popular masculine nursery game'.[3] The peace movement's biggest impact was in the 1920s and 1930s, but even in early 1914, the National Peace Council was arguing that 'there are grave objections to presenting our boys with regiments of fighting men, batteries of guns and squadrons of Dreadnoughts'; and organised an exhibition of so-called 'peace toys' — 'not miniature soldiers but miniature civilians, not guns but ploughs and the tools of industry'.[4]

Three distinct but inter-related areas of concern about the effects of war fantasies emerge in these critiques: firstly, in terms of making sense of the real world; secondly, in terms of subjective development and forms of identity; and thirdly, in terms of the mobilisation of political support for particular wars. Each of these has a contemporary relevance. The first points attention to the 'fictionalising' of war and the use of the military for entertainment: in the forms of war toys, but also in the regular use of the Armed Forces in tourist spectacles, or the coining of the Falklands-Malvinas War into comic strips and thrillers. The second questions the use of the soldier as masculine hero, as in the cult of the SAS, who offer a version of idealised British masculinity; but it also questions the privileged position of the military in national ideologies. The third suggests how the roots of a masculine pleasure-culture around war might provide a continuing source of nourishment for British (and Western) military adventurism. Put like this, the three lines of critique can be made to work together, and important connections established between fantasies and realities, masculinities and nationalism. But this only works so smoothly where war toys take a representational form, and fantasy deals with real referents. The situation in the toy shops, however, is more complicated, since many of the more 'popular' war themes (including the post-Star Wars 'wars of the future' motifs, and the 'Action Force' range found on the front page in Gamley's catalogue) eschew representational realism. To understand what is happening to the *forms* of war toys, we need to turn to developments in the toy industry.

The only major public voice raised in defence of war toys has been that of the toy industry itself. This is hardly surprising in view of their commercial success, maintained with remarkable consistency for over one hundred years since those first Britains hollow metal toy soldiers. Following its shift to mass market production in the late nineteenth century, the toy industry has participated in the massive developments characteristic of the culture and leisure industries. These have been stimulated above all by the growth of a vast American domestic toy market, 95 per cent of which was home produced by 1939. As with other culture industries, this provided the base for a take-off into the world export market; and in the twenty years afer 1945, the American toy industry quadrupled its production and began to measure its annual retail figures in billions of dollars. In 1987, sales in the United States alone (which constitutes about 50 per cent of the world market) reached $12 billion: as compared, for instance, with the film industry's $4.2 billion receipts in the United States (and roughly double worldwide) in that same year.[5]

The toy industry's defence of war toy production has been based on two main arguments. One is a version of that well-known commercial refrain, 'We are only giving our public what it wants'. Toy industry spokespersons are quoted from time to time, to the effect that 'Young consumers are pretty smart. They will not respond to something that is not value for money—or if they do, they will do it only once' (Frank Martin, marketing development and services director of leading toy maker Hasbro Bradley, quoted in 1985).[6] A second response has been to engage with the debates about toys and imagination stimulated by educationalists, and argue that war toys are, in essence, no different from other toys. In 1964, responding to worries about the ever-increasing verisimilitude of children's toy guns, the then-Director of brand leader Lone Star Products went on record to criticise the too-perfect reproduction of detail, and to defend his own company's Wild West revolvers and rifles, with this argument: 'The gun mechanism and its appearance should be simple ... An essential which applies to any toy, not just Western guns, [is] that it should stimulate rather than stultify its owner's imagination, providing the one tenth original idea round which the child can develop his (sic) private fantasy'.[7]

Both arguments are questionable. Any claim that commercial cultural production is a response to straightforward market demand must sidestep the role of marketing and advertising in actively stimulating demand for commodities that can be produced within the dictates of profitability. In this case, it also implies that boys' desire for war toys arises spontaneously from within: an expression, perhaps, of their innately aggressive masculine instincts? Any appeal to the value of that great abstraction, 'the imagination', as intrinsically 'a good thing', dodges the problem of the different *forms* of imagining and the way these change through history. A child's 'private fantasy' does not exist in a vacuum, but is deeply shaped by the (often gendered) themes and associations suggested by different forms of toy—guns and vacuum cleaners, for example—and by the discursive context that surrounds them. The toy industry itself actively contributes to that context through advertising campaigns like the Gamleys retail catalogue and, more powerfully, in TV advertising that employs all the resources of state-of-the-art 30-second film making to represent the toy at the centre of an exciting play experience.[8]

Inside the toy shops themselves, the elaborate graphics decorating boxes and other packaging and display materials also situate the artefacts on sale within a suggestive, cross-referencing web of names, images and themes for fantasy and play. The strongly gendered character of these is striking. A toy plastic gun, for example, comes attached to a card sheet that, besides proclaiming it *as* an 'AK-47 Rapid Fire Machine Gun', presents colour images of a (man) soldier and a ball of flame from an explosion, together with the following textual captions: 'A Born of Hero Glory Warrior' (sic); 'A warrior has strong strength and extraordinary talent. He completes his mission to destruct enemy bases and wins victory'.

Similarly, among the boxes of playclothes on sale can be found a 'battledress' blouse, camouflage trousers and a balaclava, to fit ages 2–10, named as 'an SAS outfit'. Add puttees and a plastic helmet with netting, and you have 'a Commando'. Here, toys are made desirable by their association with masculine soldier-hero figures, the imagined effects of powerful military technologies and the outcome of heroic adventure narratives. Outside this discursive context, the artefact looks like a rather useless and boring piece of black plastic. Once named and brought within, however, it can be transformed by wish-fulfilling fantasy into an object of magical power.

By dressing up in these outfits and playing with these toys, a boy is invited to become, in his own omnipotent fantasy, that very 'warrior' whose 'strong strength' and 'extraordinary talent' — together with the magical weapons he has given birth to! — enables him to be powerful and effective and to 'win victory' in the public world where adventures happen. Imagining himself as the soldier hero involves an acting out, in first person fantasies, of a narrative 'appropriate' to the part: a narrative of war adventure, combat and triumph over an enemy. Such hero figures — and their implied enemies — are, however, the bearers of ideological characteristics and connotations concerning masculinity (particular kinds of 'strength' and 'talent') and nationality (the resonance of the SAS soldier and the Commando for British boys is on a par with the Anzac in Australia and the Marine in the USA). Placed at the centre of wish-fulfilling fantasy, the SAS soldier and the Commando themselves become the very figure of desire. As with so many products for the consumer market, what is being sold here is as much an opportunity for fantasy and the imagining of a self as the actual artefact.

If the discursive context surrounding toys provides a set of *public* themes and associations that children draw on in their own private play fantasies, the toy industry cannot be held solely responsible for these publicly available fantasy forms. It is hard to imagine today's children, playing out in quite the same form this imperialist fantasy — 'The Game of Wonderful Islands' — described in 1911 by H. G. Wells, in his book on *Floor Games*: 'We land and alter things and build and arrange and hoist paper flags on pins, and subjugate populations, and confer all the blessings of civilisation upon these lands'.[9] In 1982 — a year when the British top ten toy best-sellers list included three different kinds of war toys and noted an increase in baby doll sales — the fantasies privately woven in play around these artefacts would have been able to draw upon fantasies articulated and amplified by the press and broadcast media around those most public occasions: the Falklands-Malvinas War and the birth of Princess Diana's first baby. Similarly, the appearance in that same best-seller list, of Action Man 'particularly in an SAS outfit', needs to be placed in the context of the SAS attack on the Iranian Embassy in Princes Gate, seen live on TV in May 1980; which stimulated a wave of popular fictions and established the SAS's current cult status.[10] In the new economic climate of the 1980s, however, the international toy industry has increasingly directed its energies towards an ever more sophisticated organisation of the discursive context immediately surrounding their products, in order to maximise sales and profits.

Until the mid-1970s, the industry internationally enjoyed as a matter of course a steady annual growth in demand in the major world toy markets, and high profit margins. Since then, in common with other sectors of productive capital, it has undergone a slump coupled with a sharp intensification of international competition. This has produced a fundamental restructuring, with many smaller independent toy companies forced into liquidation or bought out by conglomerates.[11] From 1983–85, the restructured toy industry experienced a renewed boom, with sales doubling and profits trebling in 1984. Overseas sales are increasingly important. In 1984, they accounted for 40 per cent of all sales achieved by the American company Mattel, the world's leading toymaker that year.

This restructuring of the toy industry has had a significant effect on its product. Competition for a dwindling market in the early 1980s has transformed what was traditionally a quite stable and conservative branch of production into an extremely volatile fashion industry. Britain's toy soldiers, for instance, barely changed design from 1893 until the advent of plastic in the 1950s permitted more 'realistic' modelling in action poses; and new models introduced in 1978 were virtually the same as those I played with as a boy in 1960. In the 1980s, however, these are very much residual forms, overtaken by the pace of developments.

One response of the toy industry to new market conditions has been an increased use of advertising coupled with a search for new fads and trends; notably the technological reworking of traditional themes—including war—in video games, and 'interactive' toys that use advanced microchip and sensor technologies in order to interact with TV or video images.[12] Another response has been the interlinking of toys with other media through franchising arrangements, pioneered by 'character merchandising' based on the 'Star Wars' film trilogy. Franchises worth $1.5 billion per year worldwide sold books, tapes, bedlinen, night clothes, wallpapers, posters, games, pottery—and toys worth $500 million per year to Palitoy, the General Mills subsidiary. Subsequently, much more systematic organisation of character merchandising and multi-media links has tended to reverse the spin-off, by basing fictional narratives around toys specifically designed with franchising in mind, rather than developing toys out of the narratives. in 1987, there were about seventy American TV programmes based on toy products: including, for example, the 'Masters of the Universe' cartoon series. A third response has been the refinement of 'collectables'. These are ranges of interdependent toy figures, models, vehicles and other accessories, based on the phenomenally successful 'Barbie' doll: first introduced in 1959, it topped the American toy charts again in 1987. These latter two strategies give the toy producers greater control over sales demand and also help to stabilise and sustain that demand, in an effort to contain the effects of market volatility.

The American-owned conglomerate, Hasbro Bradley, is in many ways the epitome of the new multi-national toy manufacturer. Its profits rose from under $5 million in 1981 to around $55 million in 1984: achieving in this particular year a 300 per cent increase in profits on a 50 per cent increase in sales. An important element in this success has been a design and marketing strategy based around licenced merchandising and best-selling collectables, notably 'Action Force', 'My Little Pony' and 'Transformers'. These inter-related elements in Hasbro Bradley's corporate strategy together determine not only the design of toys, but also increasingly the discursive context in which they are encountered and used by children.

Hasbro Bradley's 'Action Force' range, one of the most 'popular' toys of the 1980s, is a typical product of these developments. It is based on a set of 3¾ inch toy soldiers—or rather, 'Modern Army Action Figures'. These are smaller versions of the original military collectable, 'Action Man': made from vinyl with swivel joints at the head, shoulder, elbow, knee and waist. This gives them a slightly spastic and 'unmilitary' appearance and makes them difficult to stand upright, but enables the continual alteration of their posture, the interchangeability of items of weaponry and kit and, most important commercially, their adaptation to fit a range of special vehicles such as 'H.A.V.O.C.—the Action Force roving vehicular fortress with driver (at £12.95), and a Hovercraft (at £21.95).[13] Like Action Man, the single figure acts as a marketing bait for the purchase of those accessories without which enjoyment of the figure itself is substantially reduced. Action Force, however, represents a considerable refinement of the collectable strategy. Unlike Action Man, its smaller figures come relatively cheap (at £2.47, well within pocket money budgets); while the accessories include relatively expensive moving vehicles, aimed at present-giving adults. Then, there are 30 different figures in all, so that the single, cheap figure is marketed as one of a set (in which each becomes an 'accessory' to the others) costing £75 in all! The cost of the entire range, including the vehicles, runs into hundreds of pounds.

The figures incorporate in their very design (rather than in the detachable uniforms of Action Man) an extraordinary variety of features drawn from many different kinds of adventure narratives, and their respective hero and villain figures. It is easy to trace these representational elements to the figures of the commando and the modern mercenary soldier; to Star Wars and other space fiction characters; to the Hell's Angel and deep-sea diver; to James Bond villains, martial arts fighters, and Red Indians; to Dan Dare; and there are even echoes of the 'Long John Silver' pirate figure. These various elements are combined in a fascinating intertextual mixture which cuts the hero-villain opposition free from referential coordinates. These toy soldiers are no longer drawn, as they have been traditionally, from specific, located historical conflicts such as the American Indian Wars and Civil War. Gone are the nationalistic connotations of those Second World War goodies and baddies, the British versus the Germans. The intertextual 'Action Force' figures are '*International* Heroes', their foe the sci-fi 'Cobra Enemy': toys for a world market that now spans the Allied-Axis divisions of the 1940s.

A further development in 'Action Force' is its presentation of each of its thirty figures as named imaginary characters, such as 'Leatherneck the Marine', 'Iceberg' and even, intriguingly, 'Lady Jaye'. The construction of these characters is based on the detailed design of facial features on the toy itself, but Action Force also utilises to the full the suggestive potential of display and packaging material. Each figure comes attached, within a clear plastic box, to a 9 inch by 6 inch hanging display card, featuring the names of the brand and the particular hero-figure, together with a full colour graphic image of the character in action. This is considerably bigger and more detailed than the actual artefact, and pictures a fluidity of movement that it cannot attain. But it is recognisably the 'same' figure, from the details of uniform and equipment to the representation of facial features. This fictional persona is further elaborated on the back of the card, through the device of 'Your Action Force Command File' (with its suggestion of other entries). Each of these presents that particular character's 'file name', 'code name', 'military specialities', birthplace and brief combat history; and finally, a set of character traits given as a fictional file report, in quotation marks suggesting further, longer documents. Connections between the 'characters' (and thus the artefacts) is established by the reproduction on the card of tiny images of the whole set of characters; and secured by the inclusion, within every Action Force pack, of two 'collectors card' stickers. Similar in design to the old cigarette cards, each features another graphic image and more character details; providing a disguised source of advertising, but also helping secure the imaginative coherence of the set, upon which its narrative potential depends.

This is further exploited by franchised media spin-offs. The *Action Force* monthly comic is published by Marvel Comics under a copyright held by Milton Bradley International, which explicitly includes 'all prominent characters featured in this issue . . . and the distinctive likenesses thereof'. The November 1988 edition carries as its lead story a 'prequel' to *Action Force: The Movie*, a feature-length animation video. Modelled closely on the design of the toys themselves, these images produce additional profits from those designs and stimulate toy sales. But they also contribute a whole further dimension of meaning: both through the realised narratives they construct around the figures, and through further elaboration of the 'characters' themselves. One decisive connotation added in the comics, for example, is the association of the International Heroes with a *world state*, and their enemy as a *terrorist organisation*.

In its thoroughly 'postmodern' cross-over of fictional worlds and motifs, 'Action Force' clearly owes a debt to prior developments in comics and other media (for example, *Star Wars, 2000 AD, The A-Team*). But whereas toy manufacturers were once content to follow and then co-exist with popular narrative forms of this kind, in Action Force we see a systematic attempt to construct a sophisticated and relatively discrete fictional world of fantasy figures and scenarios around the artefacts, in order to stimulate further expenditure on the set as a whole. In this, the manufacturers are anticipating the *use* to which toy figures are put in play fantasies, and exploiting this in their design and marketing. This process, however, is not ideologically innocent. It should rather be seen in terms of the increasing investment by manufacturers in the ever-tighter *organisation* of fantasies, so as to maximise profits. This represents a further stage in the association of particular identities, tastes and imaginary worlds with 'designer' products, in order to construct differentiated market sectors. Given the primacy of *gender* difference for the toy industry, corporations like Hasbro Bradley therefore have a direct interest in reproducing these differences. It is no accident that they have developed complementary collectable ranges—'Action Force' and 'My Little Pony'—that are fiercely gender-specific both in design and discursive context. Through its design of toys for gendered market sectors, then, Hasbro Bradley actively contributes to the reproduction of gender-specific imaginary worlds; while through its organisation of fantasies around those toys, associating them with detailed sets of 'masculine' and 'feminine' connotations and stimulating particular kinds of play narratives, the corporation increasingly furnishes the contents of those worlds.

Pleasure is the basis of the toy industry's commercial activity, and its efforts are directed towards organising it in the most profitable forms. This means it must necessarily pay attention to questions about the pleasures, excitements and absorptions that children derive from play. These questions have by and large been neglected by critics of war toys, who have been more concerned with their (presumed?) ideological effects. The toy industry's defence of war toys—with its emphasis on the active 'choice' of war toys by boys (a phenomenon often lamented by anti-sexist and pacifist parents!), and the variable uses which public cultural forms can be made to serve in private fantasy—is not an adequate explanation; but it does nevertheless place on the agenda issues that must be explored if the phenomenon is to be properly understood.

They are tricky questions for adults, because they invite us to adopt a child's perspective, and this involves a shift away from the relatively safe position of the detached or worried adult critic, towards an encounter with one's own childhood self. What we experienced as children, and found pleasurable or painful, powerfully shapes what we desire for, and of, today's children. But to remember that experience is to re-assess what we have made ourselves, and been made, into. This potentially contradictory complex of feelings about oneself and one's own childhood provides the emotional fuel that makes adult assessments of children's culture such a fraught business. My own feelings about war toys, for example, are intensely ambivalent. My investments in war play and fantasy as a boy were among the most powerful of my childhood: beginning when I was two years old, and lasting into my early teens. In memory, I can still recover the thrill evoked by war play and fantasy in all its forms. These enabled the expression of many different impulses besides the obvious aggressive ones: and it is far from obvious to me that the presumed ideological outcomes are a necessary result. At the same time, I don't want to deny altogether that war play and fantasies do produce ideological effects. Retaining a critical distance on their pleasures does bring into focus a series of questions about the identifications that they may encourage and the meanings of war that they may generate.[14] Holding together both positive and negative assessments may enable both to be transformed, with important implications for the critiques of war toys.

One implication is that any effective critique must directly address the question of pleasure. The onus here should be on moving beyond a moralism that can only frown ineffectually at war toys and disavow the fantasies, desires and pleasures that have become attached to them. We need to understand more about what those fantasies, desires and pleasures are; work out coherent criteria for distinguishing their 'positive' from their 'negative' aspects; and explore what the scope might be for detaching the one from the other. The aim of this should be to stimulate and inform debate about the possibilities for influencing or regulating toy industry design, marketing and advertising; about possible responses of parents and other childcarers, confronted with the desires of their children for war toys; and about the cultural forms themselves—the artefacts, narratives and fictional characters that currently exist, and the possible creation of new ones. Unless questions of fantasy and pleasure are taken seriously across all these areas, we are in danger of witnessing the scenario satirised in Saki's 1919 story, 'The Toys of Peace'.[15] The kids in the story are provided with 'peace toys' in the form of civilians, famous people and buildings like the YMCA. Not knowing what to do with them that can be in the least exciting, they simply reimagine them as soldiers, and play at war.

NOTES

1. See, for example, Susan Isaacs, *Intellectual Growth in Young Children* (London: Routledge, 1930).

2. On gender socialisation see, for example, Elena Belotti, *Little Girls* (London: Writers and Readers, 1975); questions of identification and representation are raised in Antony Easthope, *What a Man's Gotta Do* (London: Paladin, 1986). Links between Ryan, Rambo, war toys and masculinity are explored in Rosalind Coward, 'The killing games', *Guardian*, 1 September 1987.

3. Fraser, Antonia, *The History of Toys* (London: Weidenfeld and Nicolson, 1966) p. 183. However, as the 'nursery' reference suggests, the market would have been restricted at this early period to the children of the middle class. On Britains Ltd, see Fraser passim; Leslie Daiken, *Children's Toys Throughout the Ages* (London: Spring Books, 1963), p. 141; James Opie, *Britains Toy Soldiers 1893—1932* (London: Gollancz, 1985).

4. Fraser, op. cit., p. 231.

5. For an outline of the rise of the American toy industry, see Fraser op. cit., pp. 196–212. Toy sales figures are from 'Tell that kid to shut up', *The Economist*, 12 December 1987, p. 78. Film receipts figures are from 'The Return of Hollywood', *Economist*, 29 October 1988, pp. 23–8.

6. Rodwell, Lee, 'Hard sell for soft toys', *The Times*, 29 July 1985, p. 9.

7. Quoted in Fraser, op. cit., p. 230.

8. Toy advertising has itself become a primary locus of anxieties about the commercial exploitation of children. See Maire Messenger Davis, 'Robin Hood is grounded', *Guardian*, 16 May 1988.

9. Wells, H. G., *Floor Games* (London: Frank Palmer, 1911).

10. Cross, Jack, 'How Action Man derailed a train . . .', *Guardian*, 13 December 1982, p. 8; C. Bazalgette and R. Paterson, 'Real Entertainment: The Iranian Embassy Siege', *Screen Education*, no. 37, winter 1980/81, pp. 55–67.

11. The food giant General Mills, for example, had acquired toy businesses worth $783 billion by 1985. The details in this section are taken from the following articles: 'Toys—no longer child's play', *Economist*, 25 December 1982, pp. 99–100; 'May the sales force be with you', *Economist*, 25 December 1982, p. 26; 'Playing to win', *Economist*, 19 October 1985, pp. 85–6; and 'Tell that kid to shut up', *Economist*, 12 December 1987, p. 78.

12. Mattel, for example, have launched a hand-held spaceship (retailing at $30–35) to be used like a gun to fire at enemy spaceships in the television series 'Captain Power'. Hits *on* the televised enemy are registered by a bleeping noise, and when hit *by* the enemy, the pilot figure on the toy ejects. 'Tell that kid to shut up', *Economist*, 12 December 1987, p. 78.

13. These prices were current in Beatties of London Ltd, Dyke Road, Brighton in October 1988.

14. These issues are developed in more detail in my doctoral thesis, *Soldier Heroes: War Adventure, Masculinity and Nationalism in British Popular Culture 1850—present*, to be submitted at the University of Birmingham in 1989.
15. Munro, H. H. ('Saki'), *The Toys of Peace and other stories* (London and New York: John Lane, 1919).

14

Family Affairs: Angst in the Age of Mechanical Reproduction

SHELAGH YOUNG

How do you feel? How do you really, *really* feel? If you've been experiencing a loss of the real lately then maybe its time you tuned in to some 'actuality' programming. Actuality television is the the generic term for a range of broadcast material that supposedly brings the real right into your sitting room. Recent key additions to this category are televised counselling sessions in which, as the publicity blurb puts it, 'real people talk about real life problems'. The growth of television counselling in this, Benjamin's age of mechanical reproduction, suggests that it is authenticity of emotions rather than of works of art with which we are currently most concerned. To feel is to be real.

Ros Coward argues that 'have you tried talking about it?' is one of the most frequent responses from agony aunts to their problem page letter writers but in the world of broadcast therapy 'tell me how you feel' is certainly the dominant injunction.[1] Television and radio counsellors generally ignore material conditions, preferring to explore the mysterious inner self. Yet, as Ros Coward's excellent analysis of the discourse of the agony aunt reminds us, it takes more than honest emotional discussion to resolve structural inequalities between different social groups. In her discussion of the women's magazine problem page Coward was particularly concerned to show the ways in which unequal power relations between men and women are reinforced by the nature of the agony aunt's advice. Now that agony aunts and uncles appear to be regularly plying their trade on television has anything changed? Are televised counselling sessions anything more than sheer spectacle, the latest despicable mode of expression for a prurient society obsessed with the publication of what should remain private? Surely there must be more to broadcast therapy than this?

Certainly this form of television realism doesn't simply involve us in the myth of television as an unmediated picture of external reality for it also helps to perpetuate the myth of a common human *internal* reality. Both 'A Problem Aired' and 'Family Affairs' inter-pellate the viewer as the eternal, ahistorical human subject. Broad-cast therapy holds our attention by showing us that the protagon-ists have problems just like ours. As the weekly introduction to 'Family Affairs' reminds us, these are 'real people talking about real life problems' and their ordinariness is continually reasserted. How can one watch a trained counsellor at work on these people without seeing a small part of oneself revealed? That tendency to always bring up the past when we argue perhaps? Or the way we issue ultimatums rather than agree to compromise? Or our habit of testing people because we feel insecure? Every week there will be that little hook which catches us and draws us in, inviting us to identify with the main protagonist in that week's emotional crisis.

We can speak of the discourse of broadcast therapy just as we would refer to the discourse of advertising or of the news. These discursive practices not only function to make sense of their particular areas and provide a framework within which we can make sense of our social experiences, but also enter into the construction of our own social identity. A discourse is a language or system of representation that has developed socially in order to make and circulate a coherent set of meanings about a specific topic. Discourses are power relations and they work, at the level of ideology, to naturalise meanings which serve the interests of a particular section of society. In the discourse of broadcast therapy some essence of selfhood is presumed to persist from birth to death and it is this self which we are continually urged to explore and reveal. Change, we are encouraged to believe, will come about as a result of individual growth. Social structures and economic relations are dismissed as mere barnacles on the hull of life — underneath we remain essentially untarnished.

It is all too easy to be entirely cynical about 'A Problem Aired' and 'Family Affairs'. Audience participation at this level makes exceedingly cheap television. Like a game show without any prizes or a soap-opera lacking script or stars, television counselling is a format that ought to please the accounts departments. In a period of pre-satellite pessimism media critics have been queuing up to pronounce the death of 'quality' television. It is no small coincidence that Roy Hattersley chose to include a comparison with page 3 of the *Sun* in his review of 'Family Affairs'.[2] The spectre of round the clock Murdoch beaming down from space haunts the middle classes and playing 'spot the satellite TV show' (essential qualities: cheapness and vulgarity) allows us to retain that vital sense of educated taste throughout an ordinary evening's viewing. Familiarity with the discourse of psychotherapy helps to breed contempt for the poor suckers who opt to wash their dirty laundry in public or as Paul Morely put it: 'We all need to know that everyone else is being pulverised by life's little terrors, to feel eased by a little cooling superiority.'[3] Clearly not all of us will make sense of these programmes in the same way. The very social and economic conditions which are excluded from the discourse of broadcast therapy plainly do affect the way we make sense of this phenomenon. As Fiske explains:

> Discourses functions not only in the production and reading of texts, but also in making sense of social experience. A particular discourse of gender, for example, works not only to make sense of a television program such as 'Charlie's Angels', but also to make a particular pattern of sense of gender in the family, in the workplace, in school, in social clubs—in fact, in our general social relations. Social experience is much like a text: its meanings depend upon the discourses that are brought to bear upon it. Just as two differently socially situated people may make different sense of the same text, so they may make a different sense of the same social experience.[4]

Both 'A Problem Aired' and 'Family Affairs' have been accused of fostering a spurious sense of serious social purpose. Hattersley particularly dislikes 'Family Affairs', arguing that it amounts to 'little more than televisual voyeurism at its worst'. What Hattersley explicitly objects to is entertainment masquerading as public information. Yet, as he freely admits, the revulsion that he feels for such programmes constitutes their stated *raison d'être*, 'Here in Britain', presenter Mike Smith announces, 'we rarely seem to discuss our emotional affairs until it's too late'.

These sentiments are echoed by Phillip Hodson 'popular agony uncle' and resident expert on 'Family Affairs'. Hodson also hosts a long running phone-in programme on LBC Radio and openly confirms that this has a dual purpose. While he claims that it offers a safe forum for people with immediate problems (who may at that moment be unable to leave the house let alone find a trained therapist with a short waiting list), he also recognises that he is there to entertain. Topical concerns and recently published books do influence the content of his programmes. Just like Wogan's guests, Hodson's 'experts' frequently have a book to plug and specialised sessions 'respond' to current crises. Incidents such as the ferry capsizing at Zeebrugge or the Kings Cross fire might, for example, be followed up with a programme devoted to bereavement counselling.

What others see as the vulgar commodification of feelings, Hodson promotes as a means of introducing a larger section of society to 'another way of thinking about problems' and hotly refutes Ros Coward's suggestion that media advice sessions 'have become a sort of poor person's introduction to the world of professional therapy'.[5] Nevertheless, the cost of psychotherapy is rarely mentioned and the experience of broadcast therapy for the person being counselled could hardly be compared with an hour's session in the comfort and privacy of a psychotherapist's office. On radio phone-ins the calls, no matter how harrowing, must be sandwiched between advertisements and news bulletins. Having increased his audience from 65 000 to over 400 000 in three years, Hodson has demanded the right to play the ads at an 'appropriate' moment. Thus traumatic conversations need no longer be faded out to make way for commercial jingles but he still works fast. Hodson has been complimented on his ability to zoom in on the crux of the problem in little more time than it would have taken Freud to light his cigar. Of course Hodson's field is counselling rather than analysis but presumably neither technique is really facilitated by employing a kind of psychological speed-reading.

Both very different from each other, neither 'A Problem Aired' nor 'Family Affairs' closely adhere to the format of the ubiquitous radio phone-ins. Ros Coward when contemplating the discourse of the agony aunts was particularly interested in the way they address women. It is interesting that in adapting the problem page for the broadcast media the discussion of emotional affairs has finally spilled out from the confines of the women's press. Women's magazines are no longer the exclusive sites for debates around sexual and emotional problems and even if big boys still don't cry, the discourse of broadcast therapy doesn't preclude that possibility. Ros Coward may be able to take some pleasure in the fact that, in these programmes, men are at last being expected to take on some of the emotional work which sustains their personal relationships, Phillip Hodson claims a 40 per cent male audience for his weekday afternoon phone-ins on LBC Radio and reports an increasing number of calls from men. Men are clearly now formally allowed to have problems, especially if they are prepared to discuss them in front of a live audience. Does this represent a real (if all too slight) shift in gender based power relations or has this development more to do with the need to reach parts of the market that other programmes cannot reach?

> Ted and Jean have been married for more than 40 years. Since Ted's retirement Jean has found him impossible to live with and now she wants a bit of peace and quiet . . . Ted is shocked and dismayed. The conflict is tearing them apart. Tonight Ted and Jean have come in to the studio . . . no-one knows what the outcome of this struggle will be. Keeping order is Mike Smith. . . .[6]

By traditional standards, with a ruby wedding behind them, Ted and Jean ought to be contentedly going for gold. Instead Jean is planning to leave Ted and they have less than 30 minutes in which to discover what can be done about the conflict which, as the dramatic introduction insists, is 'tearing them apart'. Unlike 'A Problem Aired', 'Family Affairs' makes no attempt to recreate the intimate relationship between client and therapist. The 'real' people featured in this show are not only required to discuss their 'real life' problems in front of a live studio audience, but are also expected to respond to their comments and questions. Ted and Jean sit between presenter Mike Smith and counsellor Phillip Hodson while the audience glares down from the encircling banks of tiered seating. In this somewhat gladiatorial setting Ted and Jean's performance is crucial. Whatever they *feel* like doing, they certainly won't be allowed to display half an hour's worth of the seething silence that apparently constitutes the norm in their relationship. In place of the awkward silences or meaningful pauses that usually punctuate the retelling of an emotional crisis 'Family Affairs' gives us questions, comments and noise from the audience. Imagine permanently sharing your marital home with two complete sets of in-laws and you begin to understand what

1. 'A Fresh Start', cover design, *Time*, Vol. 116, No. 20 (17 November 1980).

2. (*above*) Thomas Cole, 'Pioneer Home in the Woods', 1845–46, Winston-Salem, North Carolina: Reynolds House, Inc.

3. (*below*) Thomas Cole, 'A Distant View of the Falls of Niagara', engraved by I. T. Hinton and Simpkin and Marshall, *The History and Topography of The United States of America*, 1832.

4. (*above*) Emanuel Leutza, 'Westward the Course of Empire Takes its Way', 1861, National Collection of Fine Arts, Smithsonian Institute.

5. (*below*) George Caleb Bingham, 'Daniel Boone Escorting a Band of Pioneers' in the Western countryside (detail), 1851.

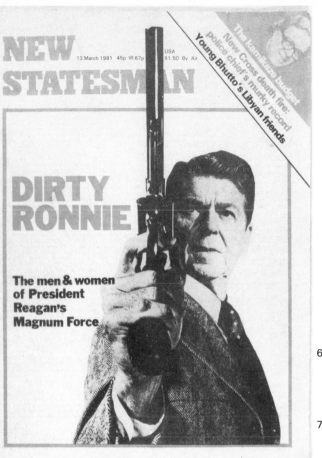

6. (*left*) 'Dirty Ronnie', c
   design, montage by Mi⟨
   Bennett, *New Statesman*
   101, No. 2608 (13 M⟨
   1989).

7. (*below*) Anon. 'In the Nu
   Age, can we afford lea⟨
   who shoot from the ⟨
   CND recruitment leaflet⟨
   (1986).

In the Nuclear Age,
can we afford leaders who shoot from the hip?

'Family Affairs' is all about. Like some nightmarish extended family, the studio audience constantly intervenes, leaving little space for either Ted or Jean to actually address the other. Hodson as the 'expert' is dethroned, after all, why should he know any better than these 'real' people with their wide experience of life?

The role of the audience can be interpreted in several ways and one suspects that comments and questions from the studio audience are considered by many viewers to be a welcome outbreak of 'common sense'. However, it is also interesting to look at the ways in which audience intervention works to disrupt certain discursive practices. As I commented above, the discourse of broadcast therapy provides us with a framework for making sense of emotional crises (and the means of resolving them) in a very specific way. Problems affecting personal relationships are primarily addressed at the level of the individual with only minor references to either the general social structure or to economic relations. Individuals are presumed to possess an inner spiritual self, to have feelings which, once spoken, will enable them to resolve their problems. For example, one of Jean's reasons for leaving Ted is that she resents his assumption that she will carry on with the tasks and responsibilities of a full time housewife now that he has retired. Though this must surely be a widespread source of friction between older couples (without a full pension of their own many women's economic dependency upon their husband's actually increases after retirement) the 'problem' is never addressed in terms of the significance of this sexual division of labour. In fact the problem is more simply interpreted by both presenters as evidence of an isolated incidence of some easily remedied thoughtlessness on Ted's part and they urge him to mend his ways in order to 'save' the relationship.

Although Ted's attitude to domestic labour is not condoned the only effort to locate his behaviour in a wider social context comes from a member of the audience when he is described as a 'bit of an MCP'. Criticism from the presenters rests at the level of the personal rather than the social and they ask not whether *women* should be expected to service their retired husbands but whether Ted cares enough about Jean to 'try and satisfy a *feeling*' she's got. It is left up to the audience (with that one small quip about male chauvinist piggery) to remind us of the more general structural shifts which the discourse of broadcast therapy obscures. Approximately twenty years of second wave feminism are the unspoken factor here as Ted struggles to comprehend his wife's curious 'feelings'.

From the look on Jean's face, her feelings for Ted clearly include contempt. Unfortunately, despite the number of 'sensible' voices hurling advice, no-one actually asks the couple to tell us why on earth they volunteered to appear on the programme. I'm also tempted to wonder the same thing about the presenters. Before agreeing to 'keep order' on 'Family Affairs', Mike Smith's involvement in social conscience twinging television was as a key figure in the BBC's AIDS information campaign. How fitting then that Mr Safe Sex himself should choose to move on to present a programme which places the emphasis on investigating problematic familial relationships rather than sexual ones. This shift is particularly interesting when considered in the light of Ros Coward's analysis of the discourse of the agony aunt. In her opinion, problem pages can be read as 'historically specific symptoms of the way in which sexuality and its emotional consequences have been catapulted to the foreground of our culture as the expression of our most intimate selves'.[7] So, what are we to make of 'Family Affairs', a programme in which sex has become the great unmentioned, if not quite the unmentionable? How can we truly express our most 'intimate selves' and deal honestly and openly with our problems if sex has been swept off the agenda?

In the case of Ted and Jean, coy allusions to 'separate rooms' and an initial wartime romance based on 'lust' are the only evidence of what others have referred to as the obsessive talk about sex which characterises Western culture.[8] In fact the discussion of Ted and Jean's 'problem' focuses not on the obvious absence of a sexual relationship, but on the 'tragic' breakdown of communications between the couple. 'You've stopped talking to each other!' exclaims a triumphant Phillip Hodson towards the end of the show, in the voice of a man who clearly believes that he has pinpointed a significant fact. He is not altogether correct—how did Ted and Jean manage to appear on the programme at all if they hadn't discussed it beforehand? But of course, I am being too flippant, for we know that Hodson is referring to *significant* talk. As counsellor and 'popular agony uncle', his injunction to talk is not to be taken lightly—merely chatting about the price of tomatoes won't do. In the discourse of contemporary broadcast therapy significant talk addresses feelings rather than material concerns and as 'Family Affairs' demonstrates, this is no longer an invitation to talk dirty: 'I think asking you what you actually do still feel is a very crucial question. What feelings have you still got for the woman next to you? Do you like her? Do you care about her? Do you love her ... ?'[9] 'Family Affairs' is broadcast during the early evening period and this provides a partial explanation for the lack of explicit sexual discussion. The IBA clearly would not tolerate frank discussion of sexual problems in a television programme being broadcast before 9 pm. However, I suspect that there are wider cultural shifts which have influenced both the style of the programmes and the type of 'problems' that are chosen for broadcasting. Perhaps our understanding of the relationship between sexual behaviour and diseases such as herpes, cervical cancer and AIDS requires us to reformulate Ros Coward's argument. Does concern about the emotional consequences of our sexual behaviour now take second place to fears about the links between sexuality and physical health? Certainly, the discourse of sexual liberation cannot comfortably accommodate the fact that sex can yet again spread diseases for which there are no cure. Suddenly it seems rather dangerous to carry on privileging sexuality as the means of 'true expression of our most intimate selves'.

In many respects I welcome this shift for it problematises the notion that sexuality is the central organising principle of our social identity. This is not necessarily a radical development for the emphasis which 'Family Affairs' places on familial relationships obviously works on some levels to reinforce the dominant ideologies which prioritise and sanctify the family. Nevertheless, the programmes are a site of contradiction; on the one hand linking comfortably with a Thatcherite belief in the supposedly fundamental importance of the family as a social unit and, on the other, exposing the less idyllic side of family life. With 'Family Affairs' London Weekend Television has provided its viewers with a prime example of the concept of 'balance'. Sandwiched between the endless happy families in their ideal adland homes, this programme offers us another version of reality and reveals the family to be what we have suspected all along—an uncomfortable site of tension and struggle.

NOTES

1. Coward, Rosalind, 'Have You Tried Talking About It?', in *Female Desire* (London: Paladin Books, 1984).

2. Hattersley, Roy, 'Indecent Exposure', *The Listener* 21 July 1988.
3. Morley, Paul, *Blitz* no. 69, September 1988.
4. Fiske, John, *Television Culture* (London: Methuen, 1987) p. 15.
5. Coward, Ros, op cit. p. 136.
6. Introductory voiceover to London Weekend Televisions 'Family Affairs' broadcast at 6.30 pm on 26 August 1988.
7. Coward, Ros, op cit.
8. This comment refers to Foucault's work in the History of Sexuality: Part One, in which he argues that 'Western culture, far from having repressed sexuality, has actually produced it, multiplied it, spread it out as a particularly privileged means of gaining access to the individual and social bodies...'. See Biddy Martin, 'Feminism, Criticism and Foucault', in Irene Diamond and Lee Quinby (ed.), *Feminism and Foucault* (Boston: Northeastern University Press, 1988) p. 8.
9. Hodson, Phillip, speaking on 'Family Affairs', 26 August 1988.

15

Is the Micro Macho? A Critique of the Fictions of Advertising[1]

MARY KNIGHT

The computer was the brainchild of male engineers and it was born into a male line of production technology. The fact that it has a keyboard rather like a (feminine) typewriter keyboard confuses no one for long. When a computer arrives in a school, for instance, boys and girls are quick to detect its latent masculinity ... It is not surprising if ... boys soon elbow themselves forward and the majority of girls retire from the field.[2]

The masculine attributes of computers have been legend in feminist critiques of technology. Men, the arguments go, have misappropriated its development over the centuries. Their machinations with machinery have led them to construct an alter ego of male proportions, manifesting itself in the persona of the computer. 'For men only.' Including their hard disk potential, the invitations offered by the computer appear as macho and exclusive to men as those offered by pornographic magazines.

But can the computer, as Cockburn suggests, be 'innately masculine'? Evidence of the masculine dynamic of computers has been found not only in boys' macho behaviour, when they're 'on the job' but also in the language and imagery of advertisements used to sell computer 'hard' and 'soft' ware.[3] Now Freud may not have recognised that multiple disk drives have a relationship to the phallus. But to acquire power in the computer world, the more you have, the better your (psychic) equipment. Of course, a 'hard' disk computer rather than one using only 'soft' ware is the ultimate attainment in this hierarchy.

But wasn't Freud's description of man's search for the phallus based on a psychic fantasy? And isn't fantasy a very real part of advertising, where definitions of 'women', 'men' and 'product' are manufactured, to entice to buy? Adverts promoting computers and computing paraphernalia applications *do* revel in stereotyped masculine imagery and sexual innuendo. So do those which use 'high tech' concepts to sell other products, such as beer. Speed, power, and durability make a great computer, together with the tools needed to do the job. Big claims are made, going hand in hand with a projected image of big businessmen, the buyers.

What interpretation other than 'masculine' could be made of advertisements which leave women as consumers out of the picture? Or which make them accessible peripherals, there to be consumed by men—or by the computer? As in one ad, where 'Desire' becomes an 'on-line service' for man and machine. In high heels and little leopard skin dress Tarzanette gets consumed by the passion of the computer's sexy messages. A pair of shapely legs are all that remain as she dives in, contained by the male monitor. But it's one thing to represent the computer as 'masculine' by showing 'woman' being 'devoured' by it, and another to interpret this event as true.

In advertising, women as objects to be consumed with the computer have been part and parcel of the sales pitch. The female persona has often been used to sexualise products of all sorts. 'Gendered', it seems they promote the male buyer's ego and confirm his control by possession of the product ('her') as the object of his desire. This is intended to provide him with sexual and social status—and might even do so at the point-of-sale, or a little longer. Yet there's something embarrassingly old hat about these representations of 'woman' and the perception of the 'manly' buyer: 'Slim, elegant, perfect vision, tilt and swivel body (and that's just the monitor)' titters the Hitachi advertisement, trying to kid us that the manufacturers are godlike in their creation of woman and machine. 'You're looking at one of two models we've designed specifically . . .' quips the copy, using a predominant theme of evolution. But they're careful to make the (white) woman who is draped around the computer in a provocative way a rich-looking business professional. Chunks of gold jewellery with the neat, feminised man's suit. 'Sex execs' as described by *Cosmopolitan* magazine. A woman at work for consumption by a man, the voyeur?

But there's no straight 'party line' in computer advertisements. When a 'woman' won't do, then it's back to the phallic imagery: protruding objects abound in pictures and captions, saying, 'look, lads, see how big yours can be if you buy this product'. But isn't this advertising 'puff', an inflated projection of masculinity masquerading as 'real' social men? Which points to a small problem. What *is* 'masculinity'? According to Anne Lloyd and Liz Newell, in 'Women and Computers', its definition is dependent on 'binary oppositions'. What one is not, the other must be:

> The term 'hardware' refers to the tangible machines and 'software' to the intangible programmes put into them ... Hard is seen as ... male ... while soft is inferior ... and female.... It is software work that women are now finding their way back into. Work on the hardware remains an almost exclusively male domain.[4]

But just because men name themselves active and women passive, doesn't mean it is true. And do we know for sure that more men than women work on hardware as they suggest?

What about the armies of word-processing women who work with computers, though in the high-skilled but low status sphere of typing support in the office? Their 'feminine' position in the workforce does not negate their engagement with the hardware—and with software. A recent commercial report recommended that women should be taken seriously as a target audience for business applications software.[5] Typists are apparently moving into areas previously understood as men's only, such as accounting programs use.

Women have also 'progressed' in other industries employing computer technology, clothing, for instance, where some have taken over 'men's work' for 'women's pay'.[6] In fact, one might ask whether we have a situation not incomparable, perhaps, with that of past histories of changing modes of production, where women prepared the industrial pathway for men? Where, with their potent little fingertips, women do the light work rejected by those who prefer the ring of hot metal pressing into print than the precision of button-pressing. Surely, a dilemma for the 'anti work of equal value brigade'?

Don't these changes alone demonstrate that 'masculinity', 'femininity' and their complimentary 'hard' and 'soft' are not what they were? Perhaps part of the problem in such an analysis as Lloyd and Newell's is that it seems to rely on rigid interpretations of 'masculinity' and 'femininity' and other 'binary oppositions'. Meanings change with age as do women and men, who are not poles apart as they once seemed to be. 'Binary oppositions' have no guaranteed staying power as permanent opposites.

So, can 'masculinity' and 'femininity' be discarded when looking at the relationship between advertisements, women, men and computer technology? Not quite, for new meanings contain old words. Haven't men, for instance, whilst maintaining an upright position in the workplace, been sold by adverts and possibly feminist demands for change, a strong but caring position in the home? Don't women, conversely, demonstrate a 'new' independence, outside?

In fact, the thesis within this paper is that there are elements of *feminisation* involved with men's engagement with (and marriage too, as we'll see later) the computer, which cause problems for 'masculinity' and representations of women, possibly to feminism's advantage. When men use computers, like it or not, they take up for all intents and purposes a position of typist—traditional 'women's work'. (Men's 'sausage fingers', as one advertiser noted, preventing men from becoming nimble and dexterous as they've been saying of women for years). Not all men have happily engaged with computers. Why? They're not all about macho power—and can be seen as deskilling 'strong' men's work. With this is the additional indignity that women can, and do, do it too.

Particularly unsettling to masculine psyches might be the fact that the 'threat' is, in part, of the advertisers' own making, and men's. Having invented images which back up their assumptions about gender and work, contemporary trends in women's entry into these spheres would surely mean they must swallow their words or re-think their patter if they're to promote sales to men *and* women. Well, they do in one ad, which might get a man going in anger. 'Woman', like Delilah, cuts off Man's strength with computer power rather than scissors: It's an 'unnamed woman' ad—everywoman? There's such sophistication in this picture, using black and white photography in a 'film noir' style. 'Everywoman' talks on the telephone, to Frank. She's a woman who is in financial control of her business and rising, '50 per cent up', *and* has a firm grasp of the technical language. She's clearly a member of the computer club, sharing its 'personal' jargon. In fact it's Frank who is on the outside. 'How's business . . . Oh dear!' is how the ad signs her off. Women too can 'master' the machine and emasculate men with two words.

Are *women* being offered a new phallic position in society, being tempted by the proposal that 'equal ops' business success is theirs for the asking? Are working women causing men to change alliances in their Oedipal complexes, in a position of envy for women's apparent success and fear of emasculation? Or are men meant to rise to the challenge set out by the advertisers with their phallic women? And where is the macho product amongst such a sex change?

There is an argument to be made for an ambisextrous computer, a 'feminine' alongside or instead of a 'macho' machine produced by advertisers, a man and woman in new form. Take 'George' for example. 'George, 45, explains why he's unfaithful' to his old computer model. A glossy double page spread: George has his back to the camera, with slicked Heselbryl hair and designer specs. He's placed in a Freudian fantasy of baroque staircase and arch-ways, leading outward and inward to himself at the centre. There for himself, a unique individual going, *rightly*, against the grain of the 'decency' of traditional business practice. No old school tie or rugger-like team work fashionable in the office for him. A picture of Thatcherite self-sufficiency, a foreign object to be admired, not desired. Yet for all George's stiff dark back view (his phallic position) he's not a man meant to be desired by other men, just envied by a buyer with just such a problem. The boundaries of 'decency' which George steps over ensure that his move towards the 'feminine' is not the 'effeminate', for how many would buy such an idea? He's master of his mistress and can't quite let go of Man's reputation. She won't be an emotional tie. She's not in the picture but absent. Quietly, as computer 'she's' the powerful resolution to an incompatible relationship, an 'ideal partner' for Man's old notions of 'woman'. A mere hint of womanhood in the mind's eye at the end of the staircase and outside the magazine. She won't turn up to embarrass George. In support of his needs she's professional, cool and discreet. The wife'll never know. But then, he's only being unfaithful to 'her', a computer system and his unadventurous and inefficient 'wife', the company for their own good. Leaving George in the controlling position of the heterosexual ménage à trois, merged with women.

Man and machine becomes an androgynous package of interdependence ('compatibility' is a keyword in computer sales) where, without him, the very fabric of society—sharp business practice in both public and private spheres, work and family, would fall apart. He is maintaining his 'lead' in 'oppositional' spheres, 'ownership' of which appears to be in doubt. For as well as the gendered, other old 'binary oppositions', such as 'work' and 'leisure', 'public' and 'private', along with the tripartheid notion of 'class' would also seem to be shifting. On the home front, the micro computer is offering men new ways of flexible working which belong more to women's traditional experience of both work and home, and within 'her' traditional sphere.

The micro, a small but potent computer has been thrusting itself into the home over the last ten years. Also called 'personal', the micro is meant to organise, rather than massage the user's identity though you might think it would do both from the sales patter.

The micro is accessible to the pockets and desires of women, men and even children. They can buy technology with a difference in reputation and use value to the domesticity of microwave ovens and electric drills. Micros are bought and used for a variety of reasons: education, toy, for work or as an all-purpose computer encompassing all three ideas. Most desirable, perhaps, is the all-purpose micro, highly profiled in advertisements and articles.[7] It's compatible with mainstream business applications, with all the gadgetry of an executive's desk. The games and doodlepads alongside the accounts and the sales charts. Micros can be found in every High Street emporium of high tech delights, where the calculating products of business 'mix and merge' with the products of leisure, TV to watch, perhaps, or a guitar to play. A labour-saving device, but not sold alongside washing machines and vacuum cleaners. A kitchen sink image might be too much for potential male consumers to stomach, although he'll quite happily read *Good Housekeeping in PC DOS* about how to manage his files by sweeping clean.[8]

In fact, is the computer one of the sites of the fine lines, if any, between participating in work and leisure and the bridging of the gap of both public and private spheres and the position of women and men, and masculinity and femininity within them? Unlike the filofax syndrome where it is worn as a symbol of wealth and efficiency, the micro *produces* equal results in an instant. Both genders buying instant gentrification? And also the myth of it as the gateway to economic and toil-free liberation. Train to use it, and you'll get a well paid job or start up your own business? Is this myth helping women pave the circuitous pathway of the phallus for a more reluctant male workforce, maybe? Blind to 'third world' women workers, no longer concentrated in Eastern countries such as the Philippines as the multinationals look to Europe for cheap female labour and find it.[9] Creating a new 'world class' of women workers? And a new illusory image of men rather than the purchase of a 'feminine' form, which can't quite be contained by the picture? What else do they buy? Enter the Professional, the Expert.

Now many men can buy and take home instant success as a do-it-yourself executive. The micro offers immediate entry into a white collar world with all the associated trappings: his micro, his secretary, for instance, a traditional female function. So, it becomes his 'right hand man' as man and computer work in harmony. Although decisive, independent management material, dynamism indeed, he works in camaraderie, a part of the fraternity, with a machine of eternal power which will maintain his lead in the market place. It is not always easy to identify which one is God: man, or machine. But as often as not Man and Machine work together to produce, at short notice, and late at night: bar graphs, pie charts and constructions looking like well-organised meccano kits of fast cars and fighter planes, showing what real male professional playsters they are. Work can be fun! And for women?

Women are not necessarily excluded from this executive board-game, their inclusion, though, sometimes depicted in a negative way. One manufacturer, announcing the 'birth' of its family range of micros, so cute, named the new portable 'Little Henrietta'. A computer carry-cot for our slick worklady who's place is in the home with the babies? Are they trying to sell women a second-best phallus, a girl child of their own? Committing the fair gender to a permanently uneasy relationship to computer technology, in Freudian terms? Expertise, 'professionalism', and late nights, is that the compensation for Motherhood that women can buy with a micro? Is this her way forward in the public sphere from the domestic domain?

But just because women don't have the necessary equipment to fill the macho role, can we exclude them from the psychic fantasy of imagining they do, or that it's theirs for the asking? In fact, loading the software, ('booting up', what a thrill!) why, the very act could be akin to impregnating it with life and knowledge, a phallic performance controlled by the user, not computer, which will give birth at the printer. For both genders, the impossible promised by the advertisers come true. 'He' becomes self-impregnated, and 'she' can be her own penetrating drive to her 'natural' end, in motherhood, an androgynous twosome.

The fantasies for sale at present are teasing prospects. The sustained idea of woman as Professional and Expert is relatively new. Although a headcount of management will not produce 'representative' equal ops numbers, it's a novelty purchase for women on such a broad social scale. 'Man' has changed his position, in some ads, showing possibilities of an image no less masculine, but different from before. He doesn't just look at women as the potential buyer, he tries to absorb them; to contain the threat of the 'feminine' of his own creation—but for how long can 'he' hope to succeed?

Feminine men and machines may have to wait under the cloak of macho advertising until they (both men and advertisers) can find a new phenomenal form of masculinity to come to grips with, in a hidden, and different shape crafted in line with new dreams for success. Waiting their opportunity to create another less confrontational 'Woman' than 'equal ops' executives permit. Waiting for the next stage of the fiction to grasp again what before seemed so certainly theirs. But why give them the chance? These ambivalent representations might have their use-value to feminism. 'The computer', it seems, has put ideas of gender and power relations up for grabs. Any attempt made by the advertisers to contain traditional extremes of 'masculinity' and 'femininity' undergoes a power failure. Skilled women as buyers and users *must* slip into the picture. As in the Carlsberg ad where the executive (for she can no longer be called a secretary in its frivolous sense) operates a 'control centre', as the expert who knows more than her boss about computers. The computer here takes a central power point and the heat out of the threat of woman's technical skill, as a fairly omnipotent neutered being leaning towards God as He.

Such sexual ambiguity in depictions and in reality may just give women a lever to upturn masculine notions of power. Whilst the images are floundering around searching for stability, it may be possible to devise some way of preventing the recontainment of 'woman'. Perhaps a starting point might be to ask the question: isn't calling the computer 'masculine' as quoted at the start of this chapter, as likely to sustain, as expose the macho mythology surrounding Man and Machine?

NOTES

1. I would like particularly to thank Lorraine Gamman, Marisa Howes, Pat Horgan, Leslie Haddon, Bryan Hutchinson and David Skinner from whom I begged or borrowed various contributions to produce this essay. The results, though, do not necessarily reflect their own points-of-view.

2. Cockburn, C., *The Machinery of Dominance. Women, Men and Technical Knowhow* (London: Pluto Press, 1985). Cockburn argues that it is 'common sense to suppose that technology, as a medium of power, will be developed and used in any system of dominance to further the interests of those who are on top' (p. 8). One of my contentions is that we can no longer be sure who, or what is on top.

3. Lloyd, A. and L. Newell, 'Women and Computers', in W. Faulkner and E. Arnold (eds), *Smothered by Invention* (London; Pluto, 1985), for example. They describe computer advertising as 'forbidden territory'. But it may do well to bear in mind that forbidden territory has been an attractive proposition to women. Eve and Satan apart, isn't this what 'equal opportunities' drives are about?

4. Lloyd, A. and L. Newell, 'Women and Computers', in W. Faulkner and E. Arnold (eds), *Smothered by Invention* (London; Pluto, 1985). Can words alone be blamed for divisions of labour?

5. Lotus and Manpower, *Secretaries and IT—Which Way to the Future?* (1988).

6. Cockburn, C., 'A Wave of Women: new technology and sexual divisions in clothing manufacture' in her *Machinery of Dominance. Women, Men and Technical Knowhow* (London: Pluto Press, 1985). Cockburn notes that women are moving into 'men's' spheres in the clothing industry (p. 73).

7. Haddon, L., 'Electronic and Computer Games. The History of an Interactive Medium', in *Screen*, vol. 29, no. 2, (Spring, 1988) pp. 69–70. L. Haddon's research into the phenomena of computing reveals that the marketing of home computers in Britain, unlike the United States, has been as 'computer' rather than 'games machine'. Likewise, home computer magazines have tended to be less hobby orientated and more sophisticated in their approach to the product and user.

8. Lawrence, D. and M. England, *Good Housekeeping in MS DOS* (London: Sunshine, 1986). The front cover shows a broom sweeping up old floppy discs.

9.   Mitter, S., *Common Fate Common Bond. Women in the Global Economy* (London: Pluto Press, 1986). Mitter suggests that: 'The creation of a new proletariat is in fact part of a wider management strategy that affects not only the Third World but also the First. It is a strategy that deliberately seeks a "flexible" workforce in order to undermine the power of organized labour'. (p. 1).

16

Pleasure and Danger, Sex and Death: Reading True Crime Monthlies

DEBORAH CAMERON

True crime literature—defined as the narrative presentation of real-life criminal cases for mass entertainment—is a staple element in western popular cultures with a long history spanning early street literature (ballads and broadsides), collections like the New-gate Calendar, nineteenth-century Penny Dreadfuls and the popu-lar tabloids of today.[1] Since the 1950s in Britain there has also been a specialist genre devoted to it—the true crime monthly magazine.

In this essay I shall describe the main characteristics of true crime monthlies and analyse their social and political significance, focusing particularly on the kinds of pleasure they offer their readers. My approach will be two-pronged, paying attention to the magazines both as *texts* (the literary/semiological approach) and as objects produced and consumed by actual persons (the sociological approach). The integration of these two perspectives is more illuminating than either would be on its own.

In Britain today three titles are widely distributed under the heading of 'true crime': *True Detective, Master Detective* and *True Crime. True Detective* is the oldest (first published 1952) while the most recent, *True Crime*, dates from 1982. All three are produced by the same editorial team and published by the same company, Argus Publications. Their combined readership is estimated at 195 000 plus, with many readers buying all the titles each month. Sociologically, the typical reader is middle-aged (over 45) and working class (group C2/D/E on the Registrar-General's scale); it appears that a large proportion are women.[2]

The format of a true crime magazine is simple. Each issue contains around eight reports, which are fictionalised accounts of real events. Although they are advertised as 'compiled from police records', the producers admit that the main source used by the freelance writers who produce them is newspaper cuttings. Material is intensively recycled — from one title to another, from the American sister-publications to the British titles and from decade to decade (thus a 1950s report can be brought back as a 'classic' crime or with new illustrations). Reports are typically illustrated with photos and/or line drawings, and are interspersed with short editorial pieces on crime-related topics such as gun control and capital punishment. There is often a space for readers' letters.

The actual stories fall into two main groups, the 'classic' (which is set in the past and emphasises period detail) and the 'contemporary', usually a recent *cause célèbre*. Contemporary stories predominate over classics. The sort of case selected for true crime magazines is interesting: the largest category are murders, and many are murders with a sexual component. Grotesque modes of killing and disposing of the corpse (boiling alive; chopping off body parts) are especially favoured. The editors often exploit the device of the 'series', where a feature with an underlying theme (for example 'Death by Poison' or 'Yorkshire Mysteries') runs over several months. The serial format, by contrast, where the story is not completed each month, is never used, suggesting that suspense is insignificant for true crime readers.

Having described the format of the magazines I shall now turn to the way their narratives are presented. The central peculiarity of true crime narratives is their complex blending of factual and fictional conventions. On the one hand, they are clearly parasitic on popular journalism: the reports are taken from 'news' sources and reproduce the wide-eyed, breathless and sensational style of the tabloids: 'Blonde was cooked alive in a sauna!'. The magazines' detailed factual information is explicitly promoted as 'true' ('*True Crime*: the great no-fiction magazine'). It is hinted, that is, that mere fiction is inferior.

Yet on the other hand it is striking that the narrative presentation is dependent on conventions from crime and detective *fiction*. The structure of reports mirrors the 'police procedural' formula in crime writing: the narrative opens with the discovery of a crime and then follows the police investigation until the truth is revealed and the criminal punished. The narrative perspective is always that of the investigating officer. Stylistically, there are obvious traces of influence from American 'hardboiled' detective fiction, which was extremely popular at the time the magazines were started and which is greatly admired by the current editors. The stories use atmospheric description, fast cutting between scenes and, most significantly, *dialogue* as a means of advancing the plot and sketching in characters. What is interesting about this dialogue is the paradox it represents: its narrative function is to provide an air of authenticity, but in fact it is the least authentic feature of true crime writing, the most obviously fictional (since all of it is fabricated) and the furthest from reportage. (Some of the dialogue is moreover, extraordinarily implausible: '"Help me!" cried the woman as she tried to hold her intestines inside her body'). These stories, prized for their truth, are actually constructed according to the codes of genre fiction.

So far I have located true crime magazines in a tradition of writing about crime itself, which encompasses several distinct forms and genres. It needs to be pointed out, however, that crime reporting and crime fiction are not the only conventional influences on true crime magazines. Since the late 1960s they have also reflected quite overtly the representational codes of *pornography*. The most obvious, uncontroversially pornographic element in true crime magazines is the visual iconography of their covers. These feature a selection of motifs familiar (and meaningful) because of their association with 'soft' page 3-style porn (naked or scantily clad women in provocative poses) or as the symbols of sadomasochism (leather, bondage, women shown screaming in terror). The scenario is frequently completed by the presence of a weapon—a gun brushing the woman's lips, a knife menacing her throat—which neatly ties together the pornographic (phallic) significance of knives and guns with their literal interpretation in the context of crime. The cover is the distinctive trademark of the magazines, and is intended to make them both instantly recognisable and alluring to the potential buyer in the newsagent's.

The content of the magazine also has certain similarities to the content of pornographic literature. As I have observed, a large proportion of cases reported are sexual murders and involve rape, torture and bodily mutilation. These events are rendered in graphic language and sometimes illustrated with photographs of corpses or of wounds close up. All of which, while overlaid with a certain 'forensic' attitude, cannot fail to remind us of the elements in the more bizarre types of pornography (descriptions of torture, representations of mangled and fragmented bodies). Given that these phenomena are eroticised in that context we might even say there is an extra frisson in the fact that true crime depicts not fantasy but *real* mangled corpses—that is, the analogy is with 'snuff' pornography.[3]

Before the 1960s, the pornographic elements in true crime magazines were less overt, since restrictions on 'obscenity' had not yet been relaxed. Nevertheless, it is arguable that the underlying structure of the true crime genre was always pornographic: it was always tacitly known to producers and consumers of this literature that the pleasure of reading it was in part a sexual pleasure. It is impossible in such a short essay to explore this point fully but it can be summarised in the following way.[4] Western culture has persistently conflated sex, violence and death; in modern times (roughly since the late eighteenth century) this has taken a novel and distinctive form—the eroticisation of what philosophers call *transcendence*, the freeing of individual subjects from social and moral constraints by conscious acts of will. Typically, transcendence is achieved through acts of *transgression*—profaning what is sacred, flouting sexual taboos, breaking the law. This allows crime to take on a new meaning as a source of excitement, liberation and pleasure. Murder in this context is the paradigmatic crime, since it transgresses not just the law but the sacredness of life itself. Thus André Gide refers to murder as 'the culminating *acte gratuité* which liberates man from the determinism of the material universe'.[5] The liberation so achieved carries with it an explicitly erotic pleasure, as writers from Sade to Genet have made clear.

The general point I am trying to make is that true crime magazines are pornographic not, or not only, because they deal with sex crime but because crime itself, and murder in particular, has been given an erotic significance by the historical discourse of transgression/transcendence. And the erotic significance has to do not merely with sex *per se* but with the self-affirmation of the transcendent Subject. In modern western society sexuality is imbricated with power and the struggle for individual identity—it doesn't just follow 'naturally', as some have argued, from particular practices or acts defined as 'sex'.

This point is important if we wish to understand why anyone would seek sexual pleasure in the form of the true crime magazine. Why read this peculiar mixture of the salacious, the moralistic and the doggedly procedural when you could be reading about sex in a less obscure form? To make sense of this we must take account of what true crime narratives do that other genres do not; first, they offer readers *extra* pleasures, forms of identity and self-affirmation, and second, through their own contradictions and ambiguities they provide a means for readers to *negotiate* relationships to the problematic and guilt-inducing pleasures of the transgressive. In other words, they offer pleasures which need not speak their name, in contrast to pornography which proclaims it from the rooftops. (In this connection it is worth recalling that many true crime readers are middle-aged, minimally-educated women.)

The question of pleasures in true crime narrative can be investigated by way of two connected issues. One is the 'implied reader': all texts position their readers in ways which assume or construct certain interests and it will be important to examine how this is done in the true crime magazine. The other issue is how real readers locate themselves in relation to the text—what they say they like about it, what the preoccupations revealed in letters to the editor suggest, and so on.

It is no coincidence that *True Detective* and its ilk are sold in newsagents alongside publications on angling, photography, railways and computers—in the section W.H. Smith labels 'leisure interest'. An interest in murder is thereby classified as one of an innocuous range of hobbies. This general approach is continued by the magazine itself: the implied true crime reader can best be conceptualised as a 'murder buff', in the same way others might be wine buffs or film buffs.

The key attribute of a murder buff is *expertise*. The magazines address their readers in a way which suggests expectations of knowledge—familiarity with the procedures of detection and forensic pathology and also with a 'canon' of famous cases (thus new material is often presented by comparisons with known material—'even more intriguing than the Manson murders' for instance). Murder buffs will have taken the trouble to inform themselves about crime; they will appreciate a 'good' as opposed to a run-of-the-mill report; and they will be able to offer their own assessments of the stories (the letters page confirms that they do this routinely). It is likely that being treated as a knowledgeable expert is a source of self-affirmation and thus pleasure in itself.

The textual characteristic that correlates with expertise is *authenticity*. Murder buffs have a right to expect that they will be given information of a quality and quantity appropriate to their special status as experts, including 'privileged' information not vouchsafed to the casual newspaper reader. Gory details (in the form of copious verbal and visual material) are enjoyed, precisely, in the name of authenticity. Readers are quick to praise the minutely detailed account of, say, methods of torture in the middle ages, and just as quick to complain about any lack of authentic detail. But if enjoying writing that dwells so relentlessly on gory details is found unacceptable, that activity can be justified in terms of expertise. The murder buff's interest in his subject is not prurient, sick, perverse and so on; it is the quasi-professional concern of a responsible expert.

Readers in their letters frequently invoke this justification, asserting that they read true crime magazines because they are true and therefore of educational value. 'Since I started to read *True Detective*', says one letter, 'I have quite lost my taste for detective fiction'. Truth is more exciting than fiction for the same reason snuff porn is more exciting than the fabricated item; but non-fiction is also 'improving' where fiction has no possible rationale besides entertainment.

In a similar way, it is important that the magazines take a high moral tone on crime. Murder buffs may wallow in salacious accounts of depraved and revolting behaviour; but if they are not to be accused of mere prurience, gory details must be offset by explicit moral condemnation in such a way as to distance the law-abiding reader from the evil criminal. The main techniques used to do this are firstly, a narrative form which allies the reader with the agencies of law-enforcement and secondly, an intrusive editorial presence which constantly interpolates a conservative perspective on law and order (rising crime rates, declining moral standards, the need for severe and retributive punishment). Readers are not just enabled but required to adopt a posture of moral superiority—and doubtless this helps to minimise any anxieties they may have about enjoying such gruesome material.

It is worth noting that the reader's moral position can only be guaranteed by an extremely conservative and indeed mystificatory view of crime and criminals, in which criminals are 'other', different from decent people, while crime itself is a fixed, timeless essence (it is the function of the 'classic' narratives to point this out: depravity is found in every age). The contradiction between this assertion and the idea that crime rates are constantly rising is less important than the underlying ideology expressed by both propositions, that is that crime is in the nature of some wicked individuals and repressive measures are therefore the only possible response. The alternative view, that crime is a *social* problem to be addressed by social change, is eschewed and sometimes explicitly denied in true crime magazines. Doubtless a number of factors enter into this, but one is the reader's need for moral certainty as a counterbalance to the ambiguity inherent in being a murder buff.

What true crime magazines thus offer readers is a balance of licit and illicit pleasures, the one defusing the anxiety of the other! The narratives are exciting *and* educational, sexually exciting *and* moralistic. This heady mix is especially likely to appeal to the conservative, low-status readers who typically buy the magazines; it confirms their social outlook and addresses their real anxieties about crime and law and order (this may be especially salient for women readers); it also offers them the status of 'expert', and allows them to partake of the pleasures of transgression without having to admit to them. Again, this may be of particular value for women readers. (One of the mysteries of the genre is why the implied reader is so clearly male, for example the gaze constructed by the cover, when the producers know full well many readers are female. The solution may be that women feel safer reading this material when they are constructed as *eavesdroppers* rather than direct addressees: their relation to transgression has to be mediated).

It is fashionable in the study of popular culture for analysts to revalue despised forms and genres, finding in the pap which the masses consume points of tension, contradictions, possibilities of subversion. It is also commonplace to celebrate 'pleasure' where we find it lighting up the dark corners of late capitalism. True crime magazines are contradictory and give pleasure. But they are also reactionary and depressing, with no subversive potential that I can discern. They are locked into a conservative view of society and crime, where traditional values of law and order (never seen in the context of class relations) are under threat from a criminal out-group; the moral panic thus generated is used to justify repressive government and judicial revenge. Furthermore—and I labour this point because it is less familiar than the first one—true crime magazines reproduce all the cultural, aesthetic and sexual values which link sexual pleasure with transgression and death. As a number of feminist critics have observed,[6] there is nothing liberating or subversive of patriarchal capitalist society in making those connections. They are part of the structure in which relations of dominance and subordination are eroticised (which helps to en-sure those same relations will be enthusiastically maintained—if inequality is 'sexy', how are we going to get rid of it?) and in which women and children particularly suffer gross abuse. The project cultural studies must address is not to revalue the pleasures of true crime but to imagine a universe in which those pleasures could be transformed.

NOTES

1. This history is traced in detail in Deborah Cameron and Elizabeth Frazer, *The Lust to Kill* (Cambridge: Polity Press, 1987). My thanks are due to Elizabeth Frazer for her contribution to this paper; the research on true crime magazines on which it is based was all done jointly with her. (I am, of course, responsible for the shortcomings of the present piece!) I would also like to acknowledge the many useful suggestions and comments made by audiences in the UK and USA when we have talked about true crime literature at lectures and conferences.

2. All information about the production, readership and editorial atti-tudes of British true crime magazines was obtained with the co-operation of the editor and staff, who gave us access to the full archive of the magazines, showed us the production centre and answered our questions; and with the co-operation of Argus who supplied information on readership profiles and circulation drawn from a recent questionnaire inserted in the magazines and responded to by 1200 people. (The titles are not included in the National Readership Survey and the results of the questionnaire must be interpreted with some caution: for instance, do women read true crime more than men or are they just more willing to fill in questionnaires?)

3. 'Snuff' refers to pornography in which a model or actress is *actually killed* during the process of producing it, for the camera; there is a good deal of evidence that it is available (imported from Latin America) and there have been cases where men have been arrested for attempting to produce it. There is also a genre of 'non-genuine' snuff movies (the most famous of which was *Snuff*). Here no-one is really killed but the film is promoted on the premiss that it does contain an actual murder. In other words, the idea of a real killing being caught by the camera is the distinctive pleasure of snuff porn. This is not altered (or indeed made less repellent) by the fact that some products are the real thing while others are cheap imitations.

4. This point is argued out at length in Deborah Cameron and Elizabeth Frazer, op. cit., chap. 2.

5. Gide, André, *Les Caves du Vatican*; cf. Coe 1968, p. 181.

6. Kappeler, Susan, *The Pornography of Representation* (Cambridge: Polity Press, 1986). Deborah Cameron and Elizabeth Frazer, op. cit.

17

A Second Byte of the Apple

GILL SIMPSON

Although the impact of computers on society can be represented (by those very computers) in terms of statistics — numbers of jobs lost, for instance, or increases in productivity — I want to propose a different way of considering it, that is, in terms of the way that people interact with computers, and to suggest that there are several aspects of this interaction that are analogous to aspects of religion. The physical aspects of computers and their accommodation, the history of man's connections with them, the beliefs that are held regarding them and the rituals that are employed in dealing with them can all be interpreted, albeit from an idiosyncratic viewpoint, as signs which support this view. In an attempt to justify this 'idiosyncratic viewpoint' I refer the reader to Roland Barthes and Umberto Eco. Concerning the 'significant features' with which the essays in *Mythologies* deal, Barthes writes 'Is this a significance which *I* read into them?'[1] In other words is there a mythology of the mythologist? No doubt, and the reader will easily see where I stand. Umberto Eco, in the preface to *Travels in Hyperreality* writes 'In these pages I try to interpret and to help others interpret some "signs". These signs are not only words, or images; they can also be forms of social behaviour, political acts, artificial landscapes'.[2]

In the church of the computer, as in other churches, there is a hierarchy and it is at the top, with the main-frame computer, that I begin. For many people the representations of film or television are the closest they will get to experiencing the physical aspects of the main-frame computer and its accommodation. A visit to the room where the main-frame is housed is a privilege, still reserved for only a few, which requires special dispensation and the services of a guide who can explain the mysteries of the computer.

On being admitted to the shrine at the heart of the temple a sense of reverence is invoked in the visitor by the litany of the guide who impresses upon him or her the wonder of the computer and the power that it represents. The furnishings of the room have been specially prepared so as to be undefiled by any trace of static and the air conditioner provides purified air to the accompaniment of a low chant of hums, whirrs and clicks. Robed in white are the acolytes who have been chosen to attend the computer and instructed in the observance of ritual and the interpretation of sayings. Although admitted to its presence, the visitor, approaching the computer itself, is not permitted to look upon the power that resides within the ark. He or she can only wonder at the metal casket, adorned with jewelled lights and strange moving symbols, which shrouds the mystery within.

Although visionaries in Europe had foreseen the birth of 'Computerism',[3] it was in the United States of America that it took hold and in a time of great need (towards the end of the Second World War) that men began to call on computers came to help them overcome the troubles which beset them. Since that time the message has been disseminated in Europe and Japan and missionaries are taking the word to the four corners of the earth. The names of the early computers roll off the tongue like those of the prophets of the Old Testament; Eniac, Edviac, Univac, Sage and Sabre ... and in each generation new miracles have been performed and even greater miracles prophesied for the future. But the texts of computers came to be written in many tongues, FORTRAN, COBOL, ALGOL, BASIC ... and followers of computerism were divided amongst themselves. Many remained true to the old faith of IBM, but others adhered to BURROUGHS, HONEYWELL, PLESSEY and other minor churches, adopting new rituals and texts.

However, in spite of their differences, followers of Computerism have retained their essential beliefs in the enabling power of computers to help mankind. Now a new message of ecumenicalism is being spread and there may come a time when members of the rival churches will come together, understanding and taking part in the rituals each of the others. Above all, they look forward in unity to the fulfilling of the prophesy that there will come amongst them a new Messiah, the thinking computer.

As computerism has spread throughout the world, the rulers of individual nations have seized the opportunity to work with the Church, using its power to control and shape the lives of their people and to defend them from their enemies. The all-knowing computer records the minutiae of the lives of individuals; their births, marriages and deaths, their credit and crimes, '. . . the very hairs of your head are all numbered'.[4] Governments encourage the spread of computerism by ensuring that children are brought up in the faith. In Britain, whilst traditional religious education is fighting to retain a place in the school curriculum, the new religion is urged upon educators so that every child may be instructed in the basic observances. Where once there was a Bible in every home, now it is prophesied that it will come to pass that there will be a computer in every home. The church of the computer co-operates by seeking to translate its texts into the language of the common people; soon we may have the New English Computer Text alongside (or instead of) the New English Bible on our shelves.

Whilst children are being brought up in the knowledge of computers (where once they coloured pictures in Sunday school now they play computer games), the conversion of adults is a difficult process for they still cling to traditional beliefs. For some it may come as a result of instruction, for others the power of a computer to solve a pressing problem may bring about a Pauline change. Many will never take computerism to heart in spite of the myriad ways in which it affects their daily lives. But the intervention of church and state will not stop and many people may suffer at the hands of the inquisition, forfeiting their jobs if they do not embrace the faith.

In the workplace, as in the school, missionary zeal is increasing and there more and more people receive instruction in the observance of the daily rituals which reaffirm belief. After a period of instruction confirmation takes place and the new lay brother or sister is admitted to membership of the Church. This means that he or she may take part in the rite of communion with the computer, through the intercession of the terminal.

Whatever a supplicant may wish to ask of the computer, certain formulaic expressions are used. Instead of 'Our Father' prayers begin with 'LOG ON' and 'Amen' is replaced by 'LOG OFF'. These rituals apart, the various problems or requests which are brought to the computer require different forms of prayer, known in the church as programmes. These are formulated for the lay person by high priests ordained for this purpose after training in seminaries of computerism. Although some of these chosen ones spend their lives as apostles or ministers, others dedicate their lives to computers in a monastic regime, keeping to their cells, perhaps fasting or keeping to special diets, and spending long hours in study.

> Wherever computer centers have become established ... bright young men of dishevelled appearance, often with sunken glowing eyes, can be seen sitting at computer consoles ... When not so transfixed, they often sit at tables strewn with computer printouts over which they pore like students of a cabalistic text. ... Their food, if they arrange it, is brought to them: coffee, coke, sandwiches. If possible, they sleep on cots near the computer. But only for a few hours—then back to the console or the printouts. ... They exist, at least when so engaged, only through and for the computers.[5]

Just as in traditional religions believers feel the need to anthropomorphise the objects of their beliefs, so in computerism followers try to establish human-like relations between themselves and their computers. Sometimes this is done by naming, so that the paternalistic relationship suggested by addressing God as 'Father' in one religion may be replaced by the avuncular one using a familiar name such as 'Ernie'. Even visual imagery may be employed, God as Father has been represented by an old man with a white beard, whereas some journalists 'draw ears and lips on their terminals and try to wheedle their way into their computers' good graces'.[6]

What is the nature of the faith that people have in computers to justify such behaviour towards them? They believe with justification that computers are a power for good. The evidence of their achievements confirms this belief: computers are used to help in the healing of the sick and the feeding of the poor. They give people aid in their defence against enemies. With their assistance people have achieved dominion over space, bringing the planets within reach and uncovering the mysteries of stars. David addressed God thus, 'For a thousand years in thy sight are but as yesterday when it is past, and as a watch in the night'.[7] Helped by computers people have also conquered time as Gerald Silver shows when he says, 'A computer is programmed to search 50 million records in little more time than it takes for us to take out a pencil and paper'.[8]

But, as in the past humans have used religion for their own gain, selling pardons and indulgences for instance, so in computerism there are those who make use of computers to defraud and steal.

The creation of computers and the evil as well as the good that can come of them are a result of the pursuit of knowledge. The original downfall of the human race was blamed on a woman, as we read in Genesis.

> And the serpent said unto the woman
> Ye shall not surely die:
> For God doth know that in the day ye eat thereof,
> then your eyes shall be opened, and ye shall be
> as gods, knowing good and evil.
> And when the woman saw that the
> tree was good for food, and that it
> was pleasant to the eyes, and a tree to be desired
> to make one wise, she took of the fruit thereof,
> and did eat, and gave also unto her
> husband with her; and he did eat.
> . . . And the Lord God said unto woman,
> what is this that thou hast done?[9]

However this time man is the instigator of a search for knowledge and is still trying to ordain reluctant women into the priesthood.

It was with the verses from Genesis in mind that I chose the title of this essay, thinking it could be no mere coincidence that 'Apple' computers were so named. I was disappointed therefore to discover that their first logo featured Isaac Newton sitting beneath his tree, a different kind of apple. However my faith is now restored by the marketers of Apple Computers since, more recently, they have adopted a new logo, an apple with a bite taken out of it. Are they trying to create some kind of myth?

NOTES

1. Barthes, R., *Mythologies* (Paris: Editions Du Seuil, 1957). Translation (London: Jonathan Cape, 1972) preface to 1957 edition, p. 12.
2. Eco, U., *Travels in Hyperreality* (London: Pan, 1987) preface p. xi.
3. Computerism: I am not aware of the existence of this word prior to my use of it here which is as the name of the 'religion' devoted to computers.
4. Matthew, chapter 10, verse 30. All biblical quotations are taken from the Authorised King James version.
5. Weizenbaum, J., *Computer power and human reason, from judgement to calculation* (San Francisco: W. H. Freeman, 1976) p. 116.

6. Banks-Smith, N., quoted in C. Berman: 'Hands-on types', *Guardian* (18 February 1988) p. 25.
7. Psalm 90, verse 4.
8. Silver, G. A., *The Social Impact of Computers* (New York: Harcourt Brace Jovanovich, 1979) p. 333.
9. Genesis, chapter 3, verses 4–6.13.

18

Illiberal Thoughts on 'Page 3'

BOB BRECHER

The first thing to avoid in thinking about pornography is trying to define 'pornography'. Trying to distinguish pornography from erotica or to define its proper limits is either misconceived or mischievous. Just as we can discuss tables, chairs, typewriters and handbags—or murder, art and responsibility—without being able to define them so we can discuss pornographic pictures, writing and advertising without being able to define 'pornography'. I am not implying that, however obscurely, 'we all know what we mean' in some (quasi-)intuitive fashion, I am simply making the point that within the limits of our fallibility and the parameters of historical and related circumstances, we can quite unproblematically discuss myriads of things which we cannot define in terms of formal ideas.

Nor have I anything to offer by way of statistical evidence, such as it is, about the relation between things like page 3 and the incidence of rape; views about the purported therapeutic value of pornography; insights about whether or not art can be pornographic; or solutions to the problems of censorship. It is not that these matters are unimportant, but that concentrating on them as 'issues' tends to obscure what I think is central: the notion of the good society, generally only implicit, in the context of which attitudes, opinions and convictions about these matters operate. Most importantly, because the basic political, social and moral values lurking in the background are not made explicit, it is all too easy to accept rather than question assumptions: in particular, assumptions about the political and conceptual role of people's wants. People *want* page 3, the story goes, and who are we to interfere? What people want is taken as the basic datum and thus accorded privileged status in argument. This chapter is largely aimed against this liberal notion of the primacy of wants, an assumption on which socialist and feminist good intentions so often flounder—and this because of a sort of shyness about operating with an explicit, albeit fragmentary, notion of a good society, with views about what it is right or wrong to want. The illiberal right understands this only too clearly, for it is what allows the likes of Mary Whitehouse and Victoria Gillick to fill the vacuum created by the left's failing to offer a positive vision of the good society, assuming instead that politics and/or morality are about what people want, rather than changing what we want. Such political floundering, one result of remaining trapped in the conceptual fleapit of liberalism, is disastrous: when political discourse—in its widest sense—remains, however unwittingly, within the limits of Adam Smith's agenda, it is hardly surprising that the left gets left behind. For example, it is not merely through her vision of a good society that Thatcher can present a substantive programme: but that, unsurprisingly after the last few years, much of what most of us in late-1980s Britain want is what Thatcher wants us to want—indeed, needs us to want. When Labour Party worthies then start bleating about the need to give people what they want they have already surrendered the debate.

But perhaps I should return to page 3. Beverley Brown has observed that:

> For liberalism, harms attach to the interests of individuals, or, less popularly, to society as a whole. Yet feminism is concerned with the interests of a constituency of women for whom pornography will have different effects on individual women. This constituency cannot be simply reduced to a collection of individuals or made homogenous with either 'reasonable people' or 'society'. Consequently the level of harm to such an interest is not amenable to liberalism either.
>
> And what is more, liberalism prefers harms to be measurable in something tangible, such as acts against individuals. Yet the harms feminism wishes to mark do not depend for their seriousness on being or resulting directly in acts. The harms indicated by pornography's relation to 'a sexist society' are serious in themselves.[1]

Such a framework offers a way of discussing, and condemning, page 3 and its look-alikes without becoming entangled in any of the diversions I have outlined. Brown's central claims are firstly that: harms are not necessarily tangible; secondly they are not necessarily acts or causes of acts; and lastly 'pornography' is in some sense a relational term. I shall attempt to suggest an understanding of page 3 and its importance in terms of these propositions, an attempt which will serve also to offer grounds for their truth. Working in this way, rather than with some definition of 'pornography' which tries, vainly, to locate it outside any particular context and/or remaining stuck in the cul-de-sac of people's present wants allows at least the possibility of a properly illiberal view of the matter.

Why take page 3 of the *Sun* as central in thinking about pornography? There are surely far worse cases, such as depictions of sexual torture in hard-core magazines; and anyway, are page 3 and its like not relatively harmless compared to other soft-core material? There are two points here: why the *Sun*, and why soft-core pornography? The first is straightforward. The *Sun*'s page 3 has become a market leader, a benchmark against which *Sunday Sport*, the *Daily Mail* and all the rest of the junk that constitutes our press measure themselves. We have all seen page 3, we know it so well, in fact, that no example need be reproduced here. The second point is deeper, and will, I hope, emerge in the course of this essay.

There is a specific pornography industry, literally and analogically producing a wide range of goods, an 'industry of images aimed at sexual arousal',[2] but of course manufacturing things other than images. It can only flourish, however, where there is a market for pornographic items; and only exist at all insofar as it is possible for items to be pornographic. The *Sun* is an epitome. It develops the market by creating the possibility at least of a certain range: and creates that possibility by developing the market. This two-way process, about which I will have more to say presently, is the root of the peculiar importance of page 3 and its ilk. The arrangement of shapes, lines or dots on page 3 gains its meaning in relation to the captions; page 3 from its place in what purports to be a newspaper and the meaning of the *Sun* comes from its place in people's lives, both literally (on the train; at work; at home) and metaphorically (in our thoughts, beliefs, feelings and convictions). Change *any* of these and you change not just all the others in my list, but also the meaning of the image on page 3—for, as Ros Coward insists, 'there is no intrinsic meaning in a visual image'.[3] The conditions of its production and the lives of its audience together make it mean what it does: it is because pornographic meanings have come to be established that page 3 can be what it is; and page 3 reciprocates the favour. Our 'images of the feminine'[4] are in large part both constructed and disseminated by such things as page 3. That is why it is perhaps more important than hard-core pornography, which depends, logically as well as materially, on this market of meanings; and why it is pornographic rather than, as many think harmless fun.

Page 3 makes inappropriate use of sexuality, inappropriate because the context is all wrong—and what is wrong can, I think, be summed up by describing it as sexist. The use of that term takes us straight to my earlier point about notions of the good life, for its justified use depends on a long story about relations between the sexes, how gender might be created and understood in a society different from ours, and so on. It is not simply a boo-word. To elaborate on this, as I would have to do to establish my argument in this essay as anything more than a prolegomenon, would be a lengthy undertaking.[5] What I hope for the moment, however, is that my methodological points might stand, whatever differences readers might have about the likely results of their application. Even if one does not think that the inappropriateness of what is on page 3 is its sexism—although I find it hard to think what else it might lie in—I would hope that its being somehow inappropriate might be agreed. For it is by means of a relational term such as this that essentialist notions of pornography can be avoided, even if the substantive question of what is appropriate where remains, waiting on the elaboration of theories of social relations and practices for its resolution: but that is precisely my methodological point. (Interestingly, I suspect it is on the basis of underlying notions of inappropriateness that some people describe things like *Rambo* as pornographic, quasi-pornographic, or at least metaphorically pornographic, whereas depiction of violence in the context of an exhibition commemorating Auschwitz might be entirely appropriate because of the ends served by it, unlike those of *Rambo*, which, if no worse, is mere entertainment.)

My objection to page 3, then, is an objection to sexist exploitation of sexuality. The images depend for their appeal on men's sexist sexuality: otherwise *that* gaze; *that* posture; and *that* caption would not arouse. Their appearance in a 'newspaper' is itself an important element: in a way impossible twenty years ago, when what is now on page 3 was being bought only under the counter, men's ownership of women is reassuringly asserted in the public domain of the paper. There is no need any longer to be furtive about it. Furthermore, such images can be produced only in conditions of economic exploitation (in a different economic order, women would not need to earn money and/or achieve status like this)—an exploitation itself predicated on sexual exploitation, since it is only because we exploit women as a class that the economic picture is what it is. This is why arguments about improving models' conditions fail. They miss the point that sexual exploitation does not depend on prior economic exploitation, but is part of the power, the wielding of which results in the latter.

Both the image and its being there constitute harm. But if I am not talking about page 3 and rape statistics, nor objecting to the sexuality of the images *per se*, or their appearing in public, what is my objection? What sort of harm is this? It might not consist in or lead to specific acts, and yet, still, it is a sort of harm. What I wish to suggest is that its harm lies in its being a symptom of our sexist society. The establishment of certain meanings make page 3 possible; but, on the other hand, page 3's being there is part of the process of such establishment. The sexism of our lives—in its relation to the sexist sexualities it both produces and consists of—makes page 3 possible, materially and psychologically and is in turn reinforced by page 3, which, in bringing into everyday contexts its sexist imagery entrenches social values more efficiently than hard porn. Page 3 is both causal and symptomatic of the attitudes and feelings which constitute a sexist society. Like filofaxes, colour supplements, videos Golf GTI's and marriage, page 3 serves to reinforce (hence a cause) just those elements of our culture which make possible its production (hence a symptom). As both cause and symptom, page 3 is a symbol: it cannot be analysed without remainder into what it symbolises and what it might be 'in itself'.[6] That is why page 3 is what it is, exemplifying our society, reminding us of it and our place as women and men in it, reiterating its structures, values and powers, and, in doing so, reinforcing them. That is its harm, recognisable as such only on the basis of a shared notion of a good society within the logical parameters of which the description of something as a harm must rest. To repeat, justification of this view requires moving on to arguments about the good society, and, specifically, discussion of gender and sexuality within it.

Meanwhile, Mr Murdoch, astute businessman that he is, continues to subvert opposition to his particular capitalist vision by giving people what they want. Sheltering behind the approval of that paragon of Tory values, Mr Tebbit, and liberal conceptions of harm limited to acts and individuals (a deep-rooted alliance) he continues to further his vision. Like the rest of the illiberal right, he knows that wants can be manufactured; and can be used. Perhaps it is time the opposition became equally illiberal.

NOTES

1. Brown, Beverley, 'A Feminist Interest in Pornography—Some Modest Proposals', in *m/f*, 5–6 (1981), pp. 12–13.
2. Coward, Rosalind, 'What Is Pornography?', in *Spare Rib*, 119 (1982), p. 52.
3. Coward, Rosalind, 'Sexual Violence and Sexuality', in *Feminist Review*, 11 (1982), p. 11—still one of the best essays available on pornography.
4. Brown, Beverley, op. cit., p. 8.
5. As I realised when I read an earlier version of this essay at a conference on 'Sex, Gender and the Family' at Gregynog in May 1987. My thanks in particular to Alison Assiter, Jean Grimshaw, Ross Poole and Lynne Segal for our discussion on 'sexism'.
6. '. . . while the sign bears no necessary relation to that to which it points, the symbol participates in the reality of that for which it stands . . . The symbol grows and dies according to the correlation between that which is symbolised and the persons who receive it as a symbol.' Paul Tillich, *Systematic Theology* (Welwyn: Nisbet, 1968), vol. 1, p. 265.

19

The Golden Age of Cricket

JOHN SIMONS

The aim of this essay is to look at some features of the game of cricket as it has been mediated to us through popular books dealing specifically with aspects of its history and through the popular imagination. My concern, however, will not be to analyse specific items — often such projects in the realm of popular cultural studies become too descriptive — rather I shall be looking at the game of cricket itself as a popular cultural form. I particularly intend to argue that, in the context of popular cricket history, the ideological load which cricket has been asked to carry may be shown, surprisingly perhaps, to constitute a consistent and deliberate set of values which appear oppositional to much contemporary social and political thought. The effect of this approach is that I will not be dealing with such well-known items as cigarette cards, though these are an undoubted proof of the popularity of the game, nor will I be dealing with the fictionalisation of cricket in such famous organs as The *Boy's Own Paper* or the *Magnet*. It is tempting to open up this area but the ethos of the school story is well understood and an analysis would do little except reinforce the themes which I will be exploring by reference to less familiar material. I am aware that this may seem to avoid the obvious areas of interest but I want, on the one hand, to make a case for the wide permeation of certain values through the medium of cricket and, on the other, to avoid speaking of artefacts and texts in isolation from the sport which generates and sustains them.

Ask anyone who is interested in cricket whether or not the game is ephemeral they will probably answer 'no' but on reflection add a 'yes'. The point is that while cricket finishes when any individual competition comes to an end, no other game is subject to such extensive reconstruction in memory or bears such cultural value. Two snatches of verse will help to illustrate the point, the first by Francis Thompson, the second by John Arlott:

And I look through my tears on a soundless-clapping host
  As the run-stealers flicker to and fro,
    To and fro:
  O my Hornby and my Barlow long ago![1]

Recorded centuries leave no trace
On memory of that timeless grace.[2]

In drawing from contemporary publications on cricket history I
will contend that this need for preservation is part of the reason for
the continued interest in the old game as continuities between past
and present become more precious and more politically charged
and the nature of our relationship with history, perhaps especially
Imperial history, becomes a topic of pressing social importance.

The 'Golden Age' of cricket is generally agreed to stretch from
c.1890 to 1914 when the War enforced a suspension of the
first-class game. To most modern enthusiasts it is presented as
being a time when the game was played only by 'characters',
before enormous crowds in endlessly hot and dry summers and
when the phenomenon of country house cricket ensured not only
a charming breadth to the career of the first-class player but also
healthy and friendly contact between the classes (as memorably
portrayed in L. P. Hartley's *The Go Between*). While, greenhouse
effect permitting, cricketers in the Golden Age suffered as much
from rain as we do currently (though playing on uncovered
wickets meant that less time was actually lost) it is indisputable
that cricket was a game with a mass following of a sort which it
does not have now (at least not for the three-day game) and that it
could still claim to be the national sport (which might now be
difficult to sustain). In 1919 the world had changed and cricket, as a
cultural form, had its share of that change. Neville Cardus, writing
in 1945 and fearing another post-war decline put it thus:

When first-class cricket was played again after the end of the
1914–1918 war, we were given yet another example of what a
sensitive plant this cricket is—how quick to respond to atmosphere, how eloquent at any time of English mood and temper. It
was an age of some disillusionment and cynicism; the romantic
gesture was distrusted. 'Safety First' was the persistent warning.
We saw at once on the cricket field the effect of a dismal
philosophy and a debilitated state of national health. Beautiful

and brave stroke-play gave way to a sort of trench warfare, conducted behind the sandbag of broad pads.[3]

An interesting comparison may be found in Ronald Mason, a writer with a far less shrewd appreciation of the bonds between cricket and society:

And the season of 1919 is not to be despised for its faults: let us remember it for its invigorating virtues, its adventurousness, its gaiety, its air of relaxation and refreshment. I do not think we should carp at its shortcomings. . . . It was high summer again, and the sun winked on the fresh paintwork at Lord's, and there was the smell of new-cut grass on the light wind; and the war was over.[4]

Mason suppresses the qualitative change in cricket by clinging nostalgically to the metaphors of the Golden Age: one does not catch Cardus's sense of a lost aesthetic, his sharing Adorno's fear that there can be no poetry after Auschwitz.

The thing which many people will call to mind when they consider Golden Age cricket is its intimate connection with the English public schools. For over half a century these establishments had progressively eschewed intellectual accomplishments in favour of muscular Christianity and the cult of games. This history is too well-known to repeat here and it would be otiose to quote Newman's 'Vitae Lampada' which for most readers, I suppose, will represent the apotheosis of the cricketer as Imperialist. The world of cricket is, at this time filled with notables like the Honourable F. S. Jackson who, in addition to captaining England and Yorkshire, fought in the Boer War, was an MP, Chairman of the Unionist Party and Governor of Bengal. But perhaps the extraordinary C. B. Fry whose career as Captain of the English cricket team, first-class player of rugby and soccer and world record long jumper did not preclude him from taking a first-class degree, attending the League of Nations as a substitute delegate, nor from being Ranjitsinhji's speechwriter, nor from being seriously considered for the vacant throne of Albania will sum up the ethic in the baldest way:

But whatever may be the defects of the English Public School, neither England, nor any other country has succeeded in inventing a better way of training a boy to be of use to himself and other people.[5]

It is all too easy at this point to see cricket becoming a mere repository of ethnocentricity and bearer of an ideology designed to cloak exploitation in the colonies and to provide a spiritual heart to an elite military and administrative corps. Certainly those headmasters who followed Thomas Arnold (who should perhaps be allowed to stand somewhat aloof from this discussion) such as Welldon (Harrow), Rendall (Winchester) or Warre (Eton) and men such as Frederick Lugard, educationalist and Governor of Nigeria give little room for manoeuvre, but the reality may not be so simple.[6] Leaving aside the fact that cricket, both as game and as spectacle, was part of a culture which extended far beyond the domain of the public schools and their old boys—though in correspondence in *The Times* Welldon attempted to improve the public image of his own school's cricket by seeking to get the Eton-Harrow match, which is played at Lord's, extended from two or three days, a move which was blocked by Warre[7]—we might listen to C. L. R. James, the most intelligent if not always the most readable commentator on cricket history (among other things):

> One afternoon in 1956, being at that time deep in this book, I sat in a hall in Manchester, listening to Mr Aneurin Bevan. Mr Bevan had been under much criticism for 'not playing with the team', and he answered his critics ... When Mr Bevan had had enough of it he tossed the ball lightly to his fellow speaker, Mr Michael Foot. 'Michael is an old public-school boy and he knows more about these things than I.' Mr Foot smiled, but if I am not mistaken the smile was cryptic.
>
> I smiled too, but not wholeheartedly. In the midst of his fireworks Mr Bevan had dropped a single sentence that tolled like a bell. 'I did not join the Labour Party, I was brought up in it.' And I had been brought up in the public-school code.[8]

James is implying that the public-school ethic and its manifestation in cricket is not purely an ideological cloaking of imperialism. He is always worth paying attention to but especially here as we try to understand what books and images of the Golden Age offer to their audience.

The period 1890–1914 was marked by urban deprivation, uncertain employment and labour unrest (in 1890 there were over one thousand industrial disputes, in 1892 seventeen million working days were lost through strikes, in 1893 thirty million) but cricket went on as if it offered a refuge from the industrial capitalism which directly exploited the masses both in the United Kingdom and in the Empire.[9] This will certainly seem a paradox given the role of cricket in the Imperial myth but it is this aspect of cricket as refuge which, I think, attracted the Headmasters who were influenced by Malory and Walter Scott as much as by Thucydides, Caesar or Rhodes as well as the thousands who thronged to the Oval in 1902 to see Gilbert Jessop hit a match-winning hundred against the Australians, with the painful South African War coming to its close, or the farm workers and servants who regularly played the game in the provinces. Cricket in the Golden Age must probably be best seen in terms of a conservative nationalism which assented to the imperial project but rejected the international capitalist just as surely as it did the international revolutionary. As James has pointed out this makes it difficult to place cricket in the conventional paradigms of history:

A famous Liberal historian [Trevelyan] can write the social history of England in the nineteenth century, and two famous Socialists [Postgate and Cole] can write what they declared to be the history of the common people of England, and between them never once mention the man who was the best-known Englishman of his time. I can no longer accept the system of values which could not find in these books a place for W. G. Grace.[10]

This declaration, however true it may be, needs to be held in mind especially since what I hope to do here is to avoid the tendency of transforming cricket from a cultural form with its own dynamic and relationships with society more generally into a mere reflection of social movement.[11] It is fundamental to my task to trace some of cricket's social relations, especially where they are mediated through the artefacts of popular culture and at the same time to keep in view the idea that cricket itself is a cultural activity.

Whether at Lord's or on the town and village pitches of Hampshire or Yorkshire, cricketers of the Golden Age appear to have been united in their dislike and distrust of the capitalist who had, in the classic formulation of Marx and Engels:

... put an end to all feudal, patriarchal, idyllic relations ...
pitilessly torn asunder the motley feudal ties that bound man to
his 'natural superiors', and has left remaining no other nexus
between man and man than naked self-interest, than callous
'cash payment'.[12]

An example of the difficulties caused to the wealthy men who
controlled cricket by these anti-capitalist tendencies can be seen in
the attempts of P. G. H. Fender to break down some of the
distinctions between amateurs (gentlemen) and professionals
(players) which had been in force since the earliest days of
organised cricket and continued until 1963. Fender (a fine and
intelligent cricketer who was seriously misrepresented by the
popular Australian TV series 'Bodyline', now shown twice on
British TV and a good example of the continuing use of cricket as
an extended national metaphor) had begun to lead his Surrey
team, amateurs and professional alike, onto the field through the
same gate. If this was not iconoclastic enough he then proposed
that all Surrey players should use the same dressing room at the
Oval. But, before the disapproval of the rulers of the game made
itself felt, opposition to the scheme came from the Surrey professionals themselves:

> He was dissuaded after talking with Hobbs and Strudwick.
> 'With respect, Mr Fender, we like to talk about you and laugh at
> what you might do next', was the gist of what Hobbs told him.[13]

It is not surprising that the professionals should have wanted this
given the cultural burden of cricket, especially its insistence on the
simultaneous maintenance of distinction and equality. It is not a
simple matter of 'knowing one's place', the world of the first-class
professional was far too sophisticated for that, though some
commentators on the Golden Age do not appear to understand this
and as Wilfred Rhodes, the doyen of professionals said, at the end
of his life, the system of segregating amateurs and professionals
was like South African apartheid, but since he said it 'without
resentment' we should see this as part of the curious balance
which allowed cricket to maintain its popularity and be a symbol of
Empire.[14] Interestingly enough Fender was, in the 1950s, himself to
become deeply involved in Conservative politics on a Free Enterprise platform and it may not be out of place to speculate that his

anti-traditional views on the relationships between players are related to his interest in modern capitalism and his participation in its administration.[15] In the Golden Age (and Fender was at the height of his career in the 1920s having begun just before the outbreak of the war) cricket seemed always to look back at an age of 'idyllic relations' where the major class encounter was between a benevolent gentry and their faithful tenants: quite different to the working relationship which Fender tried to introduce into the Surrey team and which much more nearly corresponded to behaviour in the contemporary business world of which he was a part. Cricket was, thus, an ideology in the fullest sense as it provided a set of imaginary social relations in which right-minded *men* could stage an exemplary meeting where the crude material determinations of the outside world were deflected.

Thus cricket with its stress on comradeship, chivalry, and strict integrity under the Laws (not rules: note the moral connotations of high seriousness) has since its early days depended on a developed form of nostalgia and if, in the later nineteenth century, modern thinkers used the games ethic as an imperialist and capitalist creed the game itself appears to have been able, with an admirably Hegelian aplomb, both to sustain and to deny it. Cricket still responds in this way, of course, in spite of its progressive need to turn itself into a commodity for the sponsorship industry. Spectacularly, there was the Packer affair in which the Australian entrepreneur, miffed by the lack of interest in his offers to televise Australian cricket, hired a large number of international players to run a privatised 'Super Test Series'. The legal niceties of the case are not to be reviewed here but it is interesting to see the way in which the cricketing establishment responded to this 'jet-age razzamatazz cricket'.[16] The response was essentially moral. As *Wisden* put it, when speaking of the Australian fast bowler Jeff Thomson's defection to Packer:

> Packer knew this well, and countered with a contract and a cheque book; in 1978, the two together seem to be a passport to anywhere.[17]

This moral indignation conceals the real fear that by losing Thomson, who was an important factor in the attractiveness of Test matches to the paying public, the Australian Board itself would be out of pocket. The ordinary cricket watcher had a simpler view:

> Are these posturing gum-chewing yahoos who participate in that rather poor standard television production called or perhaps mis-called World Series Cricket members of actors equity? [sic] With sadness I remember back to the days when some of them were cricketers.[18]

That an internationally organised modern sport should have had such troubles in relating to its own fiscal substructures is extraordinary but quite comprehensible in the terms of the above letter: we are not talking about sport or business here but about a way of life.

Writing after the Golden Age but celebrating a world of village cricket in which its virtues survived the mechanical scoring of Bradman and the less mechanised but nonetheless awesome feats of the later Hobbs, Hugh de Selincourt showed clearly the enmity between capital and cricket and the paradox that the amateur's money was somehow free from the taint of capital:

> 'I've rather bad news, I'm afraid: damned bad as far as I am concerned. We've been swindled out of practically all our money. We've got to let the place. Clear out. Next Saturday will be my last game of cricket for many a long day ... the bottom's out of the bucket, all right.' And as he told us of the American share-pushers' ingenious activities it seemed more than likely that it was.[19]

Presumably if the crash had not come de Selincourt's protagonist would simply have got richer and nothing said. The point could not be more clearly made but, in passing, it is worth noting that Bradman's heavy scoring and ultra-safe play was seen as symptomatic of the fall from Golden Age virtue (and indeed the occasion of the nadir of post-war cricket: the notorious 'Bodyline' series of 1932) notably by Neville Cardus who characterises him with an unflattering comparison to the genius of the past:

> Efficiency, superb streamlined efficiency! And, don't mistake me, Bradman is often grand and exhilarating to watch. But if I were asked to compare him with Trumper I should say the

difference is as that between the flight of the aeroplane and the flight of the eagle.[20]

This complaint was to be found in the Golden Age itself. As early as 1890 the Honourable R. H. Lyttleton (with W. G. Grace firmly in mind) was distressed that:

The scoring during the season of 1887 reached a pitch that, for the sake of cricket, we hope will never be seen again ... The ideal match is a match that does not last more than two days, where the wicket has got a bit of devil in it, where no individual innings realises more than 80 runs ...[21]

Nostalgia pervaded cricket even in its Golden Age and the cricket lover was caught then, as now, between admiration for the burgeoning statistics of *Wisden* and a gentle regret for a time when technical merit, the mark of the professional was, in some senses, lower but the spirit of the game thrived untroubled by the quasi-commercial dictates of seasonal averages and performance bonuses. As George Hirst, himself one of the most successful professionals of all time, was to put it in his retirement speech from the pavilion at Scarborough at the end of the season of 1921:

What can you have better than a nice green field, with the wickets set up, and to go out and do the best for your side?[22]

The values of the Golden Age are mediated to us chiefly through a flow of books which fall into four main categories: reprints of cricket 'classics' and biographies of old players, histories of the game, books of statistics and, above all, large format books of photographs and other images. It is interesting that eighteenth-century cricket and nineteenth-century cricket played before the reform of the public schools gets far less space in the popular market and I would suggest that this is because cricket, being at this time chiefly a gambling game, does not offer the cultural load for which is it now prized.[23] I propose to look briefly at one coffee-table production, Gerry Wright's *Cricket's Golden Summer*.[24] This is a book of paintings supplemented by the commentary of the well-known cricket historian David Frith. Wright's method is to take photographs of Golden Age players, paint them in authentically researched colours and then set them in imaginary gardens done in the ruralist mode. Thus, Arthur Shrewsbury, perhaps the first professional batsman to develop the modern style, who killed himself in 1903 is shown standing sadly in a swathe of poppies cut through a cornfield or Wilfred Rhodes awkwardly in a garden of unusual floridity, a comment on his long Yorkshire career in 'smokey   Sheffield   and   bricky   Bradford   and   humble Huddersfield'[25] or Albert 'Tibby' Cotter, the Australian fast bowler killed at Beersheba in 1917 with poppies at his feet, their lengthening shadows in the evening sunlight about to engulf him.

The care which Wright takes to provide his paintings with a full symbolic load redolent of the Golden Age makes Frith's Preface superfluous but it is worth quoting from as it makes such an explicit statement of the period's appeal to the present:

> In the abrasive age in which we live, where violence and cynicism, atheism and anarchy are such recurring themes as almost to be keystones of everyday life, it is excusable to seek momentary comfort in being wafted away to another age, when manners were gentle, man ruled machine, income tax was 8d (3p) in the £, and a glow of seemingly eternal summer warmed the land.... The worship of Mammon has much—no *everything*—to answer for.[26]

Of course, this is all an historical myth (not least when we see an opponent of Mammon bewailing the loss of low income tax!) but what we are being offered is, essentially, a sophisticated version of pastoral. Frith is not talking about mere escapism, he is talking about the possibility of adopting values which are clearly known to be unviable in present conditions but which do, in their consistency and firmness provide an ideological buffer to the contemporary state. I do not have space to develop a theory of the cricketer as swain but I would like to claim that the historical function of the pastoral mode and its nostalgic mythopoeia is now fulfilled by the Golden Age of cricket as mediated through such productions as Gerry Wright's. C. L. R. James has memorably compared the development of cricket with the rise of nineteenth-century romanticism:

> Civilisation had reached a certain stage of decay and they set out to offer an alternative ... To meet these new chaotic conditions, Wordsworth and Coleridge wrote about simple things with a

simplicity that sought to counteract these new dangers. Wordsworth was certain that there were 'inherent and indestructible qualities of the human mind' which would survive 'this degrading thirst after outrageous stimulation'.

That was the period and those the circumstances in which modern cricket was born. In its own way it did what Wordsworth was trying to do.[27]

If we accept this account we can see how it was that cricket remained as a pastoral idyll even at the height of its use as an imperial ideology, and if the implications of Wordsworth's philosophy when it lost its revolutionary thrust collapsed it into conservatism we can also begin to understand how the myths of cricket kept their vitality even when they plainly contradicted the social relationships which obtained in the world outside the ground.[28]

The large number of books on the Golden Age testifies to a need for Victorian values: selflessness, respect for tradition, disinterest in success or failure, communal reconciliation. These are very different from the Victorian values to which we are currently being urged to return. If the values of the Golden Age were sometimes abused I hope that readers will agree that they were often sincerely held and are not, in themselves, bad values to have. The Golden Age seems to offer a tool to be used in the political contest to define the grounds of value for our own time and its relationship to the set of possible histories. When an appeal to tradition is used to underpin social and economic policy one way of understanding this policy and, if need be, opposing it, is through the struggle for meaning which can be waged over key ideological terms. Cricket offers what might be called the 'wets' response' to contemporary politics: its values and its appeal to an historically imaginary but ideologically potent England (the national specificity is intentional), as disseminated through the kind of books drawn on here, show clear reaction against hard monetary economics, the cult of success, managerial bully-worship, and the destruction of tradition.

Cricket is not the material from which revolutions are made but I doubt that any manifestation of popular culture, in itself, could be. However, cricket does have a role to play in the quest for a coherent oppositional culture which offers a chance to unify disparate groups who share dissatisfactions. No cultural form can be understood in political innocence or neutrality and cricket, which throughout its history has attracted explicit comment on its social role, can be no exception. But it is odd that a game which, in the early part of this century, was asked to bear the burden of School and Empire should now appear to offer through its traditions an ideological bastion against radical policies which, at first sight, appear to lay claim to the same moral high ground.

NOTES

1. Thompson, Francis, 'At Lord's', in A. Ross (ed.) *The Penguin Cricketer's Companion* (Harmondsworth: Penguin, 1981), pp. 459–60.
2. Arlott, John, 'On a Great Batsman', ibid., p. 402.
3. Cardus, N., *English Cricket* (London: 1945), p. 43.
4. Mason, R., *Jack Hobbs* (London: Pavilion, 1988), pp. 115–16.
5. Fry, C. B., *Life Worth Living* (London: Pavilion, 1986), p. 44. On Fry's career at the League of Nations see also A. Ross, *Ranji* (London: Pavilion, 1987), pp. 176–8.
6. See J. A. Mangan, *The Games Ethic and Imperialism* (Harmondsworth: Penguin, 1986) for full accounts of these figures.
7. The correspondence is reproduced in *Wisden's Public School Matches* (London: Wisden, 1898), pp. 167–70.
8. James, C. L. R., *Beyond a Boundary* (London: Stanley Paul, 1963), pp. 33–4.
9. For figures on industrial disputes see J. Quail, *The Slow Burning Fuse* (London: Granada, 1978), pp. 311–24.
10. James, op. cit., p. 157. See also James's *New Society* essay, 'Cricket in West Indian Culture', reprinted in J. Bright-Holmes, *The Joy of Cricket* (London: Peerage, 1986), pp. 243–8.
11. James's line is taken up and developed in the official history of the Welsh Rugby Union, D. Smith and G. Williams, *Fields of Praise* (Cardiff: University of Wales, 1980).
12. Marx, K. and Engels, F., *Manifesto of the Communist Party*, edited by A. J. P. Taylor (Harmondsworth: Penguin, 1967), p. 82.
13. Streeton, R., *P. G. H. Fender* (London: Pavilion, 1987), p. 25.
14. Frith, D., *The Golden Age of Cricket* (London: Lutterworth, 1978), p. 12.
15. On Fender's political career see Streeton, op. cit., p. 179.
16. *Wisden Cricketers' Almanack 1980*, p. 121. Full details of the Packer case may be found in *Wisden* for 1978, 1979 and 1980.
17. *Wisden 1979*, p. 95.
18. *Wisden 1980*, p. 123, citing a letter published in an Australian newspaper. Even in the Golden Age Australian cricket had been troubled by financial and legal disputes when in 1912 six of the chief Australian professionals refused to tour England. Indeed one of these, Victor Trumper, widely acknowledged as the greatest batsman of the period, if not of all time, had been in disputes over

money with the cricketing authorities since 1899. For full details see A. Mallett, *Trumper* (London: Macmillan, 1985), pp. 117–52.

19. De Selincourt, H., *The Game of the Season* (Oxford, University Press, 1982), pp. 92–3.

20. Cardus, op. cit., pp. 45–6.

21. Steel, A. G. and R. H. Lyttleton, *Cricket*, fourth ed. (London, 1890), pp. 401–2. This interesting compendium of the lore, techniques and opinions of the Golden Age was reprinted only last year in 'The Badminton Library' (Southampton, 1987).

22. Thomson, A. A., *Hirst and Rhodes* (London: Pavilion Books Ltd., 1986), p. 79.

23. Though early works on cricket have been republished and are frequently anthologised, the chief series for the reprinting of cricket 'classics', *The Pavilion Library*, has concentrated solely on the Golden Age and the modern period. In illustrated large-format books the Golden Age also holds the field with publications such as G. Brodribb, *The Croucher* (London: Constable, 1985) and B. Darwin, *W. G. Grace* (London: Duckworth, 1978).

24. Wright, G., *Cricket's Golden Summer* (London: Pavilion, 1985).

25. Ibid., p. 26.

26. Ibid., p. 7.

27. James, C. L. R., 'Garfield Sobers', in *The Future in the Present* (London: Alison and Busby, 1977), pp. 213–25, pp. 220–1.

28. The connection between Wordsworth's Romanticism and his conservatism is best exemplified by his 1845 pamphlet on the Kendal and Windermere railway. This is edited by J. O. Hayden in Wordsworth's *Selected Prose* (Harmondsworth: Penguin, 1988), pp. 76–94. In the context of cricket and romanticism it is also amusing to recall that Lord Byron played in the first Eton versus Harrow match.

20

Bertolt Brecht and Football, or Playwright versus Playmaker

BARRY EMSLIE

We have Frederick Jameson's assurance that it is dangerous to dismiss the major debates on aesthetics that took place among radical and left-wing writers between the wars, and it is the aim of this short article to suggest a new and more contemporary framework for the theatrical theories developed by Bertolt Brecht at that time. If it is the case that the arguments surrounding a left-wing interpretation of realism in general and Brecht's 'Epic Theatre' in particular do indeed '. . . rise up to haunt those of us who thought that we could now go on to something else and leave the past behind us',[1] this might be best appreciated by placing football and Epic Theatre alongside each other and evaluating the former according to the explicit aims of the latter. The result will be to argue the case, at the very least, for the *formal* properties of football at the expense of theatre. It will be to suggest that football be taken seriously by those interested in Marxist debates on aesthetics and, above all, it will result in exposing why the Brechtian experiments in the theatre are doomed to fail within the terms of their own realist objectives.

One might begin where, more or less, Brecht did in the 1920s, though the sport he held up as a model was boxing.[2] However it wasn't only the boxers who attracted him, although he found in the German middleweight champion Paul Samson-Koerner an ideal personification of those workmanlike (matter-of-fact) qualities that he wished to introduce into theatre. More important than the seemingly exclusive figure of the 'performer' were the spectators. Brecht wrote in 1926 that: 'We pin our hopes on the sporting public',[3] and there is surely, today, yet more reason to adopt his enthusiasm as our own.

There is, firstly, the self-evident fact, clear to everyone who has regularly attended both football matches and theatrical performances, that the audiences at the former are engaged in an intellectual activity well beyond the skills and, it would at times appear, the innate abilities of the latter. Indeed, it is difficult to avoid the conclusion that, by definition, you find a better class of people on the terraces than in the stalls. Above all, the analytical talents of the regular football fan far out-distance those of the theatre or opera goer. While the football regular has at his or her fingertips a wealth of knowledge concerning the team, its history, the strengths and weaknesses of its various members and, not least, a good grasp of what the opposition can deliver, the theatre goer is trapped in the knowledge that his very presence in the building has, in essence, meaning only in so far as it is a statement that she or he is engaged in a 'special' activity; made special by the simple yet overwhelming fact that he or she is not at home with his feet up in front of the television where, it is not unreasonable to assume, he or she, in many cases, would prefer to be. Pity him or her then, obliged to display his or her appreciation of the dead object delivered up to him in the name of superior class sensibilities and 'art' (God bless the word!). For, armed in the interval with a glass of cheap yet over-priced red wine, he is duty bound to manufacture opinions, to publicly assess what he has seen even though he may have no wish to. One can leave in passing his impolite cousin who shows off by talking to his partner *through* the performance, and it would no doubt be cruel to make much of the Covent Garden consumer, both comicly honest and benighted, reading a running translation while attempting at the same time to watch the stage. Even the most extravagent display of the theatre or opera goer's opinion is of little importance to the producers and actors, except in so far as it encourages others to buy a ticket. For, basically, the theatre goer has performed his necessary task as soon as he or she has purchased a ticket. There is, beyond satisfying the egotistical needs of the performers for applause, no actual necessity that he occupy his seat. All of this changes with football.

It is the different nature of the role accorded the spectator at a sports event—the fact that he is not a spectator at all in the sense that a theatre goer is—which most clearly distinguishes sport from the so-called *performing* arts. This distinction can be approached from several angles. There is, for instance, the acknowledged influence of football fans on the destinies of their teams; something recognised by all players and statistically clear in the tendency for a side to record more wins at home than away. Interestingly, in the English League a team which manages merely an away draw is said to have got a 'result', while a draw at home is tantamount to a failure. But the special and peculiar properties of football are best seen in the light of Brecht's theory of Epic Theatre.

Now there are many ways in which to approach the complex system that Brecht called 'Epic Theatre'. However, rather than concentrate on the technical characteristics of his theatrical practice—the half-curtain, the alienation effect, and all those other tricks (once?) so beloved and fetished by 'radical' producers—it is, I think, more fruitful to try and see Brecht in the context of the overtly Marxist objectives that lay behind the development *of* those techniques. For, ironically, while Brecht's theatrical practice comes down to us as an important ingredient in the evolution of the avant-garde in the twentieth century, this is often at the expense of Brecht the Marxist. Yet theatre constituted for him a real assault on bourgeois practices and capitalist notions of Reality. It attempted, at various points in its history, to intervene in the class struggle and, above all, it was suffused by a sociological analysis that was profoundly Marxist in character. However, twentieth-century theatre, with its vulgar, consumerist middle-class status and habits, hasn't found it at all difficult to get rid of the left-wing radicalism in Brecht's work, while, in the academic world, his theories have been readily incorporated into the modern tradition of literary and semiotic analysis that calls perpetually into question the dependability of any text. If, however, we can find elements in Brecht's ideas that link directly with football we can, at least, recover something of the radical theory that lies behind his theatrical system: a theory not concerned with theatre or football as much, but rather with the much more fundamental issue of the nature of History.

Brecht's starting point is that reality is a narrative. It follows that any aesthetic practice that wishes to earn the name 'realism' must be grounded in stories. He insists time and again that to tell a story is the highest of tasks that a writer can set himself, and it is on that ground, in preference to all others, that he chose to defend himself in the vigorous and often lethal debates on theories of literature that went on among the European left in the 1920s and 1930s.

Capitalism, Brecht argues, misleads because it attempts to show all relationships as seemingly static and rational; that is, in the best interests of all classes. But Brecht insisted that what we see around us is, as an epistemological category, unstable and certain to fall apart. Oddly, in this crucial respect, he was a lot closer in theoretical terms to his great left-wing antagonist at this time, Georg Lukacs: a Marxist who was equally committed to literary forms that exposed Capitalism as axiomatically committed to treating human beings and human relationships as objects, prised out of the fluid, contradictory and narrative contexts in which they belong.[4]

One can see immediately how football is alive with that very characteristic which is so critically important for Brecht's notion of Marxism. At first sight, a football match is nothing if not a story. In fact, as we will see, it is a great deal more. But football is a story that is untrustworthy. It gives us no guarantee that the final whistle will amount to a happy end as it always, to some degree, produces losers. It is seldom the case that both teams and both sets of supporters are equally happy with a draw. Further, and more importantly, the game is a story that we know could have been otherwise. Therefore, the football fan is there not merely to consume but to participate. He or she knows that there will be closure, that the narrative(s) will be brought to an explicit cut-off point and that he or she will then leave the terraces and pour onto the streets. But whether he or she is satisfied with the result or not, he or she knows that it is transitory. Whether the team was 'magic' or whether 'we were robbed', the fan knows that the very definitiveness of the 'end' merely promises that it might all be different next week or, more significantly, the next time the same forces meet. And meet again they will, with, usually, a different outcome. Thankfully, in football it is not only every dog that has its day, but every underdog.

Brecht's theatrical practice struggles to make theatre work according to the same principles. He devised a whole recipe of techniques designed to call into question the stories he put before his audiences. Most strikingly, he attempted to distance the stage action by the use of a range of commentary effects which encouraged and enabled the spectators to consider the alternative narratives that *might* have been made manifest, but which were suppressed. And it is in the light of this fundamentally Marxist notion of reality that the whole complex of Brecht's model of Epic Theatre should be seen and from which it has been, regrettably, cut loose. At all times one must consider what Brecht would call the 'if . . . then' couplet, or what Raymond Williams has identified, as 'subjunctive action'.[5] As a result the theatrical undertaking is always focused on an objective that is, in practical terms, largely unrealisable: namely the dramatic manifestation of a multitude of contradictory, simultaneous and competing narratives.

But, of course, this *formal* consideration as to what constitutes realism in literary practice has to be invested by the particular and revolutionary values of Marx's interpretation of history in order to become a truly dialectical realism. Therefore, Brecht's emphasis on multiple narratives is only properly explicable if it is seen in relation to the mechanisms of class struggle. That is, Brecht is showing us constantly that capitalism cannot deliver on the level it claims to; that it does not and cannot function in the best interest of all citizens, and that, as a result, to think in terms of the struggle between the dispossessed and the owners, to think of winners and losers, is to come to terms with reality on a more profound level. There can be no *universal* happy ends within class based and therefore exploitative social systems. In fact, if the characters in his plays actually try and behave in a manner consistent with capitalist principles, they discover that they are obliged to pervert all those qualities most likely to encourage compassion and justice. In *Mother Courage* the 'good' capitalist mother must murder her children, while in *Herr Puntilla* the 'good' capitalist landowner can only behave in a humane way when he is drunk and has given up his wallet to his servant. These sets of contradictions come to embody, dramatically, what Brecht seems to mean by the dialectic. Everything can be turned upside down because everything contains its own opposite. Tools for the worker both enslave and liberate. The Bible is not only an ideal instrument of ruling class dominance encouraging quietism, but also an actual physical object whose ownership is cause for violent struggle. Above all Brecht employs and re-employs the images of water, rain and the stream. Indeed one day the rain may fall from below to above, symbolic of that great moment in history when those who are at the bottom, appropriating both the tools and the wallets of their masters, will supplant the ruling class.[6] Brecht invokes that day in the future when the underdog will triumph.

But, in all of this, Brecht faces an inescapable and unresolvable problem. For no matter how hard he tried to open out the drama, he remained hopelessly trapped in the overriding authority of the text. The existence of something given to the actors before the performance remains authoritative irrespective of how often the playwright calls it into question, precisely because we know that such a text *has* been given and learnt and rehearsed and that we in the auditorium had no part in this process. Most damning of all, we know that the very mechanisms by which it is called into question have also been rehearsed. Therefore, in foregrounding what must remain merely the *apparent* reality of narrative multiplicity, Brecht is engaged in a kind of fiction which is all too easy to unpick and expose, irrespective of how genuine his motives and how original the effects he produced.[7]

But football is free from the text. The activist role of the fans, without which football would degenerate into an elitist past-time like theatre, is grounded in the freedom of sport as a discourse; a discourse, moreover, characterised by an equal interaction between fans, officials and players. It is axiomatic that the discourse is, in fact, plural. For football is nothing less than the living manifestation of an infinity of stories struggling towards the goal of self-realisation. Despite the strict controls and laws of the game — or perhaps because of them — narrative possibilities are at their maximum. Moreover the experience and specialised knowledge that the fan possesses creates a situation whereby football attains meaning well beyond the passive consumption to which the theatre goer is condemned. In fact the football fan is always at work reinventing the story. The goal scored against the run of play, the injury suffered by a key player, the critical puzzle of deciding if and when to make a substitution, are only paltry examples that cannot hope to adequately reflect the perpetual stream of considerations which managers, players and fans entertain throughout the full course of the game. And there is, central to these considerations, the ideal of the creative player, usually a midfielder whom the Germans, in instinctual recognition of the creative and productive nature of football, now call the 'play maker'. Around him are centred the hopes and labours of the fans.

As a result the fan is always at work. He or she argues, insults, sings and pushes him or herself forward into the action precisely because he knows that he or she has a partially determining role in the business.[8] He attempts to disrupt the rhythm of the best players in the opposing team with the foulest and most imaginative abuse, he or she bullies the referee shamelessly, and, knowing every weakness and strength of his 'own' players, he or she cajoles, advises and forever attempts to restructure the action in the direction he or she knows to be best. And never let it be thought that all of this plays no active role in determining the drama. All of us who go to football matches have seen opposing players harried by spectators into committing fouls, referees bluffed into giving penalties that never were, and apparently beaten teams whipped into renewed effort by the collective outpouring of thousands of voices. Thus the formal properties of football can be said to realise the essential characteristics of Brechtian theatre. It is a true performing art, free from the active/passive division which is a necessary and intrinsic part of theatre. For whatever abuse may be exchanged between the fans, no one comes along and politely asks you to leave because you're spoiling the play for the other patrons.

Before looking at another crucial function that sport in general appears to fulfill, it is worthwhile noting that Brecht appears to come face to face with the problem of the text in the theatre. As he is logically obliged to involve the spectators in his dramas as much as possible in order to shatter the conventional consumerist and culinary aspects of bourgeois theatre, he throws away the curtain—both the de-mystifying 'half-curtain' he employed and the traditional full proscenium arch version—and removes the category of the spectator altogether. There are, in the so-called *Teaching Plays*, which he wrote at the end of the 1920s and at the beginning of the 1930s, only performers. Everyone takes part. But the bitter consequence of this is that it is no longer possible to engage in textual games, to overtly state that the text is not final and that we might manipulate it. The *Teaching Plays* can only work if the text is firm, authoritative and obediently followed. The result is that one is allowed to get involved in the action, as it were, but only if one accepts the unpleasant premise that there isn't anything you can do to change that action. Story and conclusion are singular, unambiguous and predetermined. Thus when students performing his play *He Who Says Yes* complained of the conclusion, Brecht could take on board their criticisms only by writing a wholly new and equally self-contained and authoritative text under the title *He Who Says No*.

Now, while I have stressed the formal properties of football in relation to Epic Theatre, there is another consideration which goes somewhat further and underlines these particular characteristics of sport in general that are especially important for anyone with an interest in Marxist aesthetics. Taking a lead from Frederick Jameson again, we might call this new consideration the *Utopian* character of all historically grounded explanations.[9] This amounts to more than just a structural element intrinsic to all narratives. It is explicitly political in its ramifications because it raises the question of, and evokes the hope of, emancipation and self-fulfilment without which the Marxist notion of class struggle and mass liberation is valueless. Although a football stadium is not, *ipso facto*, a place of *overt* class struggle, it is a site where the hopes and Utopian dreams of thousands of people take on some kind of shape. It is the true arena for those who see something ethically central to Marxism in a Marxist view of aesthetics.

In *The Political Unconscious* Jameson argues that all narratives are Utopian in character. They can be said to be 'providential fables' which, in literature, allow forms of resolution denied us on any true basis in 'real life'. He argues that it is in the very nature of Marxism to reveal the symbolic significance of narratives. This is partly because the meta-commentary of Marxism is itself overtly Utopian in that it is focused on the teleological ideal of the Communist society of the future, and partly because it has at its disposal the superior tool of dialectical analysis in the context of a theory that is wholly grounded in the primacy of history as an intellectual and explanatory category. If sport is even more narrative and dialectical in character than literature, we might, by following Jameson's ideas, come to a deeper understanding of its appeal and its role as a lived and potent force in the lives of millions.

In fact nothing is more Utopian than a sports event. Games, by definition, imply conclusions and wished-for 'happy ends'. Moreover, although such endings are not always delivered, the desire to realise these moments of seemingly perfect resolution is well-nigh overwhelming. The spectator desires that which is denied him in the mundane and often unappealing world outside the stadium. Sport implies a better world. If a leading jockey triumphs over cancer he needs to ride in the Grand National and *win* it. (Does his triumph over the disease put pressure on the other jockeys to lose?) And if the exact nature of the winner's cancer is embarrassing this can be suppressed for a few years to keep the story flawless. Of course, all the better if the hero's name is Champion. The unconscious, unwritten but desired conclusion is felt by everyone. For the sportsman must survive where we go under. He is unique, and when the fans sing his praises they tell us that 'there is only one so-and-so . . .' and that he is 'magic'. *He* makes the rest of the week bearable. If Ian Botham shows himself capable of redefining what is possible for a single player to accomplish in a Test Match his banning for drug abuse accords him a fallibility that we might share. But on his return to Test cricket he 'ought' to take a wicket with his first ball. Thankfully, the batsman obliges. Indeed, the need for most sports to defy the ordinary as a matter of principle has become very marked in recent years. Every Cup Final now has an underdog. It no longer has to be a team from out of one of the lower divisions, as both Spurs playing Coventry and Liverpool playing Wimbledon have recently discovered. The wish-fulfilment which now encourages the 'favourites' to lose is extraordinarily strong—and lose they invariably do.

But, of course, the fan is trapped. The sport is important to him in inverse proportion to the actual role accorded it in political life. Only the extreme right seems to have sensed any potential here. Today there is something bitterly apposite in the sight of English lads in Union Jack shorts variously singing 'God Save the Queen' and shouting 'Sieg Heil' in West German cities. This confused but appropriate confluence of symbols painfully reveals the degree to which both rights—the 'extreme' and the conservative—have hijacked a positive sense of national identity. It is a substantial victory. For not only is the lout permitted to debase football, about which he seldom knows anything and is often too drunk to watch even when in the stadium, he is awarded also the ironic opportunity to declare his allegiance to the very political and social apparatuses that make his escape from a dead-end life improbable. Even then his use to the conservative right is not exhausted. He can always be denied in the name of law and order and is, as a result, a convenient factor in appealing to middle-class voters.

Meanwhile the football fan, who seeks in the sport the imaginative and creative life denied him by modern capitalism, is doubly patronised and misunderstood. On the one hand, football is dismissed as debased in the very (aesthetic) terms in which it should be most celebrated; the dominant ideology seeing it only as a crude, mass substitute for the finer things of the 'arts'. On the other hand, the football fan becomes the overt representative of everything the 'civilised' Englishman most abhors and least wishes to be associated with when abroad. But it is exactly the greater *creative* potential of football which should encourage us to pay more attention to the playmaker than to the playwright.

NOTES

1. Jameson, F., 'Afterword', in Bloch et al., *Aesthetics and Politics* (London: Verso, 1980) p. 196.
2. See, in particular, Brecht's notes to *The Jungle of the Cities*, in *Plays Vol. 1* (London: Eyre Methuen, 1970) p. 118, pp. 434–5 and p. 437. There is an interesting personal recollection concerning boxing as a theatrical technique in McDowell, 'Actors on Brecht: The Munich Years', in *The Drama Review*, vol. 20, no. 3 (1976) pp. 102–16. Also of interest is L. Shaw, 'The Morality of Combat: Brecht's Search for a Sparring Partner', in R. Grimm (ed.), Brecht Heute: *Brecht Today* (Frankfurt am Main: Athenaeum, 1971).
3. Willett, J. (ed.), *Brecht on Theatre* (London: Methuen, 1984) p. 4.
4. See G. Lukacs, *Writer and Critic and Other Essays* (London: Merlin, 1970) p. 37 and passim. Re Brecht and narratives see J. Willett (ed.) 1984 p. 200, no. 65 of 'A Short Organum for the Theatre'. However, with both Lukacs and Brecht the theme is a ubiquitous one.
5. Williams, R., *Politics and Letters* (London: NLB and Verso, 1981) p. 216f.
6. See, in particular, 'The Ballad of the Waterwheel', in B. Brecht, *Gesammelte Werke 20 Vols* (Frankfurt am Main:: Suhrkamp, 1967) vol. 3 p. 1040 and pp. 1007–8.
7. NB. Brecht quite early in his career, while still in Augsburg, considered the possibility of using two clowns during a performance of one of his plays. They would not only comment on the story but, like good Brechtian sportsmen, 'take bets on the outcome'. See B. Brecht, *Diaries* (London: Eyre Methuen, 1979) p. 32.
8. Brecht is well aware of how theatre resists input from the audience. 'The Philosopher' in the *Messingkauf Dialogues* complains because he is excluded, although, as he says: 'I like ... putting my oar in'. The football fan has no such problem. See B. Brecht, *Messingkauf Dualogues* (London: Eyre Methuen, 1978) p. 18.
9. What follows is taken from F. Jameson, *The Political Unconscious* (London: Methuen, 1981). Due to space it must be seen as an extreme simplification.

21

The Woman's Realm: History Repeats Itself on the Women's Page

ANN TRENEMAN

The first women's page began not with a bang, but with a recipe—for a lamb dinner. It ended not with flourish but with a tribute to Christianity. It was sold not to its readers but to their husbands. 'The fair ones of your household will expect you to provide it for them', exhorted what was probably the first-ever newspaper promotion for a women's page. Debuting on 4 May 1896, the 'Woman's Realm' was given two columns in London's new *Daily Mail*.

Its small type, crowded columns and quaint language all bespeak an age gone by. And so it has—but the women's page has stayed with us. Now spruced up to modern standards of print and often carrying such labels as 'Style' or 'Living', these daughters of a Victorian mother have become a fixture in the fickle world of newspapers. With the venerability of age has come debate. Castigated as a ghetto of women's news, a purveyor of stereotypes, and a deeply classist institution that places wealth and power on pedestals, it has also been lauded as perhaps the only place women's issues can receive in-depth attention, and also as a possible resource for feminists. But, in turning 90 years' worth of pages, decade by decade, of the *Daily Mail*, I found much of this debate to be founded upon a myth. For, lamb dinners aside, the women's page contains some recipe of longevity, if not success, and its ingredients are the stuff of everyday, middle-class, life.

In 1896 that stuff was described as thus by the article introducing the 'Woman's Realm': 'Movements in the women's world—that is to say changes in dress, toilet matters, cookery and home matters generally—are as much entitled to receive attention as nine out of ten of the matters which are treated of in the ordinary daily papers'. This, presumably male, summing up of women's interests, dovetails with the overwhelming current perception of the women's pages of yesteryear as an icon to a 'cult of femininity'. Used specifically in analyses of women's magazines,[1] the 'cult' concept revolves around the idea that content feeds and preserves women's second-class status and, in the process, acts to counteract the winds of change.

But, while some might argue that the only way to kill the cult is to stop the presses on the women's page, there is another significant strand of thought that argues that the pages need to be transformed, not exterminated. Proponents of this view do not refute the cult concept, but see traditional content as something that must be overthrown and replaced with content reflecting the concerns and issues of the Women's Movement: that is articles that would serve to challenge the status quo instead of feed it. Pragmatically, proponents argue that the women's pages are perhaps the only place in a male-dominated news world that women's issues not deemed as 'newsworthy' can get into the paper. This position has been explored by Gaye Tuchman in particular who concludes that some women's pages in the 1970s have been a resource for the women's movement in this way.[2]

There has been a missing element in almost all of the few studies that have examined the women's page. In all the talk of the future and the near past, we have lost sight of what has come before us. Somehow, ideas of 'progress' in the women's pages have become shackled to the 1960s. As American journalist Patricia Rice enthused:

> Then, in the mid-1960s, it became the law of the land that women had to be given an equal opportunity in employment ... What happened first, the chicken or the egg? There was more to write about women now. There were more women to write about women. Women's pages, edited by women and reported by women, began articles that now could be called one long series of 'First woman does this or that'.[3]

What actually did happen first was the women's realm of one Lady Charlotte, who came to the *Daily Mail* of 1896 from the fashion press. Her wider realm was a world of expansion and seeming endless growth: the British Empire had doubled in size in

the nineteenth century. The realm of women, however, was one of
many restrictions. While the suffrage issue was to grow and grow,
women's lives were limited by the 'scientific' (but not unchallenged) belief that women were the 'weaker sex', and the near
necessity of marriage. But, whatever the strictures on a woman's
life, Alfred Harmsworth knew that women shopped and women
read. He determined to make them a part of his new *Daily
Mail*—billed as the 'Busy Man's Daily Journal'—and a part of a new
formula for journalism. 'The new journalism provided, above all,
distraction. It was out for a big circulation: and this meant, for the
first time, a working-class circulation,' states the Labour Research
Department in its 1928 study update on the press in England.[4] The
new paper's emphasis on reporting sport, crime and gossip as well
as news in a brightly written way, and its flavour for sensational-
ism assured it of the mass circulation it sought.[5] The new women's
page was certainly part of that strategy: '...a Woman's Realm
feature in the new *Daily Mail* of 1896 signalled the beginning of
newspaper's attempts to cash in on the growing readership and
advertising potential among women', noted Susanne Puddlefoot,
women's page editor of *The Times* in the 1960s. The strategy
worked.[6] The first issue sold out; its readership was nearing a
million by 1900. It would remain a circulation leader among British
newspapers for many decades. Today the *Daily Mail* is a tabloid
that oozes middle-class sensibilities from every paragraph—and it
still has a women's page.

But ninety-odd years ago there was nothing old or tiresome
about the women's page; it was new territory. At first glance, it
seems to have been home territory. Lady Charlotte had an opinion
on everything and anything homely. Here are some of her pre-
scriptions from May 1896:

> If the majority of married men were to tell what they consi-
> dered the perfect wife, they would perhaps unite in saying a
> woman whose husband dared bring home an unexpected guest
> to dinner.

> For manicuring, the lemon is absolutely indispensable.

> No girl can claim proper training who does not know how to
> pack a trunk. Mothers should be as careful to train their
> daughters in this accomplishment as they are in those other

branches which go to make a good housewife and capable woman.

A feather boa that is out of curl had far better be left at home.

Nothing is better for the purpose of reducing flesh than to exist exclusively on a meat or vegetable diet.

"A woman is known by her gloves" is an old saying often quoted. And observation testifies to the justice of the remark.

For that companion in your domestic arrangements—your maid—give her some corner of her own. Dignify it by the name of "servant's hall" if you will. Place healthy toned books, a few games and ink and paper in it and see if your efforts for her welfare are not appreciated.[7]

One article called 'Method—the Great Secret', goes as far as spelling out exactly what the woman of the house should do from the moment she awakes and how she can organise her weekly household tasks. Her advice on 'nerves' is simply to ignore them and her list of 'Some Health Don'ts' includes 'Keeping the mind in an unnatural state of excitement by reading trashy novels instead of good books'. Questions involving children, cooking, fashion and beauty are copiously advised on. Also prominent are ideas on economising—a sign perhaps that the Lady realised not all readers required her advice on servant matters.

Yet sprinkled among the recipes, dress patterns and household hints in that first month are other, less homely articles on such topics as working women, career ideas and social commentary ridiculing self-important men. Such interjections hint at a world— and thoughts—much wider than the four walls of the late nineteenth-century house. The home may have reigned supreme, but articles such as 'Where Women Fail', which appeared on 19 May 1896, illustrate clearly that non-traditional content is not necessarily a phenomenon of the late twentieth century:

Women have succeeded in all professions but one. That is the profession of law. For everything else they are admirably adapted. As cashiers and saleswomen they excel. They display wonderful aptitude in conducting a business, as the famous

Paris Bon Marché, conducted by the widow of the former proprietor, shows. Women are successful as writers and teachers. Only as lawyers they are not successful. Every woman should be thoroughly educated. While she is being educated, some specific talent usually manifests itself, and when the general education is completed, she should devote her energies to developing that specific talent. A woman's best career is that which she finds least distasteful, and for which she has talent.

Such articles as this seem all the more non-traditional when the climate of the day was so set against careers for women. Most working-class women earned their low wages through employment in domestic service or the textile industry.[8] But for the middle class, which seem to be the likely group addressed here by Lady Charlotte, the trend was quite different. 'Throughout the late nineteenth and twentieth centuries, middle-class women faced a choice between marriage and motherhood, and a career. In the early part of the period there was little choice as it was unusual even for young, single women to engage in paid employment unless family circumstances demanded it'.[9] And yet, here is Lady Charlotte with this advice on 19 May under the headline 'Women in Business':

> The majority of women who have not already embarked upon a chosen career are firmly convinced of the fact that they are fitted both in the number of brain cells and in grace of manner to adorn any professional walk in life.... Self-confidence is a desirable characteristic in business enterprise, but it will not alone and unaided launch a woman on a successful career ... The woman who can say 'Yes' to the following questions with a clear conscience may consider herself at least prepared to make a start:
>
> Is she strong-minded enough to leave personal feeling out of all business dealings?
>
> Can she accustom herself to arriving at a decision by the aid of her judgment instead of her intuitions?
>
> Can she in the course of years overcome the feeling that she is being insulted whenever her pet theories are questioned?
>
> Can she adjust her neck to the yoke of patiently receiving orders on matters about which she feels herself more than competent to dictate?

Can she discard all her petty trials and ailments, which she would secretly like to copyright, as she discards her tea-gown and boudoir slippers before starting out in the morning?

Can she sustain a cheerful exterior while labouring under the painful consciousness that the finest efforts of her life are being misunderstood, and when, probably, to cap the climax, her hair sullenly refuses to curl?

Nor does Lady Charlotte content herself with advising on career matters only. In the article 'Pin Money' on 26 May she tackled the subject of how married women felt about not having any money of their own:

The majority of women would far rather have twenty pounds a year they could call their own than twice that sum which they might or might not, as the case may be, succeed in saving out of the housekeeping.

Does a man ever consider how hard it is for a woman to have no money at all of her own to spend? He probably retorts, 'Ah, it's all very well, but what can she want? I give her clothes and food, and pay all her expense.'

That may be, yet, you have always some loose cash about you, and would think it a hard case indeed if you had not a pound to spend whenever you wanted it, and you never seem to think your wife may require a shilling.

Very often a girl marries who has had an allowance of her own at home. She may even have owned a little money or have earned it. She marries, and finds all her little incomes suddenly cut off; she must go to her husband for every penny she wants to spend or else stint the household. Every housekeeper knows what a farce 'saving out of the housekeeping' really is . . .

Other examples of articles in that first month of publication that bucked the status quo include ones on the careers of being an author, detective and teacher. In an article called 'The Best Wives' Lady Charlotte rebuts the charge that a woman who has worked makes an inferior wife: 'The fact of her being a wage-earner will not unfit her for her new role—it will aid, not hinder'. In the following article on 18 May 'Are Clever Women Liked?' she comments on the sexism of the times:

All men do not dislike clever women; still there are some who do so. For this, three reasons may be stated: one is that survival of old-time feeling when women were men's chattel, indisputably his to do with as he wished. And as this chattel showed signs of superior intellect, he grew afraid of and uncomfortable with her. Hence his preference for the simple, guileless creature who implicitly obeyed and believed in him.

Again, man is the lord of creation, he loves to strut around and flap his wings as such, but how can he pose as this superior being before a woman he intuitively sees as witty enough to weigh him in the balance and find him wanting. He cannot, so no wonder he prefers the unquestioning docility of the inferior vessel. The third reason is the false notion, prevalent even yet, that a clever woman is not a good housewife. 'Greek iambics are all very well,' said Mr Cock a Doodle Do, swelling 'but give me the woman who can make a good rice pudding.'

Such interjections into the daily diet of cult pap continue on and off throughout the decades. The years 1896, 1916, 1946 and 1976 stand out as being particularly prone to non-traditional content. But in 1906, as would also be true 80 years later, the pages revolved around entertainments of the day, gossip and royal goings-on. Again, among such articles as 'A Blue Glove Summer', could be found more serious concerns with long articles on subjects such as Christian Science, the health concerns highlighted in Sinclair Lewis's new novel *The Jungle* and the role of the husband around the house.

A decade later England was at war, and the women's pages mixed war news with fashion, food, theatre gossip and beauty tips. The result now seems rather disconcerting, with the gossipy 'What a Woman Knows' column including items such as a comment on soldiers writing from France, how to make a salad, and exhortations for women who 'as a result of war work . . . have gotten into the habit of stooping' to exercise. On 12 May, the women's page was front-page news with a special photo feature called 'Women and the War'. While just five of the 14 pictures actually showed women (and two of those were identified as fiancées), the three that did feature working women depicted them as road sweepers, bakers and munitions department workers. The war was acknowledged in other ways also. On 18 May a story notes that a woman had been 'committed for trial for attempting to murder her child and to commit suicide by drowning. It was stated that she wrote to her mother saying she was weary of waiting for her husband's return from the front.'

A feature of the page was 'Germany Day by Day'—a wide-ranging column noting everyday happenings in the enemy country. The column on 5 May included accounts of German authorities being distressed because that season's wide skirts were wasteful of fabric; the discovery of a strawberry leaf tea by scientists looking for food substitutes; the case of a woman apprentice who sued her merchant employer and won. And the column on 9 May contained this 'first woman' story: 'Saxony has just licensed the first full-fledged female butcher's apprentice, a strong-limbed girl of 19. She passed the official test with flying colours, the expert slaughter of a calf.'

The cult was firmly back in charge in the 1920s and 1930s. For during those decades—a time which could have reflected the suffrage success for women and the wider opportunities offered to some women in politics and the judiciary by the Sex Disqualification Act of 1919—there is little to be seen on the women's page that is not cloyingly traditional. Not until the Forties do the horizons of the women's page again spread into the public arena.

Main concerns in the post-war 1940s revolved around modern marriage, the rising divorce rate, the trend of 'romantic love' and 'the new status of women in modern society'. Much of the discussion of these was to be found in the advice column. 'The Human Casebook' by Ann Temple, a regular feature in the pared down women's columns that, in May 1946, included a look at how alike the fashions of 1896 and 1946 were. But styles are not the only comparison—Lady Charlotte would have approved of this answer to this reader's question to Temple on 9 May:

Nearly all the husbands I know are more domesticated than their wives. They enjoy helping with the chores and talking about rations and gadgets.

The wives loathe the endless rounds of petty jobs. They look upon their homes as cages and long to express their minds and personalities as they did in their jobs.

I'm looking for a girl with a mind like a cabbage. Isn't that the best solution for this problem of modern marriage?—PETER

It isn't a solution at all for the marriage problem. . . . It is a mistake for you yourself, but it's a tragedy for your wife if you take this limited view of marriage. The solution of the drudgery and cage problem of the modern wife lies with the husband, with his ability to give his wife enlightened and interesting companionship.

The modern girl's education is all designed to give her a wider outlook than the domestic one. . . .

For her own and her husband's and children's sake a young woman should never 'dwindle into a wife'. Let her develop as an interesting woman.

I know dozens of arguments proof against all the traditional masculine lines of thought to prove that you are the cabbage if you go looking for a girl who you think is one.

But perhaps the article that strayed the most from traditional content was one on foreign affairs — the topic of the day on 30 May for Temple. She notes, in a view echoed many times more recently, that 'international friendship among women has so far not made the slightest difference on international politics in the making of war and peace. It may not always be so. We shall go on trying.'

Ten years later foreign affairs were far too weighty a subject for the women's pages. Reminiscent of the 1920s and 1930s, the pages of the 1950s were devoted to cooking, knitting, dieting, beauty and travel. Only occasionally does it stray from home ground, as it did in an article on science classes for girls. The bar on married women working had been dropped generally after the Second World War, but it still seemed to be in place on the women's pages. The working woman receives only back-handed acknowledgements such as the 10 May article 'Six Day Diet Planned for the Girl with a Job' and Ann Temple herself seemed to have regressed: when a woman wrote that she was frightened of becoming as catty as the other wives that surrounded her in her new home, the prescribed antidote on 24 May was not a job but a hobby: 'Say one like sculpture, photography, modern embroidery that exercises the individual and gives play to the personal taste and expression to the personal way of seeing.'

The 1960s brought a bisexual character to the pages with prominent men's fashion stories and an agony column for men. Articles aimed at such concerns as raising children were sometimes scattered around the paper, and evidence of the 'sexual revolution' and the use of the birth control pill could be found in such unlikely places as an article on the history of the bra. While fashion remained a focus, other topics such as food and beauty were not in evidence and a few women's issues were aired. Columnist Ann Scott-James on 5 May deplored the new 'anti-woman' budget that levied a tax on services and asked that men 'give us the tools we need' to change how the home is run:

> We need completely mechanised homes if we are to dispense with daily help and not chuck up our own jobs ... What I dread is a hiatus with the old personal service gone and the new machinery not arriving. Then the women of Britain will strike and the protest marches will be led by me.

The same day, Monica Furlong examined another issue of the day in an article headlined 'Is a mother a nuisance? And if she isn't why does Britain insist on treating her like one?' The article endorses the ideas in the book *The Captive Wife* by Hannah Gavron and looks at the position of motherhood and its effects on working-class and middle-class women. In part, it reads:

> What's the answer to the various ills which beset the wife and mother? The suggestion of Dr Gavron's which interested me most was that young children should be much more thoroughly accepted into the community ...
>
> If they were not made to feel so wretchedly unwelcome on trains and on buses (by the other passengers I mean), in self-service stores, department stores, restaurants, cafes, hotels and a dozen other places, then their mothers would not also share their exclusion ...
>
> Dr Gavron's main proposals are about educating women to a dual role. Schools have to acknowledge that their girl pupils will be both working in the community and rearing children at various stages of their lives.
>
> Girls should be brought up to believe that it is possible for them to do both ... Working girls need a very much more adequate education than they enjoy at present ... Women need to be able to retrain and to go through refresher courses when their children are grown up. ...

The 1960s were dismissed as ancient history in 1976 in an article headlined 'You've Come a Long Way Baby but Where Exactly Are

You Now?' that was illustrated by contrasting a 1961 photo of a mother and baby with a 1976 business woman. But a look at the rest of the women's pages—now designated as such by a 'Femail' logo—shows the leap alluded to in those photos to be something less than complete. For while Anne Leslie's week-long series on the women's movement in America raises highly significant issues surrounding the status of women and is certainly non-traditional, other articles revolved around fashion, slimming, beauty and a dessert recipe. The story on 4 May on the rising cost of employing a 'daily' cleaner who now charged £1 an hour was evocative of an article that appeared in the 1906 women's page story on 'Compensation for Domestic Servants'.

Such articles as Monica Furlong's examination of motherhood or Anne Leslie's deciphering of the women's movement do not seem to have much of a place in the Femail section of the 1980s. The pages of May 1986 appear to be a testament to American research showing that the 'new' women's sections have in the main only replaced traditional content such as society news with entertainment coverage.[10] The pages of 1986 are peppered with such articles as the 'Liz Taylor Seven Day Diet', an interview with Roger Vadim and a profile of Stephanie Beecham of 'The Colby's' television soap. Another main theme of the pages is royalty—Princess Diana's eating habits are dissected and we learn 'The Secret of Fergie's Suntan'. The pages, like those of 1906, play hostess to longer feature articles, now covering topics such as a politician's wife who wrote a cookbook and the financial status of topless model-cum-singer Samantha Fox.

Occasionally the drivel is interrupted for more interesting comment. Heidi Kingstone complains on 27 May about the extra cost of being a woman in terms of services: 'A woman's dry cleaning, her underclothes and many other areas of everyday life that are directly comparable, cost the female sex more than the male'. Kingstone looks out the difficulties in using the Sex Discrimination Act of 1975 to combat such unequal charges and concludes by quoting a researcher's psychological explanation on why women don't stand up to this inequality. The conclusion and the arguments may be modern, but the general tone of airing a grievance is one that raises the ghost of Lady Charlotte and that of the officer's bride in 1906 who used the women's pages to complain about an army wife's lot in life.

Indeed, history *has* repeated itself on the women's page, and if the pages of the past have a lesson for us it is that a women's realm has long been one dogged by a fundamental schizophrenia. Again and again cult content is juxtaposed with non-traditional articles which, while not revolutionary, challenge the middle-class status quo in a variety of ways. 'Women in Business' in 1896, the 'first woman' butcher apprentice of 1916, Ann Temple's columns of May 1946 and Monica Furlong's examination of motherhood in 1966 and the 1976 series on the Women's Movement cannot be dismissed as mere aberrations. These and other like stories, standing side by side as they do with those seeking to reinforce traditional roles, give the women's pages a historic contradictory nature that reflects our complicated past and sheds light on the complexities of being a woman today.

Every era sees itself as having reinvented the 'modern woman'; every age sees its pages as superior. In 1936 Margaret Lane, in an overview of the *Daily Mail* women's pages on the occasion of the paper's 50th anniversary, wrote of the pages of 1896:

> It is easy to be condescending about those early women's features. We smile when we read in a paragraph about the care of house-plants that 'a plant imparts an air of cheerfulness and daintiness which bric-à-brac is powerless to lend' but it was, in truth, the age of bric-à-brac, and these pompous little admonitions were by no means as superfluous as they seem.

Lane's bizarre notion that the constrained women's section of 1936 was a huge step forward from those of 1896 is similar to the idea that the 'new' sections of today are vastly different from anything that has appeared in the past. Patricia Rice's dismissive comments, echoed in other commentary in England and America, on the pages of the 1950s (characterised as being mostly about charity events, debuts, trips to resorts and weddings) as if they somehow epitomised women's pages from their beginnings, are a myopic indication of our own idealistic and naive belief that today is somehow more enlightened than yesterday.

The pages of the past and the present do nothing to refute the basic arguments behind the 'cult' or the 'women's page as a resource' theories. In fact, they strengthen them by giving both a historical background. But they shatter the idea that the women's page is, or has been, solely traditional or non-traditional in content. The assumption that 'cult' content is something from bygone years while 'resource' content is a new wave brought in by the modern women's movement relies on a false sense of progress. For the cult is present today just as the winds of change were there in 1896. The idea that 'progress' is the catalyst for the appearance of non-traditional content on the women's pages can no longer be seen as sufficient.

Now, in 1988, much is being written about the 'new' integration of women's far-ranging interests in women's magazines and women's pages. *Ms* magazine has a 'Personal Appearances' column. Today's women's pages, and magazines, give their readers the chance to read about world peace, power dressing and how to make a souffle all on the same page, or issue. But there is little new here: the ingredients may be updated, but the recipe has been around almost a century. It would seem the middle-class woman's realm has always been full of such contradictions

NOTES

1. As put forward in: Marjorie Ferguson, *Forever Feminine: Women's Magazines and the Cult of Femininity* (London: Heinemann Educational Books, 1983).

2. Benet, James, Arlene Kaplan Daniels, Gaye Tuchman (eds), *Hearth and Home: Images of Women in the Mass Media* (New York: Oxford University Press, 1978) p. 187.

3. Rice, Patricia, 'Women Out of the Myths and Into Focus', in Laurily Keir Epstein (ed.), *Women and the News* (New York: Communications Arts Books, Hastings House, 1978) p. 42.

4. Labour Research Department, *The Press* (London: Labour Publishing Company, 1928) p. 18.

5. PEP (Political and Economic Planning), *Report on The British Press* (London: PEP, 1946) p. 55.

6. Puddlefoot, Susan, 'The woman complex', in Richard Boston (ed.), *The Press We Deserve* (London: Routledge and Kegan Paul, 1970) p. 75.

7. All articles from the *Daily Mail* referred to here, and throughout this piece were researched from either the original copies or microfilms of the original in the British Newspaper Library in Colindale, north London. (*Daily Mail*, London, May 1896, 1906, 1916, 1926, 1936, 1946, 1956, 1966, 1976, 1986).

8. Lewis, Jane, *Women in England, 1870–1950* (Brighton: Wheatsheaf Books, 1984) p. 156.

9. Ibid., p. 75.

10. Butler, Matilda, William Paisley, *Women and the Mass Media: Sourcebook for Research and Action* (London: Human Sciences Press, 1980) p. 119.

22

G-Men to Jar Wars – Conditioning the Public

MICHAEL WOODIWISS

In October 1982 President Ronald Reagan announced an eight-point plan 'to cripple organised crime' and 'end the power of the mob in America'. His advisers were well aware that the plan had no realistic prospect of success and therefore a crime commission to maintain public support for federal organised crime control strategy was also thought necessary. After three years selective investigation the commission found that the country's basic approach to the problem of organised crime in general and drug trafficking in particular was sound even though it was continuing to fail. So, the commission decided that a harder line was re-quired — more policemen with greater powers to arrest people and more prisons to accommodate those arrested.

The only recommendation to attract much attention was a call for a national programme to test most working Americans for drug use, in effect to force most Americans to submit to regular, observed urine tests. These tests require supervision because people might be tempted to bring in someone else's clean urine. A small number of liberals objected but a poll taken after the commission's report was issued showed that nearly 80 per cent of Americans did not oppose drug testing. In fact, many already worked for corporations that regularly tested their personnel. Most had been conditioned to accept the word of experts. The law enforcement community had announced that testing people's urine would reduce the demand for drugs and therefore hit organised crime in the pocketbook, so millions of Americans were prepared to line up and give their samples and keep the business of urine-testing labs and equipment manufacturers booming. Like most wars, jar wars has its profiteers.

Over the past half century the rights of American citizens have

187

been diminished as part of the government's war on crime. Rights to privacy and protections against self-incrimination and unreasonable search and seizure have been tampered with to produce arrest statistics and justify the existence of crime commissions. The police have been given ever more intrusive and coercive powers and ever more scope to abuse these powers. Corruption, brutality and suppression of political dissent characterises United States law enforcement more than any success against organised crime. But, there is never any sustained public opposition to these abuses—no popular questioning of the government's approach. The land of the free has become less free with the 'consent' of the people.

This article will illustrate how popular culture was reshaped after 1930 to suit the interests of the law enforcement community. These interests required significant alterations to the Bill of Rights which was not an easy task. The process was eventually accomplished in two stages. The first was to restore people's faith in the representatives of the law after the excesses of Prohibition. The second was to explain why law enforcement was still failing to combat organised crime and then offer solutions.

The first stage involved making heroes out of law enforcers and the most important medium used to achieve this was film.

To begin with some damage had to be undone. In the early gangster talkies policemen were usually inept, corrupt or irrelevant. *Little Caesar* (1930), *The Public Enemy* (1931) and *Scarface* (1932) starred dynamic actors playing criminals. Edward G. Robinson, James Cagney and Paul Muni represented American outlaws in ways which reinforced some of the country's most deeply-held myths about individual, entrepreneurial success. The way to make it in the land of free, competitive capitalism was the way Rico made it in *Little Caesar*—with dedication, determination and daring. The gangsters may have finished up dead in these films but not before they had made their mark on the world. They had achieved a lifestyle that contradicted the official dictum, 'Crime Does Not Pay'.

In 1934 a new censorship code put an abrupt end to any more glorification of the gangsters. Instead, in 1935 there was a new Hollywood campaign to glorify G-Men—the press name for agents of the Federal Bureau of Investigation. That year there were seven G-Man movies sold by Hollywood as its contribution to the war on crime. 'See Uncle Sam Draw his Guns to Halt the March of Crime' ran the ads for one of these films. In *G-Man* (1935) James Cagney played a FBI agent as forcefully as he had played gangster Tommy Powers in *The Public Enemy*. As Andrew Bergman puts it, 'exciting and benevolent law was in the hands of the US Government and in fact was the US Government'.[1]

J. Edgar Hoover, the agency's director, not only helped to create the new pro-police mythology but also became a prominent part of it. Before long his publicists had created an image for the FBI agent that lasted for decades. G-Men were dedicated, clean-cut, familiar with the most up-to-date, scientific techniques of crime detection and incorruptible. Books, newspapers, magazines even bubble-gum cards echoed the same theme as the G-Men films: 'Crime Does Not Pay' so long as the élite federal policemen were around. The FBI came to be viewed as infallible, constantly vigilant for crooks and communists who might threaten the security of American citizens. The FBI's failures and, in particular, its avoidance of organised crime until the mid-1960s did not reach the public's attention, who for the most part believed that the FBI was unrelenting in its war on crime.

The 1930s also saw the beginning of the glorification of the prosecutor. The career of special prosecutor Thomas E. Dewey in New York provided a rich source for opinion makers wanting to show the law triumphant. For a brief period Dewey became headline news because he choreographed the downfall of a succession of gangsters and some of their political protectors. However, his 'war on racketeering' was no more than a period of effective head-hunting which established dangerous precedents for civil liberties. Dewey's methods were presented to the public as the answer to the problem of organised crime. Books, newspapers and films such as *Marked Woman* (1937), *Racket Busters* (1938) and *Smashing the Rackets* (1938) sung the praises of Dewey or thinly disguised personifications and put over the message that the answer to organised crime lay exclusively in the prompt indictment and vigorous prosecution of law-breakers at whatever cost to individual liberties. Of course popular accounts of Dewey's courtroom triumphs left out such uncomfortable details as his manipulation of public hysteria, his coercion of reluctant witnesses, his illegal use of wiretaps against political opponents and his failure to make more than a marginal impact on wholesale illegal profit-making in New York.

The G-Men and Racket-busting films had established plot patterns for thousands of crime films and television cop shows in the following decades. The bad guys either finished up dead or in prison thanks to the bravery, expertise or superior intelligence of government agents or prosecutors. It all helped towards an uncritical public acceptance of intrusive and coercive policing tactics. The first stage had been completed.

It soon became apparent, however, that there was a major contradiction between fiction and fact. The good guys may have been winning on the screen but the newspapers were making it clear that they were losing badly in reality. Illegal gambling, in particular, enjoyed a wartime and post-war boom. Casino operators, slot machine distributors and off-track bookmakers were nullifying the anti-gambling laws. Journalists had a field day exposing an endless string of gambling corruption scandals. As the country got richer during the 1950s individual entrepreneurs, crime syndicates and corrupt public officials maintained the public's supply of other illegal goods and services such as drugs, prostitution and loan sharking.

For the law enforcement community the answer to crime is always the same: bigger budgets and more legal powers. But they needed to explain why they were failing before legislators would surrender people's money and rights. A second and more bizarre stage in the process of public conditioning was required.

Two tabloid journalists, Jack Lait and Lee Mortimer, first articulated what was to become the law enforcement perspective on organised crime in 1950. In a best-selling 'exposé' called *Chicago Confidential* they strung together anecdotes about Italian-American gangsters and claimed that this proved the existence of the Mafia super-criminal organisation. The Mafia, they said, was the nucleus on which all organised vice, crime and corruption all over the world, not just the US, had been built.

Lait and Mortimer had produced a formula that countless journalists have since turned to when writing about US organised crime. The trick was to describe how a secret criminal brotherhood developed in feudal Sicily, was transplanted to urban America at the end of the nineteenth century, and then took over organised crime operations in the entire country by corrupting and controlling local police and politicians. As 'proof' all editors required were unrelated anecdotes about Italian-American gangsters, with the narrative enlivened by words like 'godfather', 'tentacles', and, most essentially 'omerta'. 'Omerta' meant some kind of secret code of silence and, since no one was allowed to talk about the Mafia, it justified assertions that otherwise would appear quite ridiculous. Who could contradict them if the Mafia's code of silence could not be violated?

As an easy explanation for the country's organised crime problems the Mafia could not be beaten and government officials were more than happy to supply journalists with the 'facts' to support it. The Mafia provided the bureaucrats and politicians with an easy-to-communicate threat to the nation. The answer to this threat of course was more police and more laws to legitimise new means of control. In particular, gambling and drug taking had to be suppressed—making the prohibitions work was the only answer considered. With effective gambling and drug prohibition, it was argued, citizens would no longer be able to fill the 'coffers' of the Mafia.

By the end of the 1960s the constant repetition of the Mafia label in the Press, in films and on television and in the best-selling work of fiction producers such as Mickey Spillane and Mario Puzo ensured that most Americans had a conception of something called the Mafia as a monolithic, ethnicly-exclusive, strictly-disciplined secret society, based on weird rituals, commanding the absolute obedience of its members and controlling all organised crime. Mafia and organised crime became virtually synonymous.

A single work of fiction, published in 1969, put the law enforcement perspective into its most digestible form yet. *The Godfather* by Mario Puzo was on the *New York Times* bestseller list for 67 weeks and sold just as impressively in overseas markets. The film of the book was even more successful, breaking numerous box office records but, in the process, it fixed numerous misleading images about American organised crime for many years to come. A kind of Godfather industry has since developed with innumerable cheaper versions of the same themes turned out in every form of media communication—even Superman and Batman waged war on the Mafia in the August 1970 issue of *World's Finest Comics*—with by-products ranging from Godfather sweatshirts and car stickers to pizza franchises.[2]

For the law enforcement community the conception of organised crime as an alien and united entity had been vital. They had presented it as many-faced, calculating and relentlessly probing for weak spots in the armour of American morality. Morality had to be protected from this alien threat. Aliens were corrupting the police therefore the police had to be given more power. Compromise such as a reconsideration of the laws governing gambling and drug taking was out of the question — the only answer was increased law enforcement capacity and more laws to ensure the swift and effective capture of gambling operators and drug traffickers behind whom the Mafia was always lurking.

The message got across to the people that mattered, the legislators. By the end of the 1960s members of Congress were convinced enough by the Mafia's supposed 'threat to the nation' to enact a series of measures long sought after by the federal law enforcement and intelligence community. Organised crime control provisions in the 1968 and 1970 omnibus crime control acts included: special grand juries; wider witness-immunity provisions for compelling reluctant testimony; and the use of wiretapping and eavesdropping evidence in federal cases. The measures gave the same kind of head-hunting powers to federal police and prosecutors that Thomas E. Dewey had used to such superficial effect against organised crime in the 1930s on a local level. They inevitably tipped the balance away from such civil liberties as the right to privacy and protection from unreasonable search and seizure, and towards stronger policing powers.

The laws and concurrent anti-drug legislation have a great potential for abuse. Between 1970 and 1974, in particular, grand juries, along with the increased wiretapping and eavesdropping powers, became quite clearly part of the government's armoury against dissent. The Nixon administration abused the grand jury process in the following ways: to frighten citizens from political activity; to discredit 'non-mainstream' groups; to assist management in a strike situation; to punish witnesses for exercising their Fifth Amendment rights; to cover up official wrongdoing; to entice the commission of perjury and, finally, to gather domestic intelligence. By the time of Nixon's resignation a great deal of evidence had been accumulated to show that the legislators had bestowed an armoury of repressive crime-control powers on people who were themselves criminally inclined.

However, the law enforcers had got their way and the measures they wanted to fight the Mafia. It had taken a twenty-year campaign of disinformation. Events had been distorted, even invented, to fit an alien conspiracy theory that people were very willing to believe in. The theory was wrong and the policy based on it was counter-productive, sustaining rather than suppressing high levels of crime and corruption. Many thousands of career criminals, from every American ethnic group, have exploited the attempt to impose morality on a population too diverse and too indulgent to be dictated to. Americans continue to gamble and take drugs whether or not it is against the law, and entrepreneurs continue to supply them with the opportunities to do so.

Since the late 1960s the federal perspective on organised crime has become more sophisticated but the government continues to give the impression through its media outlets that American organised crime is still run by foreigners. However, now it's Mexicans, Colombians and Chinese—not just Italians. The solution, of course, is still the same—greater law enforcement capacity to fight crime and more intrusive powers to get the bad guys. Measures which allowed federal law enforcers to shadow and eavesdrop on people in case they were thinking about committing crimes have proved to be inadequate. So the latest crime commission recommendation is to force working Americans to give urine samples—thereby stopping them enriching drug traffickers. Organised humiliation is now the answer to organised crime and most Americans seem willing to go along with it.

NOTES

1.   Bergman, A., *We're in the Money—Depression America and its Films* (New York: Harper and Row, 1971) p. 13.
2.   Smith, D., *The Mafia Mystique* (New York: Basic Books, 1975) pp. 289–323.

23

Chaos and Order: The New York Subway

RICHARD BRADBURY

The bad news for European journalists is that the New York subway is no longer the graffiti-plastered, steamy hell it used to be. One of the fear images with which they could scare tourists from here going over there has been removed. Not, of course, that this will stop the horror stories. New York is too potent a source of material proving what hell the contemporary urban environment is to have that picture in any way eroded.

The majority of the trains have now either been cleaned up or covered with anti-graffiti paint, and air-conditioned. The impact that this latter fact has had on the statistics for violent assault in the rush hour goes unrecorded, as far as I can discover, but the effect is tangible. No longer do commuters steam and drip on each other, and in the 1988 heat wave it was a pretty good place to take shelter from the appallingly humid and airless streets above.

Not that it is a new paradise. The occasional fantastically-decorated train emerges from a tunnel when you least expect it, and the memory of how claustrophobic being in a space absolutely covered with brightly coloured patterns boldly edged in black, turns into present reality. When that train is one of the few that isn't air-conditioned (and the majority of these reminders of the recent past aren't), one is reminded of the reputation of this subway system as the worst in the world especially when the ceiling hugs down close and the person next to you sticks their armpit in your face as they grab for the handrail to save themselves from actually touching the wall of the carriage. Underneath the surfaces, the old New York is still there.

Indeed, the cosmetic work that has been done in the last few years is precisely that—cosmetic. Dingy tunnels between the different lines still wind for hundreds of yards; it still smells appallingly; the platforms are still unbearably hot and noisy in midsummer; and the beggar population is huge. In many ways, the New York subway represents a symbol of the way in which American capitalism is dealing with the longest crisis of this century; by covering up whatever symptoms it can and accusing those it can't of being the problem themselves.

This is a continuation of the role the subway has performed for many years now. Let's begin with the entrances to the stations. They vary in appearance from the majestic glass covered escalators sliding down past the skyscrapers on the corner of Lexington Avenue and 53rd Street to the excuse for, and virtual facsimile of, the British version of, a public urinal at Rector Street down below the Manhattan financial district where desolation breathes out of the stonework of every building. It's almost unavoidable to conclude that the escalators must have been installed as a way of stopping the beggars, for every station where there are steps at the entrance has its contingent of regular beggars; people who, in the richest city in the world, prostitute their poverty as a way of staying alive. Every scam that you could think of, and then several you couldn't because you've never been that desperate, operates. Dressing as nuns was the most-publicised in the summer of 1988, but the old technique of displaying one's desperation to passers by is still as effective as ever and has now been given an extra twist by the AIDS victim I saw sitting in a corner on the stairs holding a small handlettered cardboard sign which began 'whatever Ed Koch tells you this is not a scam, I have AIDS. You can't help me to live. But you can help me to eat'.

The next stage in the journey is planning a route by using the map provided free of charge at all ticket booths. Free, that is, if you've got the nerve to ask for one when the line behind you for tokens stretches away into the distance and you've got to yell the fact that you're not a New Yorker through a sheet of bullet-proof glass. On a sheet of A1 paper printed in 14 colours on both sides using 7 typefaces (plus bold imprints of at least 4) is everything you need to know about how to use the system.

Like so many other phenomena in the United States, the plethora of choice offered—you want to go local or express, on a line with a letter or a number, how many times do you want to change on the way?—in the end becomes numbing. It's like ordering breakfast in the new-style truck stops; I wanted eggs and bacon, hash browns and toast. But how did I want my eggs fried, my bacon grilled, with what kind of bread did I want my toast made? All I wanted was breakfast. At the subway all I wanted to know was how to get from Court Street to Columbia University, and they gave me this map. If Buckminster Fuller didn't say that the amount of information provided is in direct inverse proportion to the amount of knowledge acquired therefrom, he should have done.

Eventually, it is possible to understand the system; it can be explained. Either by simply standing and studying the map for an age or by asking the help of that creature which supposedly does not exist in New York City but in fact inhabits it in large numbers—the friendly native. Once it's been explained, you discover that the map is actually easy, it only looks difficult. Underneath the surface of apparent chaos is a rationale and once you understand that it is actually quite easy to get from A to B.

After these choices, though, there are other hidden ones; like the kind of train you ride in. You don't discover the difference until you try to sit down in one. There are two kinds of train: one made in the United States or Canada, and one made in Japan. You can tell instantly which kind you're on if you're my height: over six foot. But why do the Japanese cars only run on certain lines? With a system this huge and complex wouldn't it be more sensible to have rolling stock that is completely interchangeable? The answer to these questions is contained within my original observation that the New York subway is like a multiple symbol for the operation of capitalism. It appears initially as incomprehensible but when one can come to grips with some of the operations of the system it begins to make sense. Then you discover that, under the surface of rationality beneath the surface chaos, is a more fundamental chaos. It is produced by the anarchy of the market.

The New York subway began in 1870 when Alfred Beach constructed the then-revolutionary compressed air system along lower Broadway which was eventually destroyed by later developments as the technology of subway construction and power became more sophisticated. Between this year and 1900 the famous elevated lines were built by a whole number of small independent and privately-owned companies who then, under license from the Rapid Transit Commission, began to build the lines which proliferated outwards from the first route which ran from City hall up Broadway to 145th Street. Eventually, when the individual companies began to run into 'financial problems'—for which read declining profits—the whole system was consolidated into the Metropolitan Transportation Authority (or the New York City Transit Authority, it depends where you look on the map) between 1938 and 1940. The problem was that, competition working the way it does, it was impossible to integrate the different lines completely together. For example, the Red Line tunnels and tracks were smaller than the rest, and the capital investment to enlarge the tunnels would have been so vast that it was not even worth contemplating the possibilities. So, the Transit Authority imports rolling stock for this line from Japan and it therefore operates, to all intents and purposes, as a separate route within the rest of the system. This means that if, in a peak period, there's a special demand for rolling stock in a particular area, there's no possibility of complete interchangeability, and that means that you can stand and stew in the rush hour for longer than it can take a train to come at 2 in the morning.

One of the greatest ironies in the history of the New York subway, though, concerns those elevated lines which were built in the nineteenth century. According to a story told me by a New Yorker who was around at the time, many of the lines—including presumably the one terrorised by King Kong—were demolished by the Metropolitan Transportation Authority in the late 1930s and the steel collected in the process was sold to Japan, where, I suppose, it was used for the war effort.

Now, certainly, none of this is obvious when one rides the New York subway. Just as the year-by-year reduction in public welfare funding has propelled thousands on to the streets—and yet this is never discussed as one of the causes of the presences of these people on the streets—so the history which has shaped the New York subway lies hidden as you ride. The reasons for the particular shapes the subway has acquired are concealed beneath a patina of everyday acceptance.

Of all of these shapes, three are particularly striking and idiosyn-cratic—and yet in a strange way indicative of not just New York but of the whole of the United States. The first is the subway tokens, those small brass and steel 'coins' you use to pay for your ride. In recent years, alarmed by the amount of forgery, the Rapid Transit Authority have attempted to make the tokens more soph-isticated which has, each time, resulted in a very temporary decline in the amount of fare-dodging and then a rise in the level of the token counterfeiter's skill. Why not change the system, you may ask, to one similar to that employed on the E1 in Chicago—where you have to put money in the hand of a fare collector before you can get onto the trains—where fare-dodging has almost been eliminated? Because, I suspect, this is the way it's always been done in New York and this is the way it's going to stay. The increasingly sophisticated technology is directed along very narrowly defined paths, partly created by the parochialism of American local government and partly by the self-justifying and self-preserving logic which dominates it.

Second is the mythology which has been created about safe and dangerous lines. The number 2 line is always dangerous, so never ride it, but the number 5 (which in many areas follows the same route as the number 2) is safe, so use that one. The first thing to say about this is that, in true New York parlance, its bullshit. If you're going to get harassed on the subway, it can happen anywhere. A friend told me that the only place she had ever had any trouble (and she rides all over the city on the subway) was in the downtown area around Wall Street and City Hall dominated by businessmen. I'm one of the many people who have never had any trouble at all on the New York subway, but I know that that's sheer luck. After all, I've been mugged walking along the street in Royal Leamington Spa!

The point of this mythology of danger is that it's an attempt to create a system of rational explanation for something which appears to be utterly random. That route is dangerous, so I won't use it, the theory goes. The problem is that violence of that kind is contingent and the intellectual defence against it is to shore up fragments of belief and attempted understanding against that inexplicability. Except, of course, that the violence is not entirely accidental: at an individual level it may well be, but in a wider perspective it is quite clear that it is caused by the poverty and deprivation which exist continuously just beneath the surfaces of the city. This would operate as a mechanism for a geographical understanding of New York except for one problem: the city is so ghettoised and fragmented that the boundary lines between safe and dangerous areas are so thin as to be non-existent. Then, the contingent returns and without an understanding of the processes which have caused that poverty and deprivation which goes beyond geography or race or whatever, the majority turns back to that oldest and most outworn explanation—the evil of individuals.

The last is the passengers themselves who move on and off the subway in great waves that lap outwards to the end of the lines. The ability to pay the standard fare of $1 is a marker of the surface of equality. You pay, and then you ride and there is no obvious class division between the passengers. No first or second class. Yet this surface is false, concealing as it does the inequalities beneath it. The Wall Street businesswoman pays her dollar and rides home to her upper West Side apartment whilst in the same carriage an unemployed man of the same age uses his dollar to pay for a relatively safe place to sleep for the night. They may share a subway carriage for a few minutes, but in many other and more serious ways they live in different worlds.

24

'And Where Did You See *Star Wars*?' – Cinema-Going in Britain

LEZ COOKE

'Cinema—the best place to watch a film' was the clarion call of British Film Year, which ran from May 1985 to May 1986. It came at a time when cinema attendance in Britain had reached an all-time low, with three quarters of the population no longer going to the cinema at all, and only 1 per cent of the minority that was attending going every week. The total attendance at cinemas in Britain in 1984 was 54 million. This is about 3 per cent of the 1640 million that went to the cinema in the peak year of British cinema attendance—1946. In that year three quarters of the population attended the cinema at least once a year and one third attended at least once a week.

1946 was, of course, before television had entered the lives of more than a small minority of British households and it is television which is usually cited as the culprit in assessing the decline of cinema-going in Britain. By 1984 only a very small minority of households did not possess a television set, and many possessed more than one. In addition one third of British households had also acquired a video cassette recorder, the new *bête noire* which was credited with driving the nail into the coffin of cinema-going as a popular activity in Britain.

Yet, as a recent survey by the Broadcasting Research Unit has shown, watching films is as popular as ever, only, since 1946, the British public has been watching films less and less in the cinemas and more and more at home. While cinema attendances picked up after the 1984 nadir to reach 72.6 million in 1986, this figure needs to be contrasted with the 350 million video rentals of feature films in that year. When you take into account that, on average, three people watch every rented video, and add on the figures for watching films on broadcast television, it soon becomes apparent that more films are being watched in Britain than at any time during the 'golden age' of cinema-going, but today's films are not being watched in the cinemas, they're being watched in the home.

Statistics, however, only give us the bare facts. It is too easy to look at the figures for cinema attendance, television and VCR ownership and draw the simple conclusion that TV and video have been responsible for the decline in cinema-going. The situation is more complex and has as much, if not more, to do with social and demographic changes in the post-war period than it has to do with technological developments.

The growth and development of cinema-going as a mass entertainment activity was closely connected with industrial capitalism and the concentration of the working class in urban areas. In its early years cinema was patronised by the industrial working class who provided the labour for the factories and sought an escape from the daily drudgery in the 'nickelodeons', music halls and fairgrounds where the first films were shown. During the 1910s and 1920s the number of film studios escalated and production became organised along industrial lines in order to meet the increased demand for product. Throughout this period cinema-going remained essentially a working-class activity; it was 'low' culture as opposed to the 'high' culture of theatre and the opera which were patronised by the middle and upper classes. However, after the arrival of the talkies at the end of the 1920s cinema gradually became more upmarket and 'picture palaces', seating 2000 or more people, were built in order to cater for an audience which was expanding to include the middle classes.

During the 1930s and the 1940s cinema-going became a habit which was based very much upon the extended family. If children weren't taken to the cinema by their parents they were taken by aunts, uncles, brothers, sisters, cousins or grandparents, until they were old enough to go on their own—by which time they were old enough to take their own younger brothers and sisters, nieces and nephews. Parents who had grown up with the cinema in the 1920s and 1930s still attended in the 1940s, but, for a variety of reasons, this tradition wasn't to be continued by the young cinema-goers of 1946.

With the post-war boom in the economy initiating a new phase of consumer capitalism, cinema-going as a habitual activity based upon the extended family began to be eroded. As leisure time and disposable income increased new consumer durables, such as refrigerators, washing machines, vacuum cleaners and television sets, became available. With more people buying cars and their own homes, and leisure becoming based either around the car or the home, cinema-going gradually became less of a priority.

There were cultural changes too, with the advent of 1950s youth culture in the shape of rock'n'roll, clothes, coffee bars, motorbikes and scooters. This was important not because it meant that young people stopped going to the cinema – in fact with the production of youth movies to tap into this new market young people went to the cinema as much as ever – but because it marked the beginning of a significant cultural age gap. In the 1950s parents who had grown up with the cinema now tended to stay at home for their entertainment while their teenage children went out for theirs. The tradition of the extended family was breaking down and this had profound implications for the future of cinema-going.

Another contributory factor which helped to precipitate the decline was the Town and Country Planning Act of 1947 which led to the clearance of slums and the re-siting of working-class communities in suburbs and new towns. Many inner city cinemas closed as a result of these demographic changes, failing to follow their customers to the new housing estates. The cinema industry must therefore take some of the blame for its own decline, for cinema-going had been a regular activity among the industrial working-class largely because it was cheap and convenient. Denied easy access to cinemas, but granted access to a new audio-visual substitute in the shape of television, it is hardly surprising that cinema attendance declined. It is worth noting that the recent development of multiplex cinemas, situated within easy reach of urban communities, has coincided with an increase in cinema attendance in Britain. While the multiplexes may not be the only reason for this upturn in attendance, their example might suggest that if the exhibitors had been more enterprising in the 1950s and followed their audiences to the suburbs and the new towns, instead of waiting for the audiences to come to them, the decline in cinema-going may not have been as considerable as it was.

The development of multiplex cinemas (one building housing six or more screens) is a recent phenomenon, based upon the American model, which was initiated with the opening of The Point, a ten-screen complex in Milton Keynes, in 1985. It marks a more positive development on the behalf of (mainly American) companies whose belief it is that Britain is under-represented in terms of the number of cinemas for the potential audience, and the steady increase in cinema attendance in Britain in the last four years may support this theory.

But during the 1960s and 1970s the response of the exhibitors to the decline in cimena attendance (from 1182 million in 1955 to 501 million in 1960) was either to close cinemas or to embark upon a process of twinning, tripling and quadrupling the existing cinemas — which, in 1955, had seated 900 people on average. By 1985 the average number of seats per cinema was down to 400 — the days of the grand 'picture palaces' were gone. Cinemas which were not converted were either redeployed as bingo halls (ironically catering for the very audience which had comprised the cinema-going audience in the 1930s and 1940s) or else were knocked down and replaced by supermarkets or multi-storey car parks.

At the end of the war there were about 4700 cinemas in Britain. Forty years later there were 4000 fewer, with two-thirds of the remaining 700 cinemas now containing two or more screens. Furthermore, the cinemas that remain are concentrated in the major cities and in the south-east of England. In 1984 the south-east had 36 per cent of the country's screens, 48 per cent of the admissions and 53 per cent of the total box office takings. Cinema-going has become an activity which is increasingly becoming denied to the traditional working-class heartlands of industrial Britain, either because those areas have the highest unemployment and the traditional audience can no longer afford to go to the cinema, or simply because there is no longer a cinema to go to.

The recession in late-capitalist Britain which has created this situation has also been responsible for a fundamental transformation in the nature of the cinema-going audience. With the economic erosion of working-class communities and the boom in the service industries of the south-east of England helping to create a fundamental economic divide, the tendency has been for cinema to become a more upmarket leisure activity than it traditionally was in its 'golden period', taking on the status of a more middle-class leisure pursuit today, while the theatre (which previously occupied this position) has increasingly become more of an upper middle-class leisure activity. In 1977 the working-class comprised more than half of the cinema-going audience; by 1983 it comprised only a third. In the same period the managerial and professional middle-class had increased its share of the overall attendance from less than a fifth to slightly more than a quarter, while the lower middle-class share had increased from a quarter to a third. By 1983 then, the majority of cinema-goers in Britain were, in sociological terms, ABs and C1s (the middle classes) rather than C2s, Ds and Es (the working classes and those on the lower levels of subsistence).

With the rental of feature films on video cassette costing less than half the price of a cinema ticket, and broadcast television films 'free' (once the licence fee has been paid), it is perhaps not surprising that those on the lower income levels have stopped going to the cinema. Video cassette recorders (like the first television sets) were initially purchased by the middle classes and in 1980 only 2.5 per cent of households of Britain possessed a VCR. But by 1987, 55 per cent of households had one. This phenomenal increase is comparable to the rapid increase in television ownership in the 1950s. In 1950 382 000 television licences were issued. By 1960 the number had risen to 10 554 000. It would be foolish to suggest therefore that video (or television for that matter) has not had a profound effect on cinema-going in Britain. There is no escaping the fact that more people now watch films in the home than in the cinema. But the advocates of cinema as 'the best place to watch a film' will be encouraged to learn that nearly a third of the population (according to the BRU sample) believe that the cinema *is* the best place to watch a film, which is remarkable considering that only a quarter of the population actually go to the cinema. Against this, the remaining two thirds of the population feel that the best place to watch a film is in the home. It is interesting to see how these figures break down according to age and class. Two-fifths of the 16–29 age group, for example, prefer to see a film in the cinema, compared to a third of the 30–49 age group, and only one-fifth of the 50 and over age group. In terms of class 43 per cent of the upper middle and middle classes prefer the cinema, compared to 27 per cent of the skilled working-class and only 20 per cent of the unskilled working-class and those at the lower levels of subsistence, while 67 per cent of the skilled working-class and 74 per cent of the unskilled working-class prefer to watch films in the home. All of which tends to confirm the prognosis that cinema-going is becoming more of a middle-class activity.

Is this trend reflected in the type of films which are available at the box office? The biggest box office attraction in Britain in 1986 was *Beverly Hills Cop*. In 1987 it was *Crocodile Dundee*, which took $20 million at the box office, and in 1988 it has been *Fatal Attraction*. Hollywood comedies and thrillers still seem to exert their perennial appeal at the box office while the smaller-scale lower-budget 'art' movie is still a minority interest. This situation is reinforced if we take video and television screenings of films into account. While seven million people saw *Crocodile Dundee* in the cinema in 1987, 11.8 million saw it at home on video. *Crocodile Dundee* hasn't been screened on broadcast television yet but is virtually guaranteed to capture an audience far in excess of its cinema audience when it is shown. Take the example of *Raiders of the Lost Ark*. Released in the cinema in 1981, this Hollywood blockbuster had a television audience of 19.35 million when it was screened by ITV at Christmas 1984 — an audience figure for one film which was more than a third of the entire cinema-going audience in Britain in 1984. This is why the distributors are concerned that screenings of Hollywood blockbusters on television should be held back for at least three years after their cinema release; but with these films being released on video often within six months of their cinema release it is clear that the cinema is functioning more and more as an important way to promote a new film which will subsequently reap the bulk of its financial rewards through video rentals and sales to television.

Cable and satellite television offer other ancillary markets through which the major Hollywood companies can maximise their profits. This is why media moguls like Rupert Murdoch and Robert Maxwell are anxious to diversify their interests into cable and satellite television. Murdoch, for example, has acquired a controlling interest in the old Hollywood studio 20th Century Fox, which is now no longer a studio but a major film investor and distributor. Part of Murdoch's interest in the company is the library of 20th Century Fox films which he can use to supply his satellite movie channel when it starts transmitting in 1989, and he's also started holding back on the sale of recent Fox films like *Broadcast News* to the BBC and ITV so that he'll be able to compete against terrestial television with new films as well as old.

The more specialist interest lower budget art movie gets squeezed in this process which finds the bigger budget, predominantly Hollywood, film getting maximum publicity, wide distribution and saturation exhibition. The traditional alignments between the major distribution companies and the cinema circuits result in a certain type of mainstream, commercial product getting privileged on the major cinema circuits in Britain. These alignments mean that 20th Century Fox films, for example, are released initially on the Odeon circuit (which is operated by Rank Leisure), while Columbia films, for example, tend to get shown on the Cannon circuit. Only after the profits have been milked from new films in the first weeks of their cinema release will those films be made available to independent exhibitors. In fact it is written into the rental agreement between distributor and exhibitor that films will be barred from being screened at other cinemas within a certain distance of the exhibitor who has the initial contract until a certain period of time has elapsed, by which time the majority of the profits from a new release have been milked by the major exhibitors. This explains how the major distributors and exhibitors maintain their dominance over the exhibition set-up in Britain and why it is that the Cannon and Odeon circuits (which comprise 50 per cent of cinema exhibition in Britain) offer a conservative programme of mainly American product. The advent of multiplexes in the last four years has complicated this picture, but a quick perusal of the programme of any multiplex will show that much the same type of films are being screened in the multiplex as are being screened at nearby Cannon and Odeon cinemas. While part of the promise of the new multiplexes was that, with eight or ten screens, they would be able to offer a greater variety of products and programme more minority interest films, this hasn't worked out in practice, perhaps because the multiplexes don't have the experience of marketing art movies and targetting a specialist audience in the way that art-house cinemas have learnt to do. Although they have increased the number of screens available to British audiences (American Multi-Cinema UK forecasts that it will be operating 37 multiplexes—350 screens—by 1991) and offer a pleasant and comfortable environment in which to watch films—which may have contributed to the 20 million increase in cinema attendance in Britain in the last four years— multiplexes have not been responsible for any fundamental change in what the majority of people are seeing at the cinema. In fact their success is dependent upon Hollywood being able to provide the sort of films the majority of the audience wants to see, and in the multiplexes being able to provide an alternative to the home for an audience which doesn't always want to stay in and watch a video but is prepared to have a night out at the cinema, followed perhaps by a meal or a drink in the same building, provided it's convenient and not too expensive.

For the moment the multiplexes seem to have helped halt the decline in cinema-going in Britain by taking popular films to the community and enticing them with a more attractive environment than has generally been experienced in Britain since the days of the 'picture palaces'. Whether the multiplexes (and cinemas generally for that matter) will be able to fight off the cable and satellite TV revolution remains to be seen. It seems unlikely that the recent cinema-going renaissance will continue in the face of this new onslaught. On the other hand it may be that audiences are rediscovering the pleasures of cinema-going as a *social* activity. There is also the question of aesthetics. Seeing *Star Wars* on a big screen with Dolby Stereo sound far outweighs the advantage of being able to pop out for a cup of tea during the commercial break when it is screened on ITV, or of being able to stop the video when Auntie Vi telephones. But with High Definition Television on the horizon and the prospect of reproducing in the home the aesthetic experience which the cinema can now offer, will people need to go to the cinema in 10–15 years time? And with the deregulation of public service television that satellite TV is likely to hasten there are going to be fewer and fewer spaces for the minority interest movie, the type of movie which doesn't get released on video and only gets a television screening late at night on BBC 2 or Channel 4. Will there still be cinemas in which to see these films in ten years time?

So where *did* you see *Star Wars*, and where might you see it in the year 2000? Not to mention *The Draughtsman's Contract*, *Babette's Feast*, *Sarraounia* and countless other 'minority interest' films which deserve wider distribution but are unlikely to receive it in the Thatcherite era of deregulation, where maximising audiences and profits is the prime objective of the media conglomerates. Perhaps this is what cinema-going will mean in the year 2000, when 30 million upper-middle class cinema-goers a year frequent the old multiplexes, now converted into arts centres, to see the new Bill Forsyth, Terence Davies or Chantal Akerman film. . . .

25

Museums of Fine Art and their Public

ANTHONY CRABBE

In an industrial age, works of art are most often made accessible to the public in the form of mechanical reproductions. The public's acquaintance with fine art is a case in point. For example, most people in Europe and America could probably identify 'Mona Lisa'—but only that small percentage who had seen her in the Louvre could claim acquaintance with something other than photographic prints.

If 'Mona Lisa' was a famous novel then few would argue that it was better to read the original manuscript in a museum than a printed reproduction. Yet evidently, most *would* make that case when 'Mona Lisa' is an oil painting. This contrast might be explained rather as follows: the novel is an art form that has evolved in its characteristic form precisely because of technological developments that made it possible to mass produce texts. On the other hand a characteristic of oil paintings is that they have always been produced as unique objects.

It might then be argued that in order to gain the most rewarding experience of novels or oil paintings, the reader or viewer must recognise certain conventions about the practice of reading each medium. The convention concerning novels seems to be that the reader attends to the meaning of words rather than their material form on the page (given that they are easily legible). Whereas the convention concerning oil paintings seems to be that the viewer must attend just as closely to the material form of marks and shapes in the picture as to any ideas they may signify. This can be done most satisfactorily by scrutinising the original work.

Given such historical background and conventions, it may then appear self-evident why the museum of original works plays so much more of a vital role in fine art as compared to literature.

However, history amply demonstrates that conventions are not fixed canons, but can be swiftly changed or rebutted. Indeed, the notion of 'the most rewarding' reading practice is a central and controversial issue of critical practice in general. Take this into account and it begins to emerge that the experiences of the fine art which the museums offer to their visitors can be very perplexing.

We have seen that one notion which apparently underpins the *raison d'être* of the museum is that fine art is more rewardingly viewed in its original, rather than reproduced form. Yet as 'Mona Lisa' again demonstrates, it has always been possible to make very accurate facsimiles of pretty well any fine art work. The seven surviving versions of 'Mona Lisa' bear witness to the historical fact that artists of the calibre of Leonardo seemed perfectly content to reproduce their creations when required, and assign such labour to their workshop assistants as regular 'bread and butter' work. Indeed, the most painterly artist of that period, Titian, was perhaps the most outstanding exponent of this practice!

The task of reproducing pictures is incomparably more simple and reliable when using today's photographic and reprographic techniques. For at least 30 years now it has been possible to purchase at two figure sums (in sterling), very high quality prints, photographed with large format cameras to reveal the minute detail usually lost in cruder prints; enlarged exactly to original scale; carefully toned whilst printed to give faithful colour values and even printed onto canvas in some cases.

In the case of three-dimensional work, it is museums themselves that most effectively display the long tradition of reproduction methods particular to this field. The exhibits range from casts in plaster, resin, ceramic and bronze, to reconstructions of complicated mixed media pieces like Duchamp's 'Bride Stripped Bare by her own Bachelors, Even'. The practice of reproduction is so endemic to sculpture that it scarcely warrants comment when the Victoria and Albert Museum displays plaster casts of sculptures like Donatello's 'David' coated in bronze. It would seem that even among museum curators there is the view that a valuable public service can be provided by giving over space to good reproductions of famous works, even at the expense of leaving less distinguished originals hidden away in store.

Yet such seems the power of convention that this principle is not found to be applied in the case of oil paintings. Readers must ask themselves whether there is much to choose in terms of 'fidelity' between reproductions of paintings and sculptures. I would argue that in the majority of cases there is not. Furthermore, I would argue that with today's technology, far better reproductions can be made, even to the point of duplicating the surface relief of a painting through use of latex moulds and so forth. (The Boyle family of artists have demonstrated some of the possibilities in their reliefs of patches of ground).

However, we could hardly imagine museums and commercial galleries co-operating in an endeavour to make high-fidelity facsimiles of their collections, without a revolution in practices that could very well jeopardise the vested cultural and financial interests of both kinds of institution. Considering that one of the main functions of the museum is to conserve a great legacy of past 'masterworks', the museum seems obligated to play along with the credo of the special status of original work—despite evidence that many of their exhibitors seemed disrespectful of that credo and despite an implicit recognition that the dissemination of good reproductions can be culturally valuable to the public at large.

Thus the publicly-endowed museum in particular, seems caught in a conflict of interests. On the one hand it has its duty to conserve a cultural legacy. On the other, it has a clear commitment to provide its patrons with an enlightening and rewarding experience of art. Unfortunately, the museum's commitment to collecting and displaying original works seems to place severe limitations on the kind of experience it offers its visitors. The remainder of this paper will now be devoted to a discussion of this contention.

Let us begin by examining the way the museum presents itself and its exhibits. As repositories of unique historical objects, art museums are often called 'treasure houses'. We are reminded of this even before we view a collection by the presence of security guards, attendants, ropes and display cases to keep us distanced from the exhibits. In nineteenth century museums, the architectural pomp further reinforces that notion.

A major collection like that of London's National Gallery is housed in over forty galleries, each fitted with dozens of works, any one of which is likely to be worth more than all the average visitor possesses. In a society that judges the personal status of the individual so much by their material worth, it is difficult not to be impressed by ones own relative 'worthlessness' in such an environment. Such feelings all too easily distract the visitor from critical consideration of the work with puzzling questions about the phenomenon of collecting, valuing and trading, and their relevance to the *aesthetic* value of the unique object.

Furthermore, such questions impress upon the viewer that some agency more powerful than themselves has conferred a 'real' value upon these exhibits by equating them with sums of real money. Evidently, nothing the viewer thinks about the work is going to alter that value and so the status of the work is effectively insulated from the viewer's own criticism. In turn this places an onus upon the persistent viewer who still wants to participate, to discover why the work has come to acquire its worth. This is essentially an art historical task and the viewer who attempts it must then read the picture in light of what he has found *others* to think of it. Since this kind of mediated response concentrates upon the *cultural status* of the work, it effectively closes down that very debate about its artistic value which first raised it to eminence! Thus consideration of the 'value' of the original work in its treasure house setting, positively deters today's viewer from trying to extend that spontaneous, immediate, self-reliant kind of reading which 'originally' met the work.

The visitor may then be struck by the strangeness of seeing so many odds and sods of altarpieces, ceilings and incomplete canvases brought together as strange bedfellows in an environment for which they were not originally created in many cases. The classic example here is provided by the plaster cast galleries of the Victoria and Albert Museum. There, casts of statues, pulpits, gates and fountains from all over Renaissance Tuscany are packed into just one great chamber. This effect is perhaps even more striking in The Science and Natural History Museums in London, where we confront locomotives gleaming silently in a polished marble hall, rather than snorting in the filth and gloom of a railway station—or where we gasp at a life-size model of an ocean-travelling blue whale crushing the air out of a room that could contain a row of houses.

The surrealists called this kind of effect 'displacement' after Freud and valued it highly as a source of what they thought 'beautiful'. We may easily sense and enjoy this kind of beauty in museums of art. Yet as is often found in surrealist images, such beauty can often disturb and unsettle the viewer precisely because of its distortion of the everyday world. What surrealist pictures themselves demonstrate, is the way mundane objects like Lautréamont's proverbial umbrella, sewing machine and dissecting table can acquire a quite different significance when juxtaposed together. Again, such effects arouse our suspicion about the notion of a museum giving us access to art at its most 'authentic'.

The displacement effect is further heightened by the sheer volume of work on display. In even a provincial gallery, there are probably more works on display than we could realistically view in an afternoon. Such 'afternoons' stretch to weeks or months in the case of a major collection. Combine this with the fact that many viewers are temporary visitors to the metropolis where major collections are housed and we may see that they are obliged to adopt a tourist approach to viewing the exhibits.

This is particularly distressing because time seems to be a vital factor in the appreciation of all art forms. A fundamental difference between fine art and other forms is that there is no prescribed time over which a painting may be viewed. By contrast, the audience encounters the performining arts over a clearly recognised interval, which is the duration of the performance. Similarly, novels and poems are read in a prescribed temporal sequence for a duration that has a clear beginning and end.

However, even the most narrative or didactic of pictures like Nicolas Poussin's 'Bacchanal' in the National Gallery, have no clear 'beginning' at which to start viewing, nor 'end' at which to finish. A few minutes' consideration of 'Bacchanal' may persuade us that the composition of the picture establishes the central figure of the dancing man crowned with a vine wreath as the starting point of its moral instruction, and that the eventual moral degeneration of this inebriate 'finishes' with the collapse of the satyr and his female victim to the right of the picture.

Yet the temporal—and hence narrative—connection between these figure groups is not established over a period of 'real time' as it might be in a play. It is something established through an elliptical process of comparing the simultaneous conjunction of different events at different places in the picture. So it is inherent in the very act of looking at a picture, that we assimilate information about episodes in a far shorter time than when the same are successively presented over a real duration.

This seems to give extra significance to the old adage that 'a picture is worth a thousand words'. A pictorial narrative provides a kind of descriptive shorthand that promotes rapid viewing, and this leaves relatively more time to look at many more paintings in a day than we would plays or films. Thus art works themselves encourage us to view them superficially, without appreciating the richness of detail and labour that is required in the description of mere instants. Museums only serve to amplify this effect by providing greater numbers of works than we can richly appreciate in one visit.

Moreover, the viewer's uncertainty as to how long they should spend looking at pictures like 'Bacchanal' is complicated further by their historical recognition that such a work was created to be owned by an individual who could hang it at home and there appreciate it at leisure. This kind of consideration would seem to teach us something about an appropriate reading practice for fine art.

First, that it has long been conventional for the patron or client of art to experience a work over a considerable timespan—anything up to a lifetime.

Second, that a reading of a work is something that evolves out of repeated viewings, many of which may only be momentary glances at odd moments, perhaps whilst doing something else in the locality. (Indeed this practice strongly suggests that readings only ever evolve, as opposed to arrive at some final form).

Third, there seem to be works that demand to be seen in something like their original location. Certain works like Veronese's 'Jupiter Smiting the Vices' in the Louvre were created to occupy a particular place in a collective scheme of works in a particular building—the *ceiling* of the Venetian Ducal Palace in this case. To display such a composition vertically on the wall of a much smaller chamber, simply because it is a valuable original that has found its way into a national treasure trove, is not just to place the work out of context, but to distort its entire compositional structure.

Fourth, that all works should be shown in appropriate lighting conditions. Many works that are familiar through reproduction look disappointingly dull in the original. The main reason for this is the need to conserve original exhibits by lowering the ambient light levels. One of the celebrated victims here is the Leonardo cartoon in the National Gallery, London.

Museum curators are probably more sensitive than most to such shortcomings in display. Over the years much has been done to improve display and communication. Yet there would appear to be no display method that could satisfy the four practical requirements above. The obstacle is that conflict of interest which arises when museums try both to conserve works in their original physical state and at the same time make those works the subject matter of a coherent and rewarding exhibition. This may explain why so many curators these days spend much of their time organising temporary exhibitions with limited, manageable and consistent themes that seem to draw much livelier crowds than the permanent displays.

Regrettably, in the case of the latter, museum managements nowadays look to be openly fostering a tourist approach among visitors. Gift shops are strategically placed near the entrances of most art museums. There, one may acquire all the souvenirs associated with touring a strange city or country. There are postcards of the main museum sights to collect or send back home. There are posters, key-rings, mugs and most of the other goods we might expect to find offered on the souvenir stalls of Paris or Venice. And of course, there are the guidebooks, conducted parties and tape-recorded tours which inform the stranger on what they 'should', or might like to know.

Nothing is better calculated than a tourist ambiance to inculcate the credo of the original, since the major objective of tourism is to say 'I've actually been there, seen that with my own eyes...'. Those who take this to extremes, set off on a whistle-stop tour, aimed at harvesting souvenirs and rudimentary information, rather than understanding. For these people, participation in fine art amounts to a process of rapid acculturation with the institutionalised norms of their society.

The more thorough visitors might opt for the guided tours. But as discussed earlier, the extreme brevity of any such tour renders it no more than the scantest of introductions. It is all too easy to get stuck at this initial level and like so many idle students, visitors can become contented with knowing only what they think they are required to.

For this very reason, many museums have continued to eschew the display of any kind of potted commentary alongside the exhibits. Their works are left open to whatever critical practice visitors bring with them. But this returns us full circle to those problems raised by the visitor's first encounters with the museum environment. The credo of the original and its fantastic financial value gives the work a public status the visitor can scarcely alter with his or her own reading, which then becomes all the poorer if it is seen to be merely subjective.

Consequently, the dominant critical approach becomes art historical, a specialised academic approach, rather than a lay one. In most forms, art history is devoted to 'discovering the meaning' of art within its contemporary cultural context. This forms the perfect complement to the museum function, since the approach is dedicated to seeking out and conserving 'authentic', 'original' readings of the exhibits. Again, this seems to put paid to a continuity of that spontaneous, participatory criticism which can be found in abundance in literary criticism of the classics, but is absent from most 'respectable' art history.

There would of course be many literary critics who objected to the efficacy of the kind of spontaneous, evaluative, 'consumer guide' reading alluded to above. Yet it is undeniable that art does stimulate emotions as well as intellect, and so the audience need feel no shame that it actively seeks this stimulus in art works. Consumer guide criticism is an aid to this quest, if not much of an explanation for it.

The permanent displays of art museums serve as a warning of what critical practices can emerge when a continuity of spontaneous criticism is suppressed. The museum public, like any other audience, experience more rewardingly when freed of inhibition. If museum collections can be made less intimidating and more coherent by the inclusion of facsimiles which complement the legacy of originals, the public may feel somewhat less deferential. But perhaps a more satisfactory conclusion would be for appropriate works of fine art to be rendered permanently accessible to a consuming public, similar to the way literature and music are, by means of high-fidelity reproductions. Unfortunately, that may be too much to ask from the vested interests of the art establishment.

26

American National Identity and the Structure of Myth: Images of Reagan

R. J. ELLIS

This paper will contend that what Frederic Jameson calls 'the immense Utopian appeal of Nationalism' derives from National-ism's functional structure, established in what Jameson describes as the text's 'unconscious', where ideologies and myth interact.[1] It thereby constitutes a structural mechanism effecting a repression of history in a duplicit process of revelation and concealment. This process, I believe, operates with an almost emblematic potency in the United States.

An image of Ronald Reagan taken from the opening pages of a 1984 election issue of *Time* provides me with a point of departure. In a double-page spread Reagan is portrayed against an enormous painted backdrop, featuring the agrarian landscape of 'Middle America' — a farmstead nestling by a pond, fertile fields, and in the distance, rolling blue hills. Above this landscape runs the banner legend, 'REAGAN COUNTRY'.[2] Above all, however, I want to focus on the pose of Reagan in this landscape — a pose I find particularly interesting because its ingredients recur frequently in Reagan's 1984 campaign portfolio. Indeed, *Time* used an almost identical image on the cover of this same post-Presidential election issue;[3] and, even more noteworthy, another nearly identical pose appears on the cover of *Time* immediately following Reagan's first election victory, in 1980 (Figure 1). It is an image in which one can 'see very well' both 'future' and 'confidence' signified by its constitutive arrangement.[4] The front cover portraits simply add allusions to the United States flag to the otherwise unchanged, formulaic pose: a smile, a ruddy, outdoor complexion and, in particular, Reagan's head tilted slightly upwards so that the gaze is

216

directed upwards and outwards, off to the right. I wish to propose that a meaning is inscribed within this pose. In the words of Barthes what is present is 'a purposeful mixture'[5] of Americanness and confidence in the future.

Barthes, in his essay, 'Myth Today', from which I am quoting, describes such myth as a 'second-order semiological system'.[6] For Barthes, myth is 'a type of speech',[7] and therefore to be identified as an organising principle in the structure of significations contained in an image—as a 'metalanguage'.[8] By adopting this viewpoint, Barthes suggests that the type of speech of which myth consists is in itself a message: what *Time*'s image of Reagan signifies to us 'very well' is not voiced in any way, but rather exists (metalinguistically) in the image's structure. Barthes is here specifically dealing with modern myth: he calls it bourgeois, and plainly views it negatively, as freighted with ideological discourse at the metalinguistic level existing within the 'alienation of the first order semiological system'.[9] This alienation of what I shall label as 'modern bourgeois myth' is *structural*, inscribed by what Barthes describes as a 'constantly moving turnstile', in a complex process of language 'impoverishment'.[10] Levi-Strauss similarly proposes that myth's meaning emerges structurally, and that this property serves 'to provide a logical model capable of overcoming a contradiction', and further observes that myth in 'advanced societies operates in a special way'.[11] I want to analyse how this special capacity resides in the structural properties of modern myth, what Barthes describes as its 'turnstile', in which 'in passing from the meaning to the form, the image loses some knowledge'.[12] The fact that the *Time* photographs are actually of an ageing, recently re-elected President remains present, but this knowledge is robbed by the impression of 'future' and 'confidence' the image conveys.

The process by which we receive this meaning is relatively straightforward. Levi-Strauss claims that 'The function of repetition is to render the structure of the myth apparent',[13] and 1980s representations of Reagan are strikingly repetitive; the image is essentially timeless. On the *Time* covers, Reagan actually looks younger in 1984 than he does in 1980. The image's repetitive timelessness directs our analysis towards the sources of this structural organisation—towards a historical exploration of these images. Both Barthes and Levi-Strauss, arguably in spite of their structuralist allegiances, countenance such a resort, and in Barthes' essay, this acceptance is explicit: 'One can . . . imagine a diachronic study of myth ... [where] one follows some of yesterday's myths down to their present forms ...[14] It is this process that I will now initiate in search of a fuller reading of this image of Reagan.

My approach, however, given the limits of this present study, will be restricted to the identification of just one pivotal point in the evolution of the myth-structure underlying these 1980s representations of Reagan: the period 1830 to 1860. I am not representing this period as the fount of the American national myth structuring Reagan's image. Rather I regard this period as crucial, in that it witnessed the entrance of the myth-structure into representational art in a clearly conventionalised form at a particular historical juncture. Other significant periods could have been selected; I will in fact later make some reference to the 1890s. It is perhaps sufficient here to cite Helen Carr's approving quotation of Frederick Merk: 'Manifest destiny and imperialism ... were traps into which the nation was led in 1846 and 1899 and from which it extricated itself as well as it could afterwards.'[15] I do, however, confer primacy on the period 1830–60; to establish this claim, I will (albeit very briefly) examine some images in representational art of this period, their art historical co-ordinates, and the impinging historical conditions.

The art historical co-ordinates are in themselves pointers to the key contextual considerations. In this period, art historians customarily assert, an American landscape art began to emerge; Bryan Jay Wolf advances the claim: '[Thomas Cole's] three pictures in the window of a New York art dealer in 1825 mark the emergence of an American landscape.'[16] This claim can be disputed, but one must concede that something decisive happened to landscape art in America in this period. For Wolf, it became *American*, and in Cole's 1845 painting, 'Pioneer Home in the Woods', this process becomes plainly visible (Figure 2). I wish to claim that this process unconsciously carried with it an ideological freight in its very structure. To begin with, notice that, when viewing this Thomas Cole's landscape, we can hardly claim to experience sublimity as it is defined by Edmund Burke and Immanuel Kant.[17] There is no sense of a Burkean astonishment amounting almost to terror when viewing Cole's canvas. His painting offers no fearful confrontation with the Kantian alienation of the sublime. I wish to argue that these absences are critical, and involve a structured defusing of sublimity. We do not experience any splitting of consciousness into

two alienated halves, nor the consequent defensive reaction forma-
tion—the reversal of passivity (the wish to be inundated) into
activity (the wish to possess)—the Kantian process lucidly summarised by Thomas Weiskel.[18] These structural evasions demand
contextual explanation. Cole recurrently asserted that he regarded
the American landscape as quintessentially sublime, yet in his
actual depictions this sublimity is undercut. I believe that a crucial
source of this undermining resides in Cole's contemporaneous
assertion that 'the painter of American scenery has indeed privileges superior to any other. All nature here is new to art'.[19] Cole's
cultural nationalism in this key 'Essay on American Scenery' of
1835 is evident. Unsurprisingly, therefore, he turned to Niagara
Falls for early inspiration (Figure 3): 'Niagara! that wonder of the
world!—where the sublime and the beautiful are bound together in
an indissoluble chain. In its volume we conceive immensity; in its
course everlasting duration; in its impetuousity, uncontrollable
power. These are the elements of its sublimity'.[20] What interests
me here is Cole's claim that Niagara binds together the beautiful
and the sublime, despite his immediate addition of a description
that surely could qualify the Falls as undilutedly sublime.

To understand Cole's contention, we must focus on his insertion
of the figure of an Indian, wrapt in contemplation of Niagara, in
the foreground of his painting. For Cole's Rousseauvian noble
savage acts as a filter to the sense of sublimity intimated by the
landscape: our reading actively 'possesses' the 'passivity' of the
Indian, wrapt in the inundation of the negative sublime's momentary suddenness. The 'astonishment amounting to terror' which
might generate 'alienation' is here mediated by the Indian, who,
standing on a cliff-edge, assumes for us the risk of inundation,
thereby binding together the sublime's radical potential to unsettle
with the beautiful's defusing positivity. The picture, noteworthily,
was immensely popular.[21] We have then, here, I would propose, a
preliminary characterisation of how the axis of modern bourgeois
myth's turnstile evolved in American landscape painting: we can
safely read the noble savage's experience of the sublime because
our reading possesses his inundation *at one remove*. This is a
conventional strategy of landscape paintings of sublime scenery,
and of Niagara in particular. The foreground figure provides a
sense of scale, obviously, but also his/her experience of sublimity
intervenes between the reader and the scene, as a filter additional
to that of the imagination of the artist. When portraying Niagara,

however, Cole also gives it a mythic structure, stripping it of its
history in a process of impoverishment: 'history evaporates'.[22] In
fact, by 1830, when Cole painted this picture, the Falls had become
touristified, and the surrounding American wilderness had become farmland.[23] In other words, Cole's picture of Niagara was
deliberately nostalgic and sentimental; that an Indian experiences
sublimity is structurally significant. This contrivance provides
impetus to the myth-turnstile's interleaving of landscape convention and mythic speech. Cole himself was well aware of the actual
'ravages' inflicted at that time: 'I cannot but express my sorrow that
the beauty of such landscapes are quickly passing away—the
ravages of the axe are daily increasing ... and oftentimes with a
wantonness and barbarity scarcely credible in a civilized nation'.[24]
This sense of ravagement was widespread at the time, reducing the
possibility of experiencing sublimity, and it is this process that
grants a specifically nationalistic, *American* inflection to the
bourgeois appropriation of the sublime as a modern myth. The
movement is from passive inundation (Cole's Indian) to active
possession (our reading of the landscape and the inundated figure
before it), a movement precisely binding together the sublime and
beautiful 'in an indissoluble chain', closing down the sublime's
intimations of the need for radical recuperative action. This process
is a robbery. My general reflections on this mythological appropriation of the sublime within bourgeoise ideology therefore need to be
identified as specific historical articulations, in particular socio-
cultural co-ordinates, in order to account for this robbery.

The situation in the period 1830–50 is plainly transitional: the
American wilderness still existed, but was rapidly being possessed
by the United States. Indeed the process of acquiring the Indian's
lands to the west was by 1830 being cast conventionally as a source
of American national identity.[25] The claim was recurrent in the
post-revolutionary decades, and achieved additional momentum
in the general search extant in American culture in this period for a
sense of Americanness. Cole's essay on American scenery is then
culturally generic, and his landscape, 'Pioneer Home', must be
viewed in this light. The sublimity here is now not held at one
remove, but rather at two. The insertion of figures into the
landscape in itself contains the wilderness's negativity in a process
we have already analysed. But now a second, more specifically
American, removal is also occurring, and this stems from the
pioneer's physical activity. In contrast to the wrapt inundation of

the Indian at Niagara, Cole's White American has plainly progressed beyond the suddenness of sublimity; he expresses not wrapt inundation, but active *appropriation*, enacting within the landscape a process of possession that resolves the anxiety of the sublime within the picture frame. He is returning from his successful hunting foray to his log-cabin clearing in the wilderness. This activity within the vast grandeur of nature is heroic, and is part of a highly conventionalised presentation of the pioneer. Two lines from Walt Whitman's 'Song of the Broad-Axe' spring to mind:

The log at the wood-pile, the axe supported by it;
The sylvan hut, the vine over the doorway, the space clear'd for a garden.[26]

The parallels between central compositional elements of Cole's painting and these lines of poetry are precise. A definitely American subject can be identified: America was, by the 1830s, conventionally defined nationalistically by its Western frontiers, and this enables the establishment of a specifically American narrative. This, we have seen, tells of possession, but it also draws on another existing bourgeois narrative—the concept, enshrined in the famous poem by Bishop George Berkeley, 'Verses on the Prospect of Planting Arts and Learning in America' written in 1758, of the Westward course of empire—civilization's irresistible westward progress.[27] This intertwining of possession and inevitability is climatically summarised by Emanuel Lautze's immensely popular painting, its title a quote from Berkeley, 'Westward the Course of Empire Takes Its Way' (Figure 4). Here, highly conventionalised distributions are occurring. The spatial distributions mark out a narrative of imminent possession: the emigrant train travels to the right, where the virgin forest is located—it actually blocks the pioneers' progress, and has to be cleared with axes; the receding range of hills is in the process of being surmounted, and in two central tableaux this success is marked by the actions of raising a hat in celebration and indicating the future goal of the emigrant train in a sweeping gesture towards fertile western plains—again to the right. The iconographical stylisation makes the process seem irresistible.

But we must also now recall the conflicting sense of ravagement, so prevalent in the second quarter of the nineteenth century. We know that this was a period of decisive economic upheaval—a fact unambiguously revealed by the social convulsion of the Civil War, which stemmed not solely from the issue of slavery, but from a fundamental confrontation between modes of production constituted by relations of production. This reading is generally accepted; what is now being pressed by recent historians is a view of the period 1830 to 1860 as economically constitutive. This argument is most forcefully advanced by Charles Post in his 'The American Road to Capitalism'.[28] Here Post seeks to set aside the arguments of such long-established historians as Beard and Turner concerning the predominance of so-called 'natural economy'.[29] Instead, Post advocates that recognition should be given to the dominant role of commodity production:

> By the 1840s . . . agrarian self-organised commodity production in the Northeast and West was governed by the law of value. Merchant capital, through the mechanisms of land law, land speculation, and the promotion of internal improvements, was responsible for the enforced dependence of free farmers on commodity production for their economic reproduction. In particular, federal land policy promoted the transformation of land into a commodity through the public auction of the public domain.[30]

This process, instructively, runs parallel to the sense of America exhausting its potential for Westward growth, which stimulated the flood of emigrants to Oregon in the 1840s, and the acquisitions of Oregon in 1846 and California in 1848. These developments are plainly interactive — an interaction fairly summarised by Asa Whitney's application for a massive land grant in order to construct a transcontinental railway in January 1845, *prior* to the acquisition of any territory on the West Coast by the United States. 'Manifest Destiny' was in this period in full ideological flood.[31] It is at this time that an American landscape convention emerged. Leutze's painting weaves all these strands together: it was commissioned at the start of the Civil War, with all its socio-political disturbance, as a public painting to be placed in the new United States Capitol Building. Thus, it is possible to identify the social contradictions that the turnstile of the myth-structure seeks to contain. These representations of the American character as constructed by the Frontier function as mythic negotiations of contradictions in American society, a mode of discursively legitimating the rampant entrepreneurial competitiveness of commercial and industrial America. If we halt this turnstile, the contradictions in the narrative become apparent: the process is of active advance which must be historically finite, yet it is required to be spiritually infinite. And, contradictorily again, the discourse becomes more conventionally emphatic as the wilderness is progressively ravaged. So in the period 1830 to 1860 the turnstile serves to dehistoricise the shift towards commodity production and increasing class stratification. It displaces history in a reassertion of the primacy of the pioneer experience—inserting the frontiersman as hero between the reader and the anxiety generated by these contradictions.

In this iconographical process, the activity, gesture or gaze of the pioneer becomes a seminal element of the process of conventionalised resolution. The posture and gaze are characteristically not ones of passive inundated wonder, as was the case with Cole's Niagara Indian, but acts of affirmative possession. Frequently, posture or movement intimates this active possession of the land, whilst the gaze establishes a sexist discourse: possession of the female breeder, bearer of the new generation of Americans. Spatial distributions are usually unambiguous here: the female arranged beneath or behind the pioneer. Leutze's painting repeats this pattern twice; the function of repetition is indeed 'to make the structure of the myth apparent'.[32]

This seminal, possessive role of the gaze climactically emerges in the painting 'Daniel Boone Escorting a Band of Pioneers in the Western Countryside', painted in 1851 by George Caleb Bingham (Figure 5). Here, the gaze of the pioneer is the key element of the process of possession, recapitulated by the resolute stride of the pioneer forward into the wilderness. The movement is undeniably heroic in its implications—in this case an American culture-hero strides out. Although the movement is towards the picture viewer, overall spatial distributions conform to the convention: the women are in poses of passivity; Boone steps into the light, which floods from the right of the canvas, from the setting sun in the West; a bird, possibly an eagle, wheels towards the West above them. Behind, a line of mountains recedes into the blue distance. In fact, Bingham intended this painting to represent pioneers passing through Cumberland Gap. He seeks to portray a climactic historical moment in the opening of the West, just as Thomas Cole's 1845 pioneer cabin had been nostalgically portrayed as nestling under New Hampshire's Mount Chocorua long after that part of New

England was well-inhabited.

In Bingham's painting the pioneer's possessive gaze is, precisely, a gaze into some future opening of the West, an upward gaze of possessive confidence anticipating that of President Reagan in his campaign portfolios (Figure 1). This congruence is not coincidental. It is not a new idea to link 'Cold War ... patriotic and populist rhetoric ... to [the] nineteenth century ... particularly to the myths created and exploited in the westward expansion'[33]; I want now to add that it has become not concealed, but fragmentedly reliant on the convention's myth-turnstile. By the 1980s, the complete pattern cannot remain apparent in one image. This fragmentation is in large part a function of chronology. The Frontier wilderness is, plainly, by the 1980s, physically represented only by Conservation Parks. Roderick Nash traces the emergence of such Parks, which, significantly, commenced in the 1860s, when the State of California was given ten square miles of land by the United States government to establish a State Park at Yosemite in 1864. Indeed, Nash locates the origins of pressure for such parks in the 1830s.[34] In the 1980s Reagan cannot realistically pose as a pioneer striding resolutely into the wilderness, but this does not mean that the reference to the pioneer spirit is not overt; on the contrary, it is as obvious as it credibly can be. And incorporated into this representation's turnstile of meanings is the motif of anxiety-conquering active possession. The subtraction of some key features of the myth-image are compensated for by the addition of the unashamedly nationalistic allusions, themselves an indication of how the myth has become more chauvinist as it has accentuated the 'privation of history'.[35] Reagan's colonisation of the myth may even seem too overt. This it cannot be, in the sense that 'myth hides nothing',[36] but its obviousness needs again to be precisely tied down to contextual co-ordinates.[37]

The post-second world war traumas for the United States' sense of national identity need not be over-rehearsed here: its final, belatedly unambiguous entry into the international political arena, defined by the role the United States assumed in the Cold War through its economic and military involvements, is clear. Even more seminal, arguably, than the European element of this, in Western Germany, Berlin, and via NATO, are the United States' Far Eastern adventures, framed by Korea and Vietnam, and marked by the intervening graduation of Hawaii to statehood in 1959. Congruently, in the 1950s and 1960s, the United States' racial and urban problems, as they had in the late nineteenth century, entered a decisive phase, placing additional pressures on the maintenance of a coherent national identity. The consequent definitional anxieties become undeniable.[38] It is thus unsurprising to discover a sudden, decisive acceleration of the so-called Wilderness Cult in the post-war period. This cult, for Nash, found its initial impetus around the turn of the century,[39] chronologically congruent with the United States' definitive consolidation of its status as a trans-Pacific Imperialist power. It was in the 1960s, however, that a 'wilderness explosion' occurred: in 1952 only 19 people travelled down the Colorado's Grand Canyon; by 1972 the annual figure had risen to 16 428.[40] The 'Reagan Country' two-page spread, with its attendant backdrop and anchorage, makes the allusion of the gaze on the front cover of *Time* clearer. '[We] see very well what it signifies to [us].[41] This process is ideological. When Barthes speaks of it as possessing an 'imperative, buttonholing character', as 'interpellant speech,[42] he uses terms strikingly similar to those used by Althusser when talking about the constitution of the subject.[43] In this instance, the interpellation is condensed into the form of a national myth-structure, in which ideology functions not as simply false consciousness, but rather as a profoundly unconscious imposition of meaning via the functional structure of modern American bourgeois myth. Thus Barthes finds it difficult to conceive of 'Myths on the Left'.[44] Myth he views as language robbery, with history drained out of it—as 'depoliticized speech'.[45] Consequently, 'it is extremely difficult to vanquish myth from the inside'.[46]

Establishing the validity of this stricture by applying it to some satires upon Reagan's appropriation of the Frontier myth vividly illustrates modern bourgeois myth's imperative efficacy. The *New Statesman*'s 1981 cover design, 'Dirty Ronnie' (Figure 6), attempts to satirise Reagan by portraying him as analogous to a film character played by Clint Eastwood, Dirty Harry, a San Francisco detective who believes that his individual, quasi-entrepreneurial interventions produce results that more strictly conventional police procedures cannot realise.[47] The anchorage alludes to Reagan's establishment in 1981 of a rapid response force, considered to demonstrate the validity of this proposed parallel between Reagan and Clint Eastwood, both 'tough cop[s] who impose . . . rough justice on the international streets'.[48] This juxtaposition is frequently held to be amusing to left-wing opponents of Reagan. I, however, have certain reservations, when I recall Roland Barthes' adjuration about the difficulty of vanquishing myth from the inside. Conflating the two images, of Reagan and Eastwood, profits little, since the image of Reagan as Eastwood functions wholly inside the myth they both employ, and becomes its 'prey',[49] a 'promotional still', one might call it, functioning just like one of Clint Eastwood's. Publicity images of Eastwood recurrently portray him gazing outwards and slightly upwards and, in this structural characteristic, constitute a significant link between the representation of Boone in Bingham's painting and that of Reagan on the covers of *Time*. The structural congruences are indicative. Reagan's mid-century career as a Hollywood actor in Westerns simply offers one further way of making this link explicit: thus a 1986 CND recruitment leaflet's use of a B-movie still of Reagan with six-gun drawn (Figure 7) merely brings to the surface an extant metalinguistic element of his *Time* image's structure. Reagan, noticeably, is placed within mainstream conventions of the Western Movie, with a white shirt and groomed appearance that Clint Eastwood in his cowboy roles does not sustain. The collapse in the sureties of the Western genre in the 1960s and 1970s is evidence in itself of American anxieties about post-war cultural identity,[50] which Reagan's 1980s' assumption of Frontier myth conventions is motivated to contain. The turnstile of meanings in the myth-structure bear the promise of *resolution* (in both senses of the word) bound up duplicitly within them. To satirise this from the inside merely entertains the Left. Thus, I would argue, remembering Barthes' injunction 'Myth hides nothing', that in these satires nothing is being revealed, only accentuated. In fact, Barthes later goes on to add 'and [myth] flaunts nothing',[51] and it might be held that the satiric hyperbole here constitutes an attempt at disruptive flaunting. But what is flaunted is not the myth's duplicit robberies, only that which the myth does not hide, in a post hoc flaunting of what Barthes describes as the myth's 'form',[52] rather than that which it would not flaunt: the process by which myth speaks — the functional structure through which the message has been naturalised. Barthes perhaps clarifies this: 'myth essentially aims at creating an immediate impression — it does not matter if one is later allowed to see through the myth, its action is assumed to be stronger than the rational explanations which may later belie it'.[53] The image of Reagan in these satires is unrealistic, but by the mid-twentieth century the myth structure had itself evolved into an extreme conventionality bordering on pastiche.[54] In these Reagan satires the myth cannot be made to confess, it is merely confirmed; Reagan's images already represent him as Western pioneer, ambiguously placed on the frontier between noble savagery and civilisation in his myth-structural role of the heroic conqueror of the anxiety of the sublime. I would suggest that the Left has failed to find a means of effectively satirising the National myth-structure of the United States, with its 'immense . . . appeal', as described by Jameson.[55] I would consider that this appeal subsists in surmounting present anxieties by projecting into the future the conquests of the past, using the agrarian pastoral as a recurrent device. This is structured as a mediated resolution of the alienation of the Romantic sublime, recast as sublimely beautiful by the intrusion of the actively possessing pioneer. The congruence between the construction of a heroic, independent, self-determining pioneer as the intermediary between the reader and the anxiety of the negative sublime on the one hand, and other bourgeois (less specifically American) capitalist ideological ramifications on the other, such as laissez-faire individualism, creates an unusually stable, but evolving, National myth-structure, which Reagan's images exploit. If we can in this sort of way identify the structural mechanisms of a National myth's turnstile, then perhaps we can more effectively counter its imperative efficacy, what Levi-Strauss describes as its mystifyingly potent ability to generate collective endorsement.[56] In the case of Reagan, I would argue, what occurred instead was predominantly a process of complicitly continuing to 'naturalize',[57] in caricature, his pioneer image. Such satiric images helped re-cement the fragmented elements of this image, and make the pattern of the myth apparent indeed. Reagan could have asked no more.

NOTES

1.   Jameson, Frederick, *The Political Unconscious: Narrative as Socially Symbolic Act* (London: Methuen, 1981) p. 298.

2.   'Reagan Country', *Time*, vol. 124, no. 21 (19 November 1984) pp. 6–7.

3.   'Reagan's Triumph', cover design, *Time*, vol. 124, no. 21 (19 November 1984).

4.   Barthes, Roland, 'Myth Today', *Mythologies* (1957), trans. A. Lavers (London: Jonathan Cape, 1972) pp. 116, 124.

5.   Ibid., p. 116.

6.   Ibid., p. 114.

7.   Ibid., p. 110.

8.   Ibid., p. 115.

9.   Ibid., p. 123.

10.   Ibid., p. 124–5.

11.   Levi-Strauss, C., 'Response a quelques questions', *Esprit*, November 1963, pp. 628–53; Claude Levi-Strauss, *Structural Anthropology* (1958), rpt., trans. C. Jacobsen and B. G. Schoepf (London: Allen Lane, 1968) p. 209; see also Paul Ricoeur, 'Structure et hermeneutique', *Esprit*, November 1963, pp. 596–62 and Edmund Leach's summary in his *Levi-Strauss* (London: Collins, 1970) pp. 16–17.

12.   Ibid., p. 110.

13.   Op. cit., 1958, p. 229.

14.   Op. cit., p. 137. See also Barthes' description of 'myth today' as 'chosen by history', op. cit., p. 110, and Levi-Strauss's representation of modern myth as existing 'in history', quoted in Leach, p. 16.

15.   Carr, Helen, 'Race and Manifest Destiny in a Cold War Climate', *Over Here*, vol. 3, no. 1 (Spring 1983) p. 35. Carr is quoting from Frederick Merk's *Manifest Destiny and Mission in American History* (New York: Knopf, 1963), and her review-article draws attention to additional discussions of the ideological co-ordinates of 'Manifest Destiny', including, notably, Richard Slotkin's *Regeneration through Violence* (Middletown: Wesleyan University Press, 1973) and Reginald Horsman's *Race and Manifest Destiny* (Cambridge, Massachusetts: Harvard University Press, 1981). See also Slotkin, *The Myth of the Frontier in the Age of Industrialisation* (Middletown: Wesleyan University Press, 1986).

16.   Wolf, Bryan Jay, *Romantic Revision: Culture and Consciousness in Nineteenth Century American Painting and Literature* (University of Chicago Press, 1982) p. 91.

17.   Burke, Edmund, *Philosophical Enquiry into the Origin of Our Ideas of the Sublime and Beautiful* (1757) — Burke is ably summarised by Elizabeth McKinsey, *Niagara: Icon of the American Sublime* (Cambridge University Press, 1985) p. 32 and passim; Immanuel Kant, *Critique of Judgement* (1790) — a clear summary of his argument is offered by Thomas Weiskel, *The Romantic Sublime: Studies in the Structure and Psychology of Transcendence* (Baltimore: Johns Hopkins, 1976) pp. 48ff.

18.   Op. cit., 1976, p. 105.

19.   Cole, Thomas, 'Essay on American Scenery', 1835, rpt. in John W. McCoubrey (ed.), *American Art 1700–1960* (Englewood Cliffs: Prentice-Hall, 1965) pp. 98ff.

20. Ibid., 1965, p. 105.
21. Op. cit., 1985, p. 207.
22. Barthes, op. cit., 1972, p. 117.
23. Mckinsey, pp. 133ff. The United States' cultural maturation at this time is usually attributed to the emergence of a leisure class. See, for a discussion of this in relation to the American Renaissance, Robert Clark, *History, Ideology and Myth in American Fiction, 1823–52* (London: Macmillan, 1984) pp. 6ff.
24. Op. cit., 1965, p. 109.
25. My article pays only incidental attention to the strong racist strands running through the turnstile of meanings contained in the myth of the American frontier; for a discussion of this, see Helen Carr's discussion, op. cit.
26. Whitman, Walt, 'Song of the Broad Axe', *Leaves of Grass* (1856); rpt. in *The Portable Walt Whitman* (New York: Viking Press, 1945) pp. 177, 181.
27. Berkeley, Bishop George, 'Verses on the Prospect of planting Arts and Learning in America', 1758, rpt. in R. Lonsdale (compiler and ed.), *The New Oxford Book of Eighteenth Century Verse* (Oxford University Press, 1984) p. 175. Asher Durand's 'Progress' (1853), oil on canvas, 48 × 72 ins, Tuscaloosa, Alabama: Warner Collection of The Gulf States Paper Company) and F. F. Palmer's 'Across the Continent: "Westward the Course of Empire Takes Its Way"' (Currier and Ives Print, New York, Currier and Ives, 1860) each take up the conventional theme of Berkeley's poem, for example. The latter was immensely popular.
28. Charles Post, 'The American Road to Capitalism', *New Left Review*, no. 133 (1982) pp. 30–51.
29. Ibid., p. 43.
30. Idem.
31. The Phrase 'Manifest Destiny' was most probably coined by John L. O'Sullivan in this very period. See Henry Nash Smith, *Virgin Land: The American West as Symbol and Myth* (1950; revised ed. New York: Random House, 1970) p. 30 and passim.
32. Lévi-Strauss, op. cit., 1968, p. 229.
33. Carr, op. cit., 1983, p. 26.
34. Nash, Roderick, *Wilderness and the American Mind*, revised ed. (New Haven: Yale University Press, 1973) pp. 100ff.
35. Barthes, op. cit., 1972, p. 151.
36. Ibid., p. 121.
37. For a more biographically orientated exploration of Reagan's myth-colonisation, see Michael Paul Rogin, *Ronald Reagan, the Movie and Other Episodes in Political Demonology* (Berkeley: University of California Press, 1987).
38. One portrait of the anxieties created by the United States' international role in the 1960s is provided by Noam Chomsky. See *The Chomsky Reader*, James Peck (ed.) (New York: Pantheon, 1988). The perspective on Chomsky I am assuming is that of Brian Morton, 'Chomsky Then and Now', *The Nation*, vol. 246, no. 18 (May 7, 1988) pp. 646–52. For an account of the United States, domestic anxieties, see William Issel, *Social Change in the United States, 1945–1983*

(London: Macmillan, 1985, pp. 103ff. For a perspective on the consequent cultural anxieties of the Reagan era, see Frances Fitzgerald, *Cities on a Hill* (New York: Simon and Schuster, 1986).

39. Nash, op. cit., 1973, pp. 141ff.
40. Op. cit., 1973, pp. 263ff.
41. Barthes, op. cit., 1972, p. 118.
42. Barthes, op. cit., pp. 124–5.
43. Althusser, 'Ideology and the Ideological State Apparatuses', rpt. in *Lenin and Philosophy and Other Essays*, trans. B. Brewster (London: Monthly Review Press, 1971) pp. 127–86.
44. Barthes, p. 145.
45. Ibid., pp. 118ff.
46. Ibid., p. 135.
47. *Dirty Harry* (1971, Columbia Warner, dir. Don Seigel); *Magnum Force* (1973), Columbia Warner, dir. Ted Post).
48. Anon., 'Strategy for a new Ice Age', *New Statesman*, vol. 101, no. 2608 (13 March 1981) p. 2.
49. Idem.
50. Wright, Will, *Sixguns and Society: A Structural Study of the Western* (Berkeley: University of California Press, 1976).
51. Barthes, p. 129.
52. Ibid., p. 117.
53. Ibid., p. 130.
54. See, for example, Thomas Hart Benton, 'Independence and the Opening of the West, 1959–1962 (Acrylic polymer on linen mounted on panel, 19 × 32 ft, Independence, Missouri: Museum of Harry S. Truman Library); Jack Beale, 'Colonisation', 1976–77 (Oil on convas, 146 × 150 ins, Washington DC: Department of Labor Building — General Services Administration Art-in-Architecture Program).
55. Jameson, op. cit., 1981, p. 298.
56. Lévi-Strauss, op. cit., 1968, pp. 220ff.
57. Barthes, op. cit., 1972, p. 129.

Index

Acid Houses   9, 18–22
Action Force   98, 105, 107–8
Action Man   105–6
Ainslie, Alan C.   67n
Akerman, Chantel   207
Althusser, Louis   30
   Works of   31n, 229n
Apple Computers   143
A Problem Aired   113–19
Arlott, John   151
   Works of   162n
Arnold, Thomas   154
Ashley, Laura   20
A-Team, The   107
Atlas, Charles   48

Babette's Feast   207
Bakhtin, Mikhail   61–7
   Works of   67n
Barbie Doll   105
Barclays Bank   38n
Barthes, Roland   2, 75, 139, 217–29
   Works of   12n, 82n, 143n, 228n
Bazalgette, C. and Paterson,
   R.   110n
Beach, Alfred   196
Beale, Jack   229n
Beaton, Lynn   97n
Beecham, Stephanie   184
Beeton, Mrs I.   76–82
   Works of   82n
Belotti, Elena   110n
Benton, Thomas, Hart   229n
Berger, John   51
   Works of   58n
Bergman, Andrew   189
   Works of   193n
Berkeley, George   221, 229n
Beverley Hills Cop   205
Bevin, Aneurin   154
Bingham, George Caleb   223
Birds Eye   15
Black, Cilla   63
Bladerunner   33, 38n
Blanc, Raymond   82
Blind Date   63–4

Blonsky, M.   46n
Boas-Massini-Pollit   38n
Bodybuilding   49–58
Bodybuilding Monthly   48
Bodyline   156
Botham, Ian   172
Boy George   90
Boy Scouts   100
Boy's Own Paper, The   151
Bradford Exchange   46n–47n
Bradman, Donald   158
Brecht, Bertolt   59, 164–73
   Works of   168, 170, 173
British Telecom   10, 59–67
Broadcast News   205
Broadcasting Research Unit   200
Brodribb, G.   163n
Brookside   90
Brown, Beverley   146–7
   Works of   150n
Burke, Edmund   218
   Works of   228n
Burroughs Computers   140
Butler, Matilda and Paisley,
   William   186n
Butler, Rex   35

Cagney, James   188
Cameron, Deborah and Frazer,
   Elizabeth   138n
Campbell, Beatrix   94–7
   Works of   97n
Capes, Geoff   48
Capone, Al   16
Cardus, Neville   152–3, 158
   Works of   162n–163n
Carr, Helen   218
   Works of   229n
Chettle, C. H. and Charlton,
   J.   31n
Chicago Confidential   190
Chomsky, Noam   229n
Citizen's Band Radio   60
Clarke, J.   31n
Coca-Cola   14–17

Cockburn, C.   121
  Works of   129n
Cody, Colonel   14
Colbys, The   16, 184
Cole, Thomas   218–29
  Works of   229n
Coleridge, Samuel, Taylor   160
Cotter, Arthur   160
Cosmopolitan   123
Coward, Rosalind   110n, 112–19,
  147
  Works of   119n, 150n
Crocodile Dundee   205
Crosby, Bing   92
Cross, Jack   110n

Daiken, Leslie   98
  Works of   110n
Daily Mail, The   11, 147, 174–86
Dallas   16
Darwin, B.   163n
David   142
David, Elizabeth   77–82
  Works of   82n–83n
Davies, Terence   207
Davis, Marie Messenger   110n
Dean, James   21
De Tocqueville   14
Dewey, Thomas E.   189, 192
Dews, P.   31n
  Works of   31n
Diamond, Irene and Quinby,
  Lee   120n
Dick, Philip K.
  Works of   38n
Dickens, Charles   14
Donatello   209
Down, Lesley-Anne   81
Draughtsman's Contract, The   207
Duchamp, Marcel   209
Dynasty   8, 16, 81

Eastenders   8, 90
Easthope, Anthony   110n
Eastwood, Clint   225–6
Eco, Umberto   139
  Works of   143n
Economist, The   110n
Eliot, T. S.   14
Engels, Frederick   155, 162n

Family Affairs   113–19
Family Fortunes   85
Fatal Attraction   205
Federal Bureau of
  Investigation   188–93
Fender, P. G. H.   156–7
Ferguson, Marjorie   186n
Filofax   12n
Fiske, John   114
  Works of   120n
Fitzgerald, Frances   229n
Flex   48
Foot, Michael   154
Ford, Henry   14
Forsyth, Bill   207
Fox, Samantha   184
Frake, C. O.   75–6
  Works of   82n
Fraser, Antonia   110n
Freud, Sigmund   38n, 121–2
Frith, David   159–160
  Works of   162n
Fry, C. B.   153
  Works of   162n
Furlong, Monica   184, 185

Gamleys   100–2
Gavron, Hannah   183
  Works of   183
Generation Game, The   86
Genesis   143
Genet, Jean   134
Giacometti   33–8
Gide, André   134
  Works of   138n
Gillick, Victoria   146
Good Housekeeping   126
Graburn, M.   46n
Grace, W. G.   155, 159
Grosz, E. A.   38n
Guardian   74n, 110n, 144n
Guinness   21, 50

Haddon, L.   129n
Hampton Court   10, 23–31
Harmsworth, Alfred   196
Hartley, L. P.   152
Hasbro, Bradley   101, 105, 108
Hattersley, Roy   114
  Works of   120n
Hepworth, Barbara   34

Hirst, George   159
Hodson, Phillip   114–19
Honeywell Computers   140
Hoover, J. Edgar   16, 189
Horsman, Reginald   228n

IBM   140
Irving, Sir Henry   14
Isaacs, Susan   110n

Jackson, F. S., The Hon.   153
James, C. L. R.   154, 160
   Works of   162n–163n
James, Henry   14
Jameson, Frederick   164, 171, 216,
   227
   Works of   171, 173n, 228n
Jessop, Gilbert   155

Kant, Immanuel   218
   Works of   228n
Kappeler, Susan   138n
King, Stephen   90
Kingstone, Heidi   184
Koch, Edward   195
Kongman   98
Kristeva, Julia   64–5, 67

Labour Research
   Department   176, 186n
Lacon, Jacques   58n, 67
Lait, Jack   190
Lane, Margaret   185
Laplanche, J. and Pontalis,
   J. B.   38n
Lautze, Emanuel   221–9
Lawrence, D. and England,
   M.   129n
Leslie, Anne   184
Lévi-Strauss, Claude   14–17, 21,
   217, 223
   Works of   229n
Levy, Paul   82
Lewis, Jane   186n
Lewis, Sinclair   180
   Works of   180
Little Caesar   188
Lloyd, Anne   123–4
   Works of   129n
Lone Star Products   101
Lotus and Manpower   129n

Lugard, Frederick   154
Lukács, George   167
   Works of   173n
Lyons Maid   15
Lyttleton, R. H., The Hon.   159
   Works of   163n

MacDonald's   9, 13–17
Mafia   190–3
Magnet, The   151
Mail on Sunday   80–1
Mallet, A.   163n
Mangan, J. A.   162n
Marcuse, Herbert   72
Marked Woman   189
Martin, Biddy   120n
Martin, Frank   101
Marvel Comics   107
Marx, Karl   155, 162n
Mason, Ronald   153
   Works of   162n
Master Detective   131–8
Mastermind   84, 88
Masters of the Universe   105
Maxwell, Robert   205
McKinsey, Elizabeth   228n
Merk, Frederick   218
   Works of   228n
Mills and Boon   90
Milton Bradley International   107
Mitter, S.   130n
Moi, Toril   67n
Monkhouse, Bob   85
Mona Lisa   208–9
Monroe, Marilyn   21
Moonlighting   16
Moore, Henry   33–8
Morely, Paul   114
   Works of   120n
Morris, William   20
Mortimer, Lee   190
Morton, Brian   229n
Ms   186
Muni, Paul   188
Murdoch, Rupert   16, 114, 149,
   205
Muscle and Fitness   48
My Little Pony   105, 108

Nash, Roderick   224–5
   Works of   229n

National Gallery 212, 213
National Peace Council 100
National Westminster Bank 38n
Nerina, Zia 79
Newell, Liz 123–4
 Works of 129n
New English Bible 141
News of the World 80
New Statesman 225
Newton, Isaac 143
New York Times 191
Nixon, Richard 192

Observer 46n–47n, 81–2
Opie, James 110n
Orwell, George 90
 Works of 97n
O'Sullivan, John L. 229n
Oughton, E. 31n

Packer, Kerry 157
Palitoy 105
Pavilion Library, The 163n
People, The 80
Play Your Cards Right 84
Plessey 140
Political and Economic
 Planning 186
 Works of 186n
Pople, Alexander 27
 Works of 27
Popular Culture 1–12
Post, Charles 222
 Works of 229n
Pound, Ezra 14–15
Poussin, Nicolas 212
Price is Right, The 86
Public Enemy, The 188
Puddlefoot, Susanne 176
 Works of 186n
Puzo, Mario 191

Quail, J. 162n

Racket Busters 189
Radio Times 89
Raiders of the Lost Ark 205
Rambo 56, 99
Rank Leisure 206
Readers' Digest 13–17
Reagan, Ronald 187, 217–29

Rhodes, Cecil 155
Rice, Patricia 175, 185
 Works of 186n
Robinson, Edward G. 188
Rodwell, Lee 110n
Rogin, Michael Paul 229n
Royal Bank of Scotland 38
Ryan, Michael 99

Sade, Marquis De 134
Saki 109
 Works of 110n
Sale of the Century 86
Samson-Koerner, Paul 164
Sarraounia 207
Scarface 188
Science and Natural History
 Museum, The 211
Scott-James, Ann 183
Scott, Ridley 38n
Scott, Walter 155
Screen 129n
Screen Education 110n
Selincourt, Hugh De 158, 163n
Sex Discrimination Act 1975 184
Sex Disqualification Act 1919 181
Shakespeare, William 27
 Works of 27
Shaw, L. 173n
Shrewsbury, Arthur 160
Silver, Gerald 142
 Works of 144n
Sinden, Donald 81–2
Slotkin, Richard 228n
Smashing the Rackets 189
Smith, Adam 146
Smith, D. 193n
Smith, D. and Williams, G. 162n
Smith, Mike 114–19
Spillane, Mickey 191
Star Wars 104, 106, 200, 207
Stoker, Bram 14
Streeton, R. 162n
Sun, The 11, 114, 147–50
Sunday Express 46n–47n, 80–2, 83n
Sunday Telegraph 81, 83n
Sunday Times, The 82
Sunday Sport 147

Tattinger, Claude 81
Tannahill, Reay 76

Taylor, Elizabeth   184
Tebbit, Norman   150
Temple, Ann   181–2, 185
Thackeray, William   14
Thatcher, Margaret   146
Thomson, A. A.   163n
Thomson, Jeff   157
Thompson, E. P.   71
Thompson, Francis   151
   Works of   162n
Thompson, J. Walter   38n
Thucydides   155
Tillich, Paul   150n
Time   216–29
Times, The   110n, 154, 176
Tiny Tears   98
Today   18
Tommy   33
Town and Country Planning Act
   1947   202
Townsend, Peter   38n
Transformers   105
True Crime   131–8
True Detective   131–8
T-Shirts   19, 68–74
Tuchman, Gaye   175
   Works of   186n
TV Times   89
Twentieth-Century Fox   16, 205–6

Vadim, Roger   184

Van Gogh, Vincent   44
Victoria and Albert Museum   209,
   211
Veronese   213

Walls   15
Warner Bros.   38n
Weiskel, Thomas   219
   Works of   228n
Weizenbaum, J.   143n
Wells, H. G.   103
   Works of   110n
Whitehouse, Mary   146
Whitman, Walt   221
   Works of   229n
Willet, John   67n, 173n
Williams, Raymond   26, 59–60,
   71–4, 168
   Works of   31n, 67n, 74n, 173n
Wimpy Bar   14–17
Wisden   157, 159, 162n
Wolf, Bryan Jay   218
   Works of   228n
Wordworth, William   160–1
   Works of   163n
World's Finest Comics   191
Wright, Gerry   159–60
   Works of   163n
Wright, William   229n

You (Mail on Sunday)   46n, 83n